Taking a Career Break

Taking a
Career Break

by Katrina McGhee

Taking a Career Break For Dummies®

Published by: **John Wiley & Sons, Inc.,** 111 River Street, Hoboken, NJ 07030-5774, www.wiley.com

Copyright © 2024 by John Wiley & Sons, Inc., Hoboken, New Jersey

Published simultaneously in Canada

For general information on our other products and services, please contact our Customer Care Department within the U.S. at 877-762-2974, outside the U.S. at 317-572-3993, or fax 317-572-4002. For technical support, please visit https://hub.wiley.com/community/support/dummies.

Wiley publishes in a variety of print and electronic formats and by print-on-demand. Some material included with standard print versions of this book may not be included in e-books or in print-on-demand. If this book refers to media such as a CD or DVD that is not included in the version you purchased, you may download this material at http://booksupport.wiley.com. For more information about Wiley products, visit www.wiley.com.

Library of Congress Control Number: 2023947186

ISBN: 978-1-394-19759-0 (pbk); ISBN 978-1-394-19761-3 (ebk); ISBN 978-1-394-19760-6 (ebk)

SKY10056757_101223

Contents at a Glance

Table of Contents

Introduction

Career breaks, sabbaticals, and gap years are finally having their moment and gaining popularity among those looking for a more sustainable way of living and working, as well as those who want more time to fully enjoy and appreciate their lives.

There's a powerful alchemy that occurs when you pause to focus intently on your own well-being and happiness. It can help you reconnect to joy and excitement and ultimately return to work feeling steady, inspired, and excited to contribute.

If you've spent decades endlessly sprinting on the hamster wheel of life and are wondering when you're going to get to the good part. . . you're almost there! This book guides you to prepare for the break that will help you reclaim your life. The world needs you to bring your light and gifts into being, and taking a break can help you do just that.

About This Book

This is a how-to book. It's action-oriented, and I hope you'll interact with the information in this book by doing the activities and reflecting on the questions. You don't have to tackle every step; choose the ones that apply to your situation and feel free to skip the ones that don't. While you can move through this book at your own discretion, you may find that working through it from start to finish creates the best results.

This book breaks down the process of designing, navigating, and returning from a break in an easy-to-follow format. You'll discover the unique frameworks and coaching tools I developed supporting dozens of successful breaks. You'll even get an inside look at some successful career breaks and sabbaticals so you can see what a break is like and learn from others' experiences.

By demystifying the exciting world of career breaks and sabbaticals, I hope to make you feel confident and clear about how to move forward. In fact, you can apply many of the tools in this book even before your break begins. You don't have to wait to start creating the change and personal growth you want to experience in your life.

To make the content more accessible, I've divided it into five stages of a break, plus a section with helpful rules and examples.

Foolish Assumptions

My biggest assumption about you is that you're desiring a change in your life — temporarily or permanently — and you're ready to experience a life that feels more spacious, joyful, and fulfilling. You want to reclaim your time to focus on important things outside of work and think that taking a career break or sabbatical can help you achieve this goal. Perhaps one of these descriptions comes close to describing your circumstance:

>> You've never taken an extended break or leave from work and want to make sure you do it right and don't end with regrets.

>> You want to create a more joyful and fulfilling life and are hoping the break will provide the personal growth and transformation you need to make this happen.

>> You're thoughtful when approaching significant changes and want to make sure you've designed a break that will allow you to have the best experience *and* create the best outcome possible.

>> You've been working for a number of years and are beyond ready to leave the rat race for a while, but you don't want to jeopardize all the progress or sacrifices you've made along the way.

Note: I have NOT assumed that you have zero responsibilities. You can have an amazing and life-changing experience even while you're managing obligations and responsibilities. Many of my clients have done this successfully!

I know I'm biased, but I believe that everyone can benefit from the information in this book. We all need a break sometimes, and learning how to prioritize and incorporate a respite into our lives (whether brief or extended) greatly enhances our quality and enjoyment of life.

Icons Used in This Book

Throughout this book, I place icons in the margins that call your attention to certain types of valuable information. Here are the icons you'll encounter and a brief description of each.

TIP

The Tip icon marks tips and shortcuts that will make planning and navigating your break much easier.

REMEMBER

A Remember icon marks the information that's especially important to know. When you see this icon, be sure to pay close attention.

WARNING

The Warning icon tells you to watch out! It highlights potential missteps I want to help you avoid.

ACTIVITY

The Activity icon highlights the tools I use with my clients. This is your chance to apply and personalize the concepts covered in this book.

ANECDOTE

The Anecdote icon points out true stories that show you how certain career break concepts have been applied in the real world.

Beyond the Book

In addition to the abundance of information and guidance related to planning and navigating career breaks and sabbaticals that I provide in this book, you get access to even more help and information online at www.dummies.com. Check out this book's online Cheat Sheet, which covers prompts to determine if you need a break, the five steps to design a plan (and the big benefits it provides), ways a break can improve your life, and more! Just go to https://www.dummies.com/ and search for "Taking a Career Break For Dummies Cheat Sheet."

Where to Go from Here

This book contains information that will help you create a successful career break, from beginning to end. You may want to skip around if you're curious about what to expect throughout the process. Feel free to check out the table of contents or index and search for a subject of particular interest. For example, if you're worried about finding a job when your break is over, Chapter 14 may be your first stop. If you're concerned about having health insurance while on a break and want to know what your options are, Chapter 8 can help.

If you're considering a break and trying to decide if it's the right choice for you, start with Chapter 1 and then check out Chapter 3.

If you want to take a break but are worried you can't afford it, jump to Chapter 5 for help figuring out your finances and a simple process that will help you save money more quickly.

If you're already in the planning stages, start with Chapter 4 to confirm you have a solid plan in place and haven't missed anything vital.

If you're already on a break, congrats! You can start with Chapter 10 to make the most of your experience and avoid the most common pitfalls.

Note: If your break started involuntarily, you can still choose to embrace your time off. Design a break that will create a big personal benefit by starting with Chapter 4.

Wherever you begin, welcome to the next step of your fantastic journey!

1

Deciding Whether a Break Is Right for You

Learn the basics of a career break. Discover what a break entails, understand and overcome your biggest objections, and learn what waits for you at the end of a break.

Discover the benefits a break offers with real-life stories that illustrate the life-changing impact of a break.

Determine whether a career break is a viable option for you. Find out how to assess your situation and examine the risks involved without letting fear hold you back.

Chapter **1**

Getting Acquainted with Career Breaks

Welcome to the exciting world of career breaks, sabbaticals, and gap years! Jumping off the hamster wheel to take a break is an exciting adventure, but it can also feel like approaching a void of uncertainty — scary and overwhelming. If you find the idea appealing but aren't sure where to begin, you're in the right place!

This chapter covers the basics to get you up to speed quickly. You'll gain a better understanding of what a career break entails, why you should consider one, and how to reframe the objections that could prevent you from taking a break. Are you ready to discover a new world of possibility that could change your life for the better? Then let's get started!

Examining Your Options for Taking a Break

While sabbaticals have existed for centuries as periods of rest, renewal, research, and travel within academia and religion, the idea of taking an extended break from work recently has been gaining momentum in the corporate world and beyond. With the relentless pressures of work and an "always-on" culture taking its toll, many are left searching for a more sustainable way of living and working. Career breaks, gap years, and sabbaticals are helping to fill this need, especially for those suffering from burn-out and extreme imbalance. Along with their rising popularity, new names and terms have been popping up to describe these extended breaks, which can get a bit confusing. This section clarifies your options and explains the nuances among them.

Defining the term "career break"

So, what exactly is a career break? A career break is when you quit your job to begin a period of intentional unemployment. It's far more than just an extended vacation. A career break presents an opportunity for deep rest, personal growth, and exploration. It's similar to a company-approved sabbatical or leave absence, with a few notable differences. Don't worry — these adjacent terms are explained in more detail in the section, "Exploring other types of breaks."

Partly due to the misconception that career breaks only refer to large employment gaps taken for caregiving duties, many people refer to career breaks by a different name:

>> Adult gap year, golden gap year

>> Career pause, career hiatus

>> Mini-retirement

>> Sabbatical, personal sabbatical, work sabbatical

If you're considering any of these options, this book's advice on planning, navigating, preparing for, and returning from a career break is a perfect fit for you.

WARNING

If your only goal for the break involves trading one full-time job for another — such as launching a business or becoming a digital nomad — it might technically be a career break, but it won't feel like much of a break at all. Consider incorporating some personal interests or self-care into your plan to receive the full benefit of taking this time off.

TIP

If you've become involuntarily unemployed and are actively searching for your next role, you're experiencing more of a career gap than a career break. If you have the financial means to extend your time off and set personal goals, this could be a great time to get yourself back on track. You can turn this unexpected break into an intentional hiatus and use this book to help create a productive and rewarding experience with life-changing results.

While I highly recommend taking a career break at some point in your life, it's not the right choice for everyone. If quitting your job feels extreme, nearly impossible, or just plain unappealing right now, you have other options like taking a sabbatical or a leave of absence through your employer, both of which I explain in the next section. You can also visit Chapter 3 for a self-assessment to determine if a break is right for you; if you discover it's not, consider the list of alternatives suggested there.

CAREER BREAKS BY THE NUMBERS

While there's no specific time limit, career breaks typically range from 3 months to 2 years, with the majority of them lasting between 6 to 12 months.

An abbreviated career break lasts less than 3 months and is preferable for some due to financial and/or time constraints.

Among my clients, the majority of career breaks have started mid-career, ranging from ages 30 to 55 with an average age of 41. You can see a breakdown, by age bands, in the figure.

The average cost of a career break, among my clients, is $3,650 USD per month, and 50 percent fall within the $2,000 to $4,500 USD range.

(continued)

(continued)

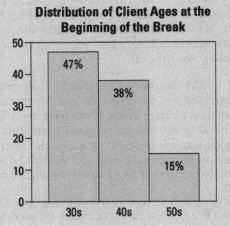

Distribution of Client Ages at the Beginning of the Break

CHOOSING A TERM FOR YOUR BREAK

You have a ton of options when it comes to labeling your break. In this book, I'm very intentional about using the term *career break* to describe an intentional break that begins by quitting your job.

My aim is to help remove any lingering stigma around this term. Taking a break from a decades-long career to enjoy your life and restore your well-being shouldn't be controversial or a decision that's looked down upon. My goal is to empower you to feel good about taking a break and not feel the need to use other terms to disguise or diffuse it.

Ultimately, though, when it comes to choosing a term to refer to your break, the most important thing is picking a term that makes you feel comfortable and excited about the idea of taking a break so you can share your news confidently and joyfully.

Exploring other types of breaks

To help you avoid confusion and better understand your options for taking a break, this section walks you through the different types of breaks.

Sabbaticals

A sabbatical is a benefit granted by your employer. With it, you'll take an extended leave of absence to pursue personal goals and then return to your employer when it's over. There are several ways that it differs from a career break:

>> A minimum number of years of service are required to be eligible for this benefit (if provided by your employer).

>> It requires your employer's permission (if your company offers it and you qualify, you must still be approved).

>> The length of your break is fixed and agreed upon before the break begins.

>> You may retain some, or all, of your employer-provided benefits while you're on a break.

>> You will not quit your job. You will return to work with your same employer when it's over.

The benefit of a sabbatical over a career break is that it eliminates the added stress and uncertainty involved in quitting your job. You may also receive some employer-provided benefits, like health insurance, while you're away, which can lighten your financial load. If, however, you're looking to change employers, pivot your career, or take a long or indefinite leave, this option doesn't provide as much flexibility and freedom, so you might be better served by taking a career break.

You may hear many variations of this term (personal sabbatical, work sabbatical, travel sabbatical), but in this book, the term *sabbatical* refers only to the traditional, employer-provided benefit.

Gap years

A gap year is a specific type of career break — one that is primarily project and/or travel-focused. This term also has several nuanced variations:

>> **Adult gap year:** Adults leaving their jobs to take a project- or travel-focused career break (also referred to as a "grown up" gap year)

>> **Golden gap year:** Adults ages 50+ leaving their jobs to take a travel-focused career break (but not retire)

>> **Student gap year:** Students taking a project- or travel-focused break before (or during) college to aid in their professional and personal development

Gap years are career breaks in disguise. If you're considering a gap year, this book's advice for planning and navigating a break is exactly what you need.

Retirement

Retirement is another break–related term with variations. Some variations involve exiting the workforce, and one is just another career break in disguise:

>> **Traditional retirement:** Stepping away to permanently leave the workforce. Through a mix of savings, benefits, and passive income, retirees can enjoy a life free of professional obligations.

>> **Semi-retirement:** When you're semi-retired, you've divorced yourself of a full-time job but entertain professional obligations on a part-time basis.

>> **Mini-retirement:** A temporary exit from the workforce that involves quitting your job to take some self-directed time away from work (this is another term for a career break).

Leaves of absence

If you have an unusual set of circumstances that requires extended time away from your job, you may want to inquire about a leave of absence. Leaves are unpaid and provided at your employer's discretion. Common reasons for submitting a request include

>> Bereavement

>> Burnout

>> Moving or relocation

>> Providing care for a family member

>> Pursuing higher education

>> Serious health conditions

TIP

Be sure to check your employee handbook to see what types of longer unpaid leaves are offered and for what circumstances. Your employer may refer to it as a sabbatical, leave of absence, unpaid leave, or life leave, or there may be a unique company-specific term. If you need a break, you may find an option to take extended time off.

TIP

Burnout is a common reason for requesting a leave of absence. If you're struggling with burnout, you may qualify for a medical leave of absence to address your mental health. In the United States, this type of leave is supported under the Family and Medical Leave Act (FMLA).

Considering a Career Break or Sabbatical More Closely

Taking a break can be an exciting idea to consider. Who knows — it might even be exactly what you need! To help you form a more informed perspective, this section provides an overview of the main motivations and most common objections when it comes to taking a break, and also maps out your options once the break is over.

Looking at the motivations for taking a break

Why might you decide to take a break? You could have an infinite number of reasons, but the desire is usually born from one (or more) of the following motivations:

>> **Achieving a big goal:** Complete an ultra-marathon, write a book

>> **Caregiving duties:** Provide palliative care, care for aging parent or loved one in crisis, raising children

>> **Connecting with loved ones:** Spend more time with aging parents, children, extended family, friends

>> **Addressing health-related issues:** Attend to your needs to recover from burnout, address ongoing issues or illness

>> **Launching a business:** Start a company, create a new product, become self-employed

- **Coping with crisis or loss:** Divorce, death, job loss, health crisis

- **Pursuing personal development:** Rediscover your passions and interests, transform your relationship with productivity, create an identity outside of your job

- **Pursuing professional development:** Pursue upskilling to acquire new skills or to enhance your current skillset, fellowships, certifications, short-term projects

- **Practicing self-care:** Slow down, develop healthier habits, rest deeply

- **Reconnecting with fun and joy:** Rediscover hobbies, explore new passions, renew your zest for life

- **Traveling or undertaking bucket list pursuits:** Hike the Camino de Santiago, take a world-wide family adventure

- **Volunteering:** Create a positive impact in a neighborhood or community

TIP

If want to consider taking a break more seriously, be sure to read Chapter 2 for a detailed explanation of the many benefits and rewards that await you on a break, and Chapter 3 to explore the risks involved in this big decision.

If you're curious to know the most common motivations for taking a break, see Figure 1-1 for the reasons my clients chose to take a break. (Note that many clients cited more than one reason.)

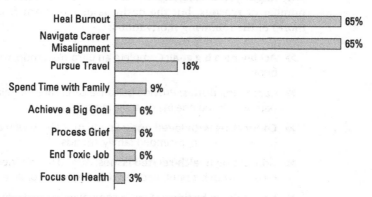

Reasons for taking a break

Heal Burnout	65%
Navigate Career Misalignment	65%
Pursue Travel	18%
Spend Time with Family	9%
Achieve a Big Goal	6%
Process Grief	6%
End Toxic Job	6%
Focus on Health	3%

FIGURE 1-1: Clients' reasons for taking a break.

REMEMBER

When it comes to planning your break, I *highly* encourage you to put yourself at the center of it all. Even if you're taking a break to care for others or pursue hefty professional goals, create space to give yourself the rare gift of time focused on fulfilling and exploring your own needs and desires. Plus, when you fill your own cup, you're able to show up more fully for others, too. Chapter 4 guides you through a simple process to uncover your needs and desires so you can incorporate them into your break and get clear about your personal motivations and purpose for taking a break.

Addressing the biggest objections

You probably have a lot of great reasons to consider a career break or sabbatical. But I'm sure you have some big concerns and apprehensions about it, too, as you should. It's important to think through the pros and cons of big decisions, and now feels like the right time to tackle the big objections you may have about taking a break.

This section includes the doubts and objections I hear most often. Whether they're your own or those of a friend or family member, I have suggestions to help you logically work through each one so you can decide whether it's a valid reason to pass on a break.

TIP

Having doubts and fears is a very normal part of this process. For the best outcome, allow them to inform you but not dissuade you. Use them to uncover the potential roadblocks and dangers ahead and make a plan to overcome them, but don't let them fool you into believing you can't move forward.

You're being irresponsible

If you're worried that it would be massively irresponsible to take a break, you're not alone. For example, I was once in your shoes, and many of my clients have been, too. You're likely juggling a lot of balls right now and can't imagine dropping any of them (let alone most of them). You've probably sacrificed and worked hard to get to where you are today, and taking a break could feel like you'd be throwing it all away. You're steady, dependable, and successful; you don't make rash or ill-advised decisions. If this sounds like you, here are three things I want you to consider:

>> If you feel a strong desire to slow down and pause, spend more time with your loved ones, or have a grand adventure, it may be irresponsible to ignore this desire and continue pushing through a life that isn't fulfilling or nourishing you.

>> Responsible is defined as "being able to choose for oneself between right and wrong." Pay attention to who's choosing your right and wrong. Is it you? Or are you influenced by people with different lives, goals, and priorities than you?

>> Taking a break can create new possibilities in your life and lead to an even better future. It might be more irresponsible to delay taking this detour to better health, expanded joy, and greater impact.

REMEMBER

Taking a break doesn't have to be a rash decision. A well-planned break can improve your life and usher in more success. Chapter 4 is dedicated to helping you create a thoughtful plan and strategy for your break.

WARNING

Not taking care of your health and well-being is not acting responsibly. If you feel that you truly need a break, I urge you to start planning a break before you're forced into one.

It's likely that some of your responsibilities will need to be managed through your break (family, home, debt, pets). This is totally doable. For a breakdown of the responsibilities my clients have carried during a break, see Figure 3-1.

You'll ruin your career

If you think taking a break means "taking a step back" from your career, I've got a surprise for you . . . a well-designed career break can actually support your career progression! Whether you return to your same job or seek out a new one, a career break or sabbatical can pave the way to more success, fulfillment, and opportunity after it's over.

REMEMBER

Using a break to nourish yourself, fulfill your goals and dreams, and have some fun creates a version of you that is better, bolder, and happier. This new version of you has the same advantages that you've always had — same education, work history, and network — but the post-break you also has more energy, inspiration, and a unique perspective.

I've witnessed countless success stories of career breaks propelling career changes, company changes, and promotions, in addition to launching self-employment journeys. When you're able to stop and give yourself what you need most, you'll find yourself restored and ready to tackle even bigger challenges and goals.

ANECDOTE

After returning from a 20-month break, I landed five job offers in just five weeks, including a dream job, a new career option, and a promotion with a 30 percent raise. I used my break to create a professional advantage. To find out more about my exact process for securing job offer(s) after a career break, visit Chapter 14.

You can't afford a break

"Must be nice, but I could never afford a break" is something I've heard many times. As much as you may doubt your ability to afford a break, you might be surprised to know it's more achievable than you think. If being able to afford a break is one of your current objections, consider the following:

>> **A break is an investment — in you!** It's a chance to prioritize and invest in your well-being, your dreams, and your enjoyment of life. We're taught to invest large sums in many things (mortgages, cars, education) but often overlook the importance of investing in ourselves.

>> **Before deciding if you can afford it, make sure you know how much a break would cost.** Estimate how much money you'd need to take a break before dismissing the idea. Chapter 5 helps you estimate the cost. It might be less than you think!

>> **Revisit your priorities.** Are you spending money on things that will provide a meaningful improvement in your future and your current well-being? If not, consider how you might redirect and reprioritize your expenses to invest in a break.

>> **You can always save for a break.** I started with a dream of taking a break with just $1,500 in my bank account and more than $50,000 in debt. But 18 months later, I'd saved $40,000 and left to take a 20-month break. If you want help saving money, you can discover my four steps to saving for a break in Chapter 5.

>> **Your break doesn't have to be expensive.** You can "downgrade" your expenses without sacrificing your experience. You can move in with loved ones to save on rent, reduce the length of your break, or travel to more affordable places. If you're willing to be creative and resourceful, you can create an affordable plan.

Many people have the money for a break but they struggle to give themselves permission to spend it. They're used to collecting a steady income, with a healthy amount diverted to savings and investments. And after years of building wealth, it's unimaginable to consider pausing that. If this is you, I hope you'll take an honest look at your finances. While you're doing an excellent job of investing in the future, make sure you know what you're saving it all for. You've spent years trading your time for money. Maybe it's time to flip that equation and buy back some of your time.

You should wait for a better time

"I'll just wait until . . . the market improves, I deal with my health issue, pay off my car, land the promotion, etc."

Now might not feel like the best time to start planning a break, but there will always be *at least* one good reason to postpone doing the big things you want to do. If you're waiting for the right conditions, I've got a spoiler for you: Life won't create a perfect space for you to chase your dreams or unplug and recover. You have to create that space yourself.

WARNING

Waiting to start planning the break you want and need also means delaying the benefits and positive changes that will come from taking a break. Do you really want five more years of feeling exhausted, misaligned, or just generally stuck in life? If you start planning now, you'll reach your goals much sooner.

Many of my clients have planned and launched a break during uncertain times, like a global pandemic, an international conflict, a potential recession, and more. While their circumstances created more uncertainty, they were certain about their desire to take a break. By starting early, they were able to prepare their finances, develop a plan for their break, and get clear on their personal goals. Now is always a great time to start planning your break!

You're not the "career break type"

Have you fallen for any of these common misconceptions about career breaks and sabbaticals? They might have you believing that a break isn't right for you, when it really is. To clear things up, I'm going to set the record straight on three of the most common misconceptions out there:

SHOULD YOU WAIT UNTIL YOU RETIRE?

Some of my clients are less than a decade away from retirement when they start considering a break. A part of them thinks they should keep their head down and push through, while another part realizes they don't want to.

Taking a break in the last years of your career can create a wonderful new chapter full of possibilities. Tomorrow is never promised, so making the most of what you have today (like your health) is imperative. Plus, breaking for a few months can be a restorative and rejuvenating experience that provides a more expansive vision for what your life can be.

A break can also be a great trial run for your retirement. You'll gain experience managing unstructured time and navigating a life full of freedom and possibility. You can also explore your identity separate from the work you do or the title you hold. If you're considering a break, don't feel you have to wait until retirement to claim it — you can start sooner than you think!

>> **You can't like it "too" much.** If you have a fear that you'll enjoy your break so much you'll struggle to return to your old life, think about how limiting that belief is. You're essentially pre-disappointing yourself to try to avoid potential disappointment later. When you take a break, it will set a new bar for your life and push you to change what wasn't working. You won't resign yourself to the same-old-same-old when your break is over — you'll set out to create something even better.

>> **You don't have to travel to have an eventful and beneficial break.** Almost one third of my clients opted not to travel abroad during their breaks. If your finances, health issues, family life, or personal preferences make staying close to home a better option, travel is not essential for a successful break experience.

>> **You won't die of boredom.** If the idea of downtime feels uncomfortable, it may be a sign that you're equating busyness and productivity with worthiness (a recipe for

burnout). Boredom isn't toxic. It's just a temporary state — one that can give birth to creative ideas and support a deeper level of rest.

Outlining options for returning to work after a break

Part of considering a career break includes envisioning your future beyond the break. What might be waiting for you after it's all over? There are so many possibilities for what could come next!

You can use a break to explore and discover new options or return to a better version of your previous role (with a better company, better pay, or both). You could blaze a new trail for yourself and start living as a digital nomad. Or you could launch your own business and become your own boss. To help you imagine the possibilities, I'm including client examples of how you can return to the workforce after a career break.

Returning to your previous career path

Many people elect to return to their former career after a break, putting their expertise and previous experience to use. The good news is that they often jump back into a better opportunity. It might be a more interesting role, offer a better compensation package, or a more desirable location. For some, it's an opportunity to work with a company or industry that's more aligned with their values. As they return to their original career path restored and excited to start fresh, they often zoom ahead and land in a much better spot than when they left.

Following are some examples from my clients who've found themselves in improved situations after their breaks:

ANECDOTE   Lili was a successful entrepreneur and business owner, which made creating a separation from her work and company quite difficult. But Lili was determined to give herself a break and did an incredible job of growing her team and adjusting her processes to support her taking significant time away from the business. She returned feeling inspired and restored and with better systems and support in place. Both Lili and her company benefitted from her sabbatical.

Juliana used her previous expertise and network to land an exciting opportunity with a startup near the end of her break. She parlayed her relevant and valuable skillset into an opportunity to experiment with her career in a new capacity and try a different approach to work. After a couple months, she realized the startup was no longer a good fit, so she re-entered the job market and landed a more aligned opportunity. (She credits her break with empowering her to more easily and quickly leave a job that wasn't a great fit.)

Hollis left his senior leadership role for a two-month career break, before starting as the CEO of a new company. He used his break to reset, restore, and connect more deeply with his family, before leaping into the new adventure ahead of him. The break provided a necessary pause that allowed him to show up fully for this greatly expanded role.

Embarking on a new career path

If you're considering a career pivot, a break can pave the way for this transition. You can use time during your break to upskill or gain new certifications, complete a fellowship for professional development, expand your network, or shore up any weaknesses (building fluency in a new language, learning a new program or tool). With ample time off, you can experiment with new ideas and pursue passions and interests. When you're ready to re-enter, you can integrate your interests with your previous experience and skillset to make yourself a standout candidate as you launch your new career.

ANECDOTE

Misha used her break to fulfill a long-held dream of relocating to the Pacific Northwest. The time off gave her an opportunity to explore her new surroundings and build a new community. She had several big adventures, like learning to surf in Hawaii, and eventually realized she was ready to return to the workforce. She didn't have a desire to revisit her previous career, so she opted to apply for new jobs and roles. She quickly landed one, just a few weeks after starting the application process, and settled into her third career.

Becoming self-employed

Breaking free of the rat race may leave you wanting to give self-employment a try. Whether you took a break to launch your own business or discovered the desire during your time off, a career break can be a great time to try out being your own boss. You could become a contractor, consultant, or freelancer or start your own company.

I most commonly see career breakers approach self-employment while on a break in these three ways:

» Becoming inspired by an idea during their break and wanting to offer a new service or product

» Experiencing the freedom and autonomy of a break and deciding to continue living and working on their own terms

» Meeting interesting people who are doing innovative things and feeling inspired to do the same

ANECDOTE

Heidi's previous career in education wasn't fulfilling her anymore, so she decided to give self-employment a try during her break. She had a few possibilities floating through her mind, so she opted to plant seeds for several ideas at the same time and see which bloomed first. She became a medical interpreter, Airbnb manager, and a vacation planner and launched an export business for women's accessories. Each pursuit began generating income as Heidi applied her previous skills in new ways and integrated them with her passions and interests.

Creating a more desirable lifestyle

After leaving the unsustainable and fast-paced working world behind, you may decide to pursue a lifestyle that better suits you. A career break can be an optimal time to design a lifestyle that reflects your desired pace, rhythms, and priorities. When you're ready to return to work, your break can provide an opportunity for you to approach your work and life differently. For example, you could

» **Become a digital nomad or remote worker:** If you desire location independence and love to travel to new places, you can explore remote work and create a more nomadic lifestyle.

» **Incorporate more breaks into your life:** You might enjoy the contrast of intense work sprints followed by long periods of recreation and leisure and decide to take more breaks in the future.

>> **Return to work part-time:** If you enjoy your work but desire more time to focus on your life outside of work, returning part-time could be an option.

Taking a break allows you to break your life apart and put it back together in a new and exciting way. As you begin the process of returning to work, you can give yourself time to consider your options and design a lifestyle that will support and align with the new you, instead of defaulting to the one you previously had.

Jess had settled into her break when she was contacted by an old manager and asked to accept a new contract position. Realizing that she wasn't ready to return to full-time employment, Jess happily accepted the part-time position, which allowed her a much slower transition out of her break. While she would eventually ramp back up to full-time, starting with a part-time role allowed her to continue focusing on her other career break goals.

Rita had worked hard for many years and was feeling tired when she started her break. Luckily, the space her break provided allowed Rita to collect herself and nourish her mind and body. She eventually accepted a freelance position during her break that allowed her to explore the option of remote working. After she started, Rita realized this lifestyle really suited her and she decided to become a contractor freelancer and remote worker. She even developed some helpful resources to share her experiences and journey with others.

health

» **Realizing personal goals**

» **Creating more professional success**

Chapter 2
Embracing the Benefits of a Career Break

A career break can improve your life by providing time to recover, realize big dreams, explore exciting ideas, advance your career, and much more. Many benefits are provided by taking a career break, and in this chapter, I highlight some of the biggest and most impactful because understanding the benefits is an important step in deciding whether a career break is right for you. You'll also get to look behind the scenes of several different career breaks and sabbaticals, as I share anecdotes to help illustrate the benefits.

If you've decided you want to take a break, this chapter provides the affirmation you need to keep moving forward. And if you're on the fence, or have recently started thinking about a break, this chapter's real-life examples will help you understand the impact a well-designed career break can have on your life. So many benefits are waiting for you at the end of the career break rainbow!

WARNING

You may want to gloss over the benefits and focus solely on the potential drawbacks, but don't make this mistake! The drawbacks are important to consider (I cover them in Chapter 3), but it's equally important that you also consider the benefits – they are what you stand to gain from taking this leap.

Restoring and Improving Your Physical Well-Being

Imagine feeling stronger, healthier, and more energized than you've felt in years. Good health is invaluable, but you may find that you often neglect it as you race toward your professional and financial goals. Luckily, improving your physical health is one of the biggest benefits a career break can offer. A break provides an opportunity to slow down, fully recharge, and hit the reset button on your health — it's a chance to prioritize your well-being.

During a break, you can extract yourself from the many distractions competing for your time and potentially sabotaging your health goals. It's challenging to adopt and maintain healthy habits when you're fully immersed in the working world. But power naps, healthier meals, reasonable bedtimes, daily movement, and more are suddenly within reach when you're on a break. And if you have lingering health issues that require more time and attention, you'll have ample time to resolve them during this time off, too.

Recharging your batteries

We've normalized running on empty for extended periods of time, with only a quick recharge when absolutely necessary. But when you accept the bare minimum of what's needed to get your system back up and running, you eventually crash and find yourself in need of a system reboot.

Taking a break provides time for a complete recharge. You'll have the luxury of waking up sans alarm clock and starting your day at a slower pace. It's a sharp contrast to several rounds with the snooze button and a burst of adrenaline, as you hustle your way into the start of your work day. When you're on a break, you'll have space for the deep rest and ease a full recharge requires.

ANECDOTE

I had a client who half-jokingly worried that giving themselves permission to rest all day would be the gateway to a life spent sitting on the couch, eating bonbons. But they were exhausted and in need of deep rest, so they cautiously gifted themself "do nothing" days — days during which their only requirement was to eat and sleep. And after several weeks, they gained enough energy to add in fun activities like hikes with their spouse, dinner with friends, and dance classes. Several months into their break, they had more energy and motivation than they'd experienced in a long time.

TIP

Taking time to step away from the daily grind will restore your energy and renew your motivation. When you're on a break, you choose the speed and your activities. You'll have the freedom to exchange many of your energy-draining activities for things that give you energy instead, which leads to rejuvenation. The power of rest is underrated, but it's essential for renewing your energy and enthusiasm.

Following are some ideas to help recharge your batteries while on a break:

» **Eat well.** Be sure to incorporate nourishing foods that will restore your energy and support your body and immune system.

» **Get adequate sleep.** Sleep is essential for maintaining good health and supporting your body's ability to repair itself.

» **Move your body.** Stillness and rest might be required for the first few weeks of your break, but after you've rested it's time to add movement. Whether it's walking, hiking, dancing, stretching, yoga, etc., incorporate gentle movement to support your recovery.

» **Breathe intentionally.** This one is incredibly simple but also important. Incorporating pockets of deep, slow breathing into your day will support your body's ability to repair itself.

» **Embrace play.** Play relieves stress, reduces tension, and promotes relaxation, among other health benefits. Plus, it's fun! This makes play a win-win.

» **Spend time outdoors.** Spending time in nature can have a calming effect on your body and increase feelings of vitality. It can also be a mood-booster that supports and improves your overall well-being.

Recovering your physical health

A break can help you reclaim your health and improve your quality of life, with benefits that last well beyond your break. Whether you want to get into better shape or desire a deeper level of healing and recovery, a break provides time for you to get your health back on track (or on track for the very first time).

You might see this benefit begin soon after your break starts. With more time for healthy meal prep and daily movement, plus less time being tied to your devices every day, an immediate reduction in your stress levels and a healthier body are more accessible.

Here are several ways people pursue health improvement while on a break:

» Addressing significant changes in their bodies due to aging and/or stress

» Experimenting with approaches to achieve a higher quality of sleep (meditation, going to bed earlier, reducing or eliminating caffeine, etc.)

» Exploring alternative health practitioners (chiropractors, acupuncturists, functional medicine, reiki healers, etc.) for support

» Finding a specialist to help resolve complex health issues

» Incorporating consistent daily movement into their life (e.g., yoga, walking, running, Pilates, stretching, pickle ball, tennis, swimming, hiking, etc.)

» Preparing more meals at home, experimenting with new recipes, and incorporating more nutrient-dense foods

» Undergoing necessary surgery with ample recovery time

» Working with a dietician, nutritionist, or health coach to improve their diet

If you need to resolve a more serious health issue, a break can be incredibly beneficial. Significant health issues require a lot of time, patience, and support to resolve. Being on a break means having more time and energy for things like doctor or specialist appointments, medical tests, research, new treatment protocols, surgery, recovery time, and more. With the extended time off that a career break provides, you'll be able to properly address your health issues and create a more nurturing environment to support your recovery.

ANECDOTE

One of my clients struggled with declining health before her break began. She worked a very demanding job, which made it difficult to take good care of herself. It also made it challenging to manage doctor visits and get answers about her worsening symptoms. With no diagnosis, she wasn't sure how to get ahead of her mystery illness. While saving and preparing for a career break, her body crashed and forced her into an early start. During her break, she had time to find a new doctor and finally receive a definitive diagnosis: Lyme disease. After years of uncertainty, she had an answer. This career break set her on a path to heal her body and manage her symptoms — she credits the break with saving her health.

Creating a healthier lifestyle

Even if you aren't struggling with health issues, a career break can provide a reset that makes living a healthier life easier. With fewer competing priorities and more time freedom, you can develop supportive habits and routines that will lead to a heathier, more vibrant life. This is a gift that will keep on giving!

TIP

Creating a healthier lifestyle doesn't have to feel like work — start simple so you can keep it fun and stay consistent! Don't overload yourself in the beginning — choose one or two new habits to start. View this as an experiment with no right or wrong answers. Stay curious and be willing to adapt and change as you learn more about yourself and your body. Try new foods and new activities — keep the ones you like and replace the ones you don't. Be patient; you're learning how to take excellent care of yourself in this process.

TIP

A break is the perfect time to let go of the habits that have been working against you (hello, late nights and social media–scrolling marathons) and to replace them with habits that support your well-being and help you feel more relaxed, stronger, and more motivated to get out into the world and live fully. Using this time to reset your health habits can improve the quality of your life for decades to come.

Here are some examples of what you can include in a health reset.

>> Adding movement and physical activity into your day (e.g., dance, yoga, walking, hiking, etc.)

>> Stretching daily

>> Improving the quality of your sleep and sleep hygiene (e.g., earlier bedtime, blackout shades, app with soothing nighttime sounds, earlier end to screen time, etc.)

>> Meal-prepping with healthier recipes

- >> Napping and practicing non-sleep deep rest (a state of calm and focus similar to hypnosis that provides your brain with a burst of intense rest)
- >> Taking cooking classes with themes that interest you
- >> Starting a supportive daily morning routine (see Chapter 12 for ideas)

ANECDOTE

I had a client who didn't believe in morning routines and struggled to trust her body after surviving a serious health incident. When her break began, she wasn't sure she could adopt and stick to the healthier habits necessary for a true reset. But six months later, she was a morning routine queen. Even on the busier days amidst the chaos of mom life, she made time for the morning routine essentials (the most critical items). Her secret? Keep it simple. She realized how much better and more grounded she felt with her routine, so she held those essentials sacred even when she was too busy for the full routine. This helped her create a healthier lifestyle that she incorporated into her life after the break ended.

Supporting Your Mental and Emotional Well-Being

A career break is like a deep breath of fresh air for your heart and mind. It's an opportunity to eliminate the mental clutter and find more ease. This is one of the biggest reasons for taking a break — 65 percent of my previous clients listed "burnout" as a key reason they decided to take a break.

When you take a break, you'll have time to recover from your burnout and the emotional energy to process big life events that you might have pushed aside to meet your work demands. Plus, if you've been feeling down or just in need of a pause, a break will help you feel lighter and clearer about the direction of your life. With this time, you can process unresolved feelings, answer deep and reflective questions about what you want in life, and finally have the space to celebrate the life you've worked so hard to create. One of the best benefits of taking a career break is the chance to support your mental and emotional health so you can enjoy your life more deeply.

Addressing mental and emotional challenges

Some seasons of life can be especially challenging. In a tough season, a break creates a safe space to navigate difficult life situations without worrying that you may lose your job or ruin your reputation. During this time, you can seek support (e.g., a therapist, coach, grief counselor, spiritual leader, etc.) to work on emotional or mental obstacles that you've encountered. It can be scary to imagine loads of free time spent focusing on your problems, but if you create themes for your break (as recommended in Chapter 4), you'll have plenty of exciting and nourishing plans to infuse into your break.

Taking a break means having time to address anxiety, depression, mental fatigue, and/or a diminished capacity to handle stress. Your difficult life season might be prompted by grief due to loss (of a loved one, a marriage, or a job). Grief is a journey, and the healing process can take far longer than expected. Sometimes you need a break to heal and come back as your best self. Recovering from this loss will require time — time to be sad, time to process your feelings, time to get adequate support, and time to move forward.

If you lean into your break and take time to address and support your mental and emotional well-being, you'll create an entirely new reality when your break is over. You'll move through difficult feelings, heal old wounds, and find a new perspective that helps you feel more grateful and excited for what's to come. And when you arrive at the end of your break, you'll bring a better version of you into your next chapter.

ANECDOTE

One of my clients was a high achiever who'd pushed through the loss of both parents in her early 20s. But the unresolved grief caught up with her a few years later and she was unable to perform at the high level she was used to. She decided to take a break and regroup. During the break, she focused on supporting her emotional and mental health. She connected with loved ones and gave herself time to heal, rest, and explore new things. One of those adventures led to an in-person visit with a death doula, who was able to help her process her fear of dying and resolve some of her lingering grief. She also discovered the Enneagram (a system that identifies patterns in how you interpret the world and classifies you into one of nine personality types) and learned more about herself in the process. Her healing journey during the break helped her see things from a new perspective and make big, bold decisions: She and her spouse decided to move across the country and start a family.

ANECDOTE

Another client used a sabbatical to recalibrate her life. Releasing her work commitments provided time to reconnect with herself and put her own needs and desires first. Near the beginning of her break, she and her spouse started divorce proceedings, and she was able to support her emotional well-being as she navigated this big transition. She focused on achieving several goals during her break, but having the space to deal with difficult days and tough emotions as they arose was an invaluable gift and sped up her healing process. She was able to move forward and returned to work feeling refreshed and excited to contribute again.

Building yourself back up

If you're looking for an opportunity to build yourself back up and emerge with renewed energy, motivation, and focus, a career break could be the answer. You might be experiencing excruciating misalignment at work — the kind that arises when your role doesn't match up with your skillset, strengths, or values. Maybe you're ready to escape a toxic work environment that's left you depleted and burned out, or you're dealing with a life circumstance that has shaken your confidence. You might be working in a job that goes against some of your core values, or you could be entering a break involuntarily, after being let go from your job. Whatever the case, the mental exhaustion and self-doubt these situations create can feel crippling, but a well-designed break can bring you back into balance and help to restore your confidence.

TIP

During your break, you get to stop worrying about how others perceive you and the need to pretend that everything is fine. It's a chance to let your guard down, admit things are not okay, and fully decompress, creating distance from your stressors. This is exactly how you create space to rebuild your confidence and come back stronger than before.

ANECDOTE

At the beginning of my break, I was feeling mentally and emotionally rundown and wondered if the "rock-star" version of me still existed somewhere or had been lost altogether. Although I was once a high-achiever, I'd started to wrestle with intense self-doubt after years of being numerically rated and ranked against my also high-achieving peers. My sparkle dimmed from years of working jobs that didn't value my strengths nor align with my personal values. As my break began, I put myself in environments that felt nourishing and affirming and allowed my strengths to shine, like using my positivity to help me connect more deeply with strangers while traveling. Removing myself from the stress of competition and always needing to measure up helped me shift to focus onto things I did well and channel my energy into things that felt personally rewarding and meaningful. This changed my perspective and helped me rebuild my confidence. When I was ready to return to work, I leapt into a dream job that aligned with my values, excited to shine bright. My manager confirmed during my annual review that I'd wowed them with my talents and created a positive impact on the business.

Pursuing new experiences and stepping outside your comfort zone during a career break can help build your confidence and resilience. This is valuable for your personal and professional life. Navigating the uncertainty of a break will provide evidence that you're resourceful and capable of figuring things out. And healing your burnout will allow you to operate at a higher level and start feeling on top of things again. As you recuperate, you'll increase your capacity to handle and manage stress, which will improve all facets of your life.

REMEMBER

Your break is a gateway to the excitement, joy, and passion for life you've been missing. Your break will help you reignite your spark, reconnect to your passions and strengths, and remember what makes you unique.

ANECDOTE

Another client came to me feeling burned out after performing in a role that felt beyond his scope and that wasn't aligned with his strengths. The desire to detach from that work situation, mingled with a desire to travel the world before starting a family, led him to plan a career break. As he moved through his break, he discovered new interests like learning Spanish. Because he followed this new interest, he was offered a short contract job in a Spanish-speaking territory and later landed an incredible fellowship opportunity near the end of his break. He was passionate about his field but needed time to step back, focus on personal goals, and have some fun. When he felt restored, he jumped right back in and landed a well-suited role at a new company.

Shifting into a better mindset

Here's an uncomfortable truth: Sometimes *you* are the one stand-ing in your own way. It's not that you want to hold yourself back, but old programming and habits are working against you and subconsciously creating more of the same results that you don't like. If you want to change this, you'll need a new perspective — and a career break provides an incredible vantage point.

Maybe you want to live a bolder life and make braver decisions. Or you're stuck in a vicious cycle of overwork and exhaustion that appears in every role you've had. Whatever shift you're longing for, a break puts you in new circumstances and reduces distrac-tions and demands, so you can see things more clearly and with a fresh perspective.

In this unique moment where the familiar has disappeared, you'll stop operating on autopilot. Here, it's easier to see your life from a different point of view and to consciously choose new thoughts, habits, and routines that support that life you want to create. The power of changing your environment is amplified when you include travel to new places, cultures, and/or countries.

A break is a natural reflection point to consider your relationships (to yourself, your loved ones, your friends, etc.) and thoughtfully choose where you want to invest your time going forward. You'll also have space to incorporate more of what you want in your life: playfulness, creativity, fun, adventure, gratitude, etc. These actions will help you feel better about life and shift into a more positive mindset.

ANECDOTE

Adopting a better mindset was the biggest benefit for one of my clients. His job involved striving to maximize efficiency and productivity in healthcare, in which lives were literally on the line. Several weeks into his break, he panicked about the empty space in his days. He felt this bursting need to "do something." We explored the source of his stress and he realized that he was chronically rushing through life, even when he didn't need to. As exhausting as it felt, he was unconsciously creating this sense of urgency himself. When he let go of the belief that he needed to do more to be worthy and valuable, it completely shifted how he showed up in life. He could allow himself to relax more, enjoy his life, and be present to the wonderful things happening around him. He's now back at work and loving his job, without burning himself out.

You have to be selective about thoughts you choose to accept as facts. A break will have you seeing things in a new light and questioning things you've never questioned before. This is really good! It's giving you the chance to improve things that aren't working and that are causing you pain. You can design a life that supports you, instead of working to support and maintain your life (e.g., your home, lifestyle, job, etc.)

ANECDOTE

One of my clients saw herself as the "good girl." She followed rules, even when they didn't make her happy or match up with what she really wanted. But the act of planning for her break broke the good-girl mold and pushed her to step up and make different, bolder choices in her life (before her break even began!). She started speaking up more and making choices that felt good to her, even if others disagreed. One of her biggest moments was co-leading a teacher's strike with her fellow teachers. At the time of this writing, she's living abroad as an expat and challenging herself with new and exciting adventures every day. The version of her that emerged from her break is unrecognizable to the "good girl" she once was.

REMEMBER

Stepping away from your routine gives you new perspective on your career, your priorities, and your goals. It offers a chance to create a new approach to life — one with more joy, alignment, connection, and beyond!

Celebrating your life

Gratitude is potent. It can reduce stress and symptoms of anxiety and depression, promote better sleep, and boost your immune system. And it feels good, too — when you're connected to it, you'll notice feeling more abundance, safety, and love. Which leads us to another wonderful career break benefit: sidestepping the chaos of life to appreciate all that you have and more fully enjoy the life you've worked so hard to create. And when the break is over, career breakers can use this celebratory experience to catapult into a new level of success in life.

When you imagine taking a break, you might initially have visions of annihilating your bucket list. But in reality, you don't need a series of epic adventures to have an epic experience overall or to justify taking a break. Stepping away from the daily grind to admire and celebrate the life you already have and to feel more connected to the good things already in it can be life-changing.

TIP

You can load up on adventure but don't pressure yourself to have an endless stream of once-in-a-lifetime experiences. Your life is literally a once-in-a-lifetime experience, and if you're letting it pass by without stopping to celebrate and appreciate it, that is the far bigger tragedy.

ANECDOTE

One of my clients was a successful executive who wanted a break to enjoy time with his family and recover from the hectic demands of his successful career. When we started working together, he was focused on his break having "epic" experiences — the Instagram-worthy kind that come with a big splash. But while mapping out his true priorities, quality time with loved ones and a deep restoration of spirit and body rose to the top. So we put the "epic" adventures on the shelf. He slowed down, enjoying the simple pleasures in his life and being fully present for himself and his loved ones. And in this space, he could celebrate life and enjoy the fruits of his labor. This time also granted him a change in perspective that helped him create a more sustainable approach to juggling the responsibilities of life and work. At the end of it all, he realized that just the act of taking a break to enjoy his life was epic.

On a break, you're finally free of the usual work stress and demands. You'll get to focus on relaxing and enjoying life. Take up new hobbies, discover new passions, and connect with your loved ones; in the process you'll infuse more joy, gratitude, and inspiration into your daily life.

You can use a break to enjoy and appreciate many aspects of your life, including:

>> **Community:** You can congregate with others who share your passions and interests or create an impact by volunteering.

>> **Friends and family:** Use this time to reconnect and make memories with your friends and family. You can try new things together or make time for your old favorites.

>> **Interests and passions:** Explore new interests and hobbies. Try things you might not be good at and let your curiosity lead you or revisit passions and interests you haven't had time to pursue in years.

>> **Home and neighborhood:** Enjoy the house you've made feel like home. Take walks in your neighborhood, hang out

with your neighbors, and celebrate your little neck of the woods and the things you love about it.

>> **Physical health:** Whatever your body is currently capable of, make time to enjoy it. Take walks or practice yoga, if you're able. Or sit quietly and practice a few rounds of deep breathing to appreciate your aliveness. Make the most and celebrate whatever you've got!

Pursuing Personal Development and Interests

One of the most life-changing benefits of taking a break is having the opportunity to live your wildest dreams and experience personal growth. These pursuits are an integral part of having a great experience and achieving a new level of success when your break is over. The benefits you'll learn about in this section are focused on refilling your cup, restoring your spirit, and sparking excitement. Here is where you'll pave the way to an even better you and a more rewarding life.

The opportunity to pursue personal growth is one of the aspects that distinguishes a career break from an extended vacation. During this time, you can indulge your passions, fulfill your dreams, deepen relationships (with yourself and others), and move leaps and bounds toward the life you want.

Discovering new parts of yourself

If things are feeling stale or you're feeling "stuck," a career break can help you shake things up in a meaningful way. A break opens the door to discovering and cultivating new parts of yourself to admire and enjoy. It's also the perfect opportunity to re-establish your identity beyond your career and the work you do.

It's not uncommon to double down on old goals that a younger you set, only to realize they're no longer aligned with the life you want to live. At the time, they were exciting and motivating, but as you've achieved them and continued growing and changing along the way, they just don't fit anymore. Sacrificing for more promotions and responsibility might not light you up the way it used to — and that's totally ok! Taking a break will help you pursue endeavors that stimulate your mind, spark new and exciting ideas, and reveal new strengths and interests. The insight and discovery you'll experience on a break will help you get clear on the new goals you want to set and the path you want to follow.

A career break also invites you to reflect on who you are beyond just the work you do or the career you've had. It helps you create a richer and more colorful life and to expand your self-identity. It can be disorienting to take a step back from something that you've invested the majority of your time and energy into (especially if you love it), but in this uncomfortable space you will be surprised and delighted by what you discover. You'll explore new parts of yourself that will make life more joyful and can help you maintain better balance when you return to work.

ANECDOTE

It's never too late to discover and cultivate new interests and passions. One client who illustrates this point quite well was in her early 50s when she started her break. Coming from a male-dominated industry, she wanted to reconnect with her femininity and slow down to savor the sweet moments in life. On her break, she discovered new things about herself like her passion for partner dances (kizomba, bachata, salsa, etc.) which she now refers to as a "requirement for living her best life," and she's embraced a nomadic lifestyle, learning more about her preferences and abilities as a traveler. Her break has been a springboard into becoming the person she wanted to be.

How can you pursue self-development while on a break? You can discover and cultivate new strengths and talents in many ways. The key principle is to follow your curiosity and go where it leads you. Following are some activities and resources to inspire your growth, learning, and exploration:

>> **Books and podcasts:** Explore topics that pique your interest and immerse yourself in stories that intrigue and inspire you.

>> **Adventure:** Try new things, especially if they are outside your comfort zone. Put yourself in new situations and test long-held theories about what you do and don't like. Be willing to learn something new about yourself!

>> **Create without expectation:** Use any medium (words, paint, pencil, song, dance, food, etc.) and create without trying to become an artist or do it flawlessly. Enjoy this form of self-expression and let go of perfect.

» Life coaching: Coaching can be a great way to explore and discover new parts of yourself. With a coach, you'll have the opportunity to examine old beliefs that might have limited your happiness and replace them with more empowering thoughts and ideas.

» Courses or classes: Go where your interests lead you! You can take a class or join a course on almost any topic: cooking, painting, singing, languages, entrepreneurship, investing, etc. Even if the class doesn't lead to a new passion, it will introduce you to new ideas and new people that might direct you to even better ideas.

» Explore your surroundings: Gain a fresh perspective by viewing your town or city through the eyes of a tourist. You can explore new places you've been meaning to check out or take an extended stroll through your favorite neighborhood. Even if travel isn't part of your break, you can embrace the mindset of an explorer to make new and interesting discoveries.

» Journal: Journaling for self-reflection can be a great way to build awareness and discover new things about yourself. If you need help with determining your preferred method and/or coming up with prompts, grab a book on the topic (*Journaling For Dummies* by Amber Lea Starfire (Wiley) may be a great option).

» Meditation: Meditation can help you quiet the chatter of your mind and explore new thoughts and ways of approach-ing life. You can do it guided or unguided, with music or in silence. You can explore this topic in more depth with meditation apps (like Insight Timer, Headspace, or 10% Happier) or a book for self-guided study, such as *Meditation For Dummies*, 4th Edition, by Stephan Bodian (Wiley). Meditation retreats are a popular choice for those who want an immersive experience. Choose one that sounds good to you and dive in!

» Physical activities: A break is a wonderful time to explore recreational sports and other physical activities more deeply (like yoga, swimming, tennis, running, trampolining, pickle-ball, weight lifting, or golf). This is a great time to experiment with new ways of moving your body.

>> **Meet new people:** Encountering new people can be a great way to learn new things. If you try some of the activities on this list, you'll find yourself in new places with new faces. This is the perfect time to extend a "hello" and start a conversation with someone new. You never know where it will lead you.

>> **Travel to new places:** Travel teaches you a lot about yourself. Travel, especially to a new country, exposes you to new foods, cultures, languages, and customs. Through travel, you'll discover new ways of thinking and living, which will reveal new strengths and skills and expand your perspective on life

Building deeper connections with others

A career break can bring more connection into your life. Humans are social creatures who thrive on connection, and during your break, you'll have lots of time to build community, make new friends, reconnect with people you haven't seen in ages, and spend quality time with loved ones. Focusing on connection will support your emotional well-being and enhance your career break experience.

ANECDOTE

When I started my own 20-month career break, my first mission was a 3-month road trip around the United States. I designed my trip to incorporate bucket list locations (e.g., the Grand Canyon and the Pacific Northwest) and to revive old friendships. Because many of my friends lived in other states and had families with small children, travel wasn't something they could easily do. But they were excited to host an old friend and often treated me like royalty, going out of their way to make me feel welcome. These visits were a highlight of my career break experience and provided a chance catch up after years apart. I ended my trip feeling incredibly loved, connected, and supported.

ANECDOTE

"Donut Day" was a creative idea one client came up with to build connection and spread joy among his friends. Knowing their dietary restrictions, he loaded up on regular, gluten-free, and vegan donuts and then drove around the city delivering donuts to his friends' doors. They were delighted and surprised at this fun way he decided to reconnect with them.

NURTURING YOUR FAMILY AND CARING FOR OTHERS WHILE ON A BREAK

Whether it's your main focus or one of several goals, a break can provide you with more time and energy to support and care for loved ones. For instance, you can use a break to

- Look after small children
- Foster or adopt a child
- Spend more quality time with your family
- Care for a sick family member

Whether you want to nurture your family, support a loved one through a difficult time, or create new memories with those you love, a break offers an opportunity to invest in the well-being and development of others, in addition your own.

TIP

If you don't already have a strong community, this is a great opportunity to build one! You can try volunteering, join a meet up, or take a class to find others who share common interests or values.

Fulfilling your big life goals and dreams

Here comes the one you've likely been waiting for — a career break grants you time to fulfill your big goals and dreams! This benefit often comes to mind when thinking about a break, and with good reason — using your break to realize your goals and dreams is a great use of your time.

You'll need more than the annual allotment of paid time off to live out your big travel fantasies, finally write that novel, or to dive into entrepreneurship. Taking a break provides you with the space you need to make these amazing things happen.

If you've been working for a while, you likely have a backlog of goals you want to pursue, places you want to see, and dreams you want to realize. It's easy to fall into the trap of thinking that taking a career break is irresponsible. You might even feel guilty about leaving your job to relax, have fun, and live a (mostly) care-free life. But taking a break to go after your dreams and goals is actually a powerful way to celebrate and honor your life. It would actually be irresponsible to never explore your potential and aim for big goals, because you were too busy maintaining the status quo. You have to make the most of your one precious life.

Using a break to go after your dreams creates pivotal moments — the kind that will play on the highlight reel of your life. You can scratch items off your bucket list, relocate somewhere new (temporarily or permanently), start a new a career, study abroad, and so much more. The possibilities are truly endless.

If you're in need of inspiration, here are examples of some epic experiences my clients have had while on a career break:

>> Moving across the country and starting a new career

>> Writing a novel that gets interest from publishers

>> Completing a Spanish language immersion in Guatemala, while living with a host family

>> Becoming a certified yoga teacher at a retreat in Bali

>> Launching a travel blog for mid-life women

>> Hiking 400 miles of the Camino de Santiago in Spain

>> Watching the world cup in Buenos Aires as Argentina wins

>> Fostering a newborn, with hopes for adoption

>> Moving to France to study abroad for a year (in their late 30s)

>> Starting an animal sanctuary for aged animals

ANECDOTE

One of my clients dreamed of living in the Pacific Northwest. She'd spent her life in Texas, where the rest of her immediate family resided, but longed to give this new location a try. Although her initial thoughts about what to do on her break involved elaborate travel experiences, she soon realized that she really wanted to use this time to move to Seattle. So she sold her house, packed up her pet, and relocated. Being on a break gave her 10 months to explore the city at a leisurely pace, make new friends, and have a comfortable homebase for her smaller career break adventures. When it was finally time to return to work, she landed multiple interviews, accepted a new job, and started her third career in a matter of weeks.

Boosting Your Professional Success

This might be the most surprising benefit when it comes to taking a career break. Thinking about a break might induce panic, as you imagine struggling to find a good job when your break is over — this is a common career break fear. But actually, it's the opposite: Taking a well-designed career break can be one of the best career moves you'll ever make. Truly. And in this section, I share several specific ways it can contribute to your professional success, whether you return to the same career or venture into something new.

Exploring new career possibilities

If you've been struggling with professional discontent, boredom, or a foreboding sense that your current path isn't heading in the right direction, you're not alone — more than half of my clients listed career misalignment as a reason for taking a break. A career break is the perfect way to explore your options. You can use it to try new things, pivot your career trajectory, and ultimately land a better-suited career, role, or opportunity when it's over.

TIP

If you want to explore a new career path, here are five ways you can approach this while on a break:

>> **Dabble in your interests and passions.** Use this time to lean into things you're good at and enjoy doing. Hone your skills and explore how you might turn this into a side hustle, new business, or freelance opportunity. *Example: Start an Etsy shop to experiment with selling your creations.*

>> **Network with old and new contacts.** Being on a break makes you a very interesting person to catch up with — use this to your advantage! You can ask for coffee chats with people you admire and enjoy or those doing cool and interesting things. You'll expose yourself to new paths and roles. *Example: Send a personal thank you note to a podcast host or author that you admire and request a brief chat to learn more about their journey.*

>> **Try a new workstyle/lifestyle.** If you're curious about starting a new business, becoming a freelancer, going fully remote to become a digital nomad, or testing the waters of semi-retirement, a break provides time to explore these new workstyles and lifestyles. *Example: If you're interested in freelancing, pitch yourself on websites like Upwork and notify friends and old colleagues that you're currently open to work.*

>> **Take a course or get a certification.** Hone your skills and talents by taking courses or gaining a certification. You can expand your current career options, pivot into an adjacent career, or open a new avenue of income starting your own business. *Examples: Take a bookkeeping course to add to your accounting knowledge and explore bookkeeping for new entrepreneurs as a side hustle; complete a Spanish immersion to create new opportunities abroad in your original career.*

>> **Travel to new places.** If travel is on your career break wish list, leave time for meeting new people! It's often easier to do while traveling — people are more open to chatting with strangers and making time for spontaneous conversation. This can expose you to new ideas and approaches to making money. It can also expand your network, which might be very beneficial down the road. *Example: While on a local walking tour, chat up the person next to you and learn more about their interests and travels.*

WARNING

While pursuing new career options might be a key part of your career break plan and one of your four themes (see Chapter 4 to learn more about themes), don't jump into this at the beginning of your break. You need adequate time to decompress, recover, and have fun before launching into a career exploration; otherwise, you'll jeopardize receiving the full benefit of this experience.

ANECDOTE

One of my clients pursued her acting dream while working a demanding corporate job at a Fortune 100 company. One of the big motivations for her career break included time to go all in on her dream of becoming a full-time actor. Regardless of how it works out, she planned to use her break to take her best shot.

Returning to work even better than before

For some, taking a career break evokes fears of getting "rusty" and falling behind on relevant trends. They worry this time will mean re-entering the job market with a professional deficit. But the opposite is actually true — a thoughtfully designed break increases your professional value. Think about it this way — who wouldn't want to hire a happier, well-rested, more motivated, more inspired version of you? You'll return ready and excited to dive back in, bringing innovative ideas and new skills with you.

Instead of focusing on the areas in which you aren't keeping up with your peers, it's important to consider all the ways you'll be zooming past them. Healing burnout, recharging your batteries, acquiring new skills, enhancing your existing skillset (upskilling) and expanding your perspective all mean that you'll have more to give and to share — more energy, innovative and creative solutions, better approaches, etc.

TIP

If your profession is becoming redundant due to new and emerging technologies, you can use a break to future proof your career by acquiring new skills and/or enhancing existing ones. This can expand your future career opportunities and possibilities.

Taking a break is a demonstration of courage. With all those career break adventures under your belt, you'll likely be the most interesting person in the room. You'll easily stand out in a crowd of job applicants, and your break experiences will provide fun and easy topics for interviews and colleague conversations. It will make it even easier to connect with others and offer a unique perspective on things. If you were struggling with misalignment and/or burnout in your last role, a break can also help you refresh your personal brand and emerge as a new version of yourself.

For this very reason, I returned from my break and received five exciting job offers in just five weeks:

>> A job that offered a 30 percent raise and promotion from my prior one

>> A career change opportunity as a flight attendant

>> A job in my dream industry (natural and organic products)

>> An opportunity to relocate closer to my family

>> A part-time, remote job that would allow me to pursue my interests and create alternative sources of income

Many career breakers return to better work opportunities after their break. They feel clear on who they are and what they want — they're no longer willing to settle.

Having a more enjoyable and harmonious work–life blend

This is one of the most invaluable benefits of taking a break, because it can positively affect and improve the rest of your life. A break will teach you a lot about your values and priorities, especially with regard to how you spend your time. After you've experienced the deep joy and peace that a career break can offer, you'll be very selective about what constitutes a worthy sacrifice.

A break provides a fresh start as you return to the working world and the chance to design a healthier and more balanced life. Admittedly, you'll have less free time once your break ends, but you can bring those healthy habits and supportive routines into your new chapter. Add in the new interests and passions you've nurtured and the personal relationships that you've deepened, and you're set up for a more harmonious and well-blended life.

DEFINING WORK–LIFE BLEND

One of my clients introduced me to the term "work–life blend." They offered it as an alternative to the commonly used "work–life balance." Work–life blend suggests an integration of the different aspects of our lives instead of a stark separation of them. This approach is more expansive and permissive. It offers a holistic perspective of how the important parts of your life are being included, instead of a weekly tally of hours spent on personal matters versus hours spent working. As you prepare to return from a break, it's more realistic to aim for a healthy mix and integration of priorities than a perfect weekly distribution of your personal and professional commitments.

As you begin the process of returning to work, you can search for opportunities that support your ideal work–life blend. You can find options that are more engaging, fulfilling, and aligned. Your break will demonstrate that when you meet your own needs, everyone around you benefits, and this will make it easier to avoid losing yourself in your work, no matter how meaningful it is. It will also inspire you to continue prioritizing your own well-being and other aspects of your life, such as your health, relationships, and personal growth. You'll enter your next chapter feeling empowered and have a deeper sense of fulfillment.

ANECDOTE

One of my sabbatical clients started her break unconvinced of the benefits. Her default mode was to put everyone else's needs first, and because she strongly believed in the mission of the non-profit where she worked, she found herself feeling burned out by this approach. Once her break began, she pursued new interests (like making pottery), started supporting her well-being, and deepened her connections with others. Her time off left her energized and in great spirits. She felt protective over the balance she'd worked hard to reclaim and so she returned to work better equipped to maintain a healthier and happier work–life blend.

Chapter **3**

Determining whether a Break Is an Option

It can feel luxurious to imagine an extended break filled with rest and freedom. But the reality of the effort and finances required to make a break happen may create some angst as you wrestle with the question, "Is taking a break really something I can do?" In this chapter, I help you analyze your situation and explain key steps that will help you make an informed decision about taking a break.

After reading this chapter, you'll be able to assess your current situation and understand if a break is feasible, and you'll have a better understanding of the risks involved. If all signs point to "yes" but you're feeling terrified at the idea of taking a break, in the last section of this chapter, I describe how to manage those big fears so you can make a brave decision.

TIP

If a break feels impossible, please resist the urge to give up without exploring the possibility. Of my clients who were undecided about taking a break when they hired me, 55 percent felt a break might be impossible. They each went on to create a life-enhancing break.

Can you really take a break? Let's find out!

Assessing Your Current Situation

"There's no way I can take a break" is a common reaction when people first consider the idea. In fact, I initially had a similar response, as did many of my clients. But a career break is more feasible than you might think.

As you work through the activities in this chapter, you'll collect key pieces of information that will help you determine if a career break is an option for you.

Whether you're unsure of taking a break or already know you want one, this section helps you reflect on your current situation so you can make a regret-proof decision.

Knowing your why

Your first step to determine if a career break is right for you is getting grounded in why you want to take a break. "Knowing your why" means understanding your reasons for taking a break — why you feel like you want or need this experience. Having this knowledge is an important step that will become your foundation for making a good decision.

Chapter 2 explores many of the amazing benefits that come with taking a break, but there are also risks involved, which I discuss in the "Examining the Risks of a Career Break" section later in this chapter. Knowing your why helps you determine if taking a break is worth the risk and sacrifice that may be required and gives you more perspective as you evaluate your options to make this big decision.

TIP

When you move into the planning stage (Part 2 of this book), you find out how to distill your reasons down to a clear and succinct purpose statement for your career break. If you struggle to articulate your why in one or two simple sentences, see Chapter 4 for two questions that will help you create a clearer why and develop your career break purpose statement.

TIP

When it comes to understanding why you want to take a break, it's sometimes easier to start with what's missing or isn't working in your life right now. This approach highlights the gaps that a career break could help you fill. In the next section, I share an activity to uncover this important information and get clearer on your why.

Reflecting on your life and measuring your satisfaction

If you want to thoroughly assess your situation, start by reflecting on what is and isn't working in your life right now. Getting clear on what you'd like to change or improve helps you understand whether a break could be a satisfying solution and evaluate its potential impact on your life and well-being. The following activity leads you through a self-reflection on several important aspects of your life and helps you assess your satisfaction with each.

ACTIVITY

Work your way through the aspects of life listed here and rate each one based on your current satisfaction level, with 1 being completely dissatisfied and 10 being completely satisfied. After you score each aspect, go back through the list and describe what each category would have to be like for you to score it a 10. This activity uncovers what's working well and what's not, and the difference between your current reality and your ideal vision reveals what's missing or could be improved in your life. With this information, you can better evaluate whether a break is right for you or a different solution may be a better fit (alternatives are covered later in this chapter).

>> Career
>> Community
>> Friends and Family
>> Fun
>> Health
>> Learning
>> Money
>> Romance

Evaluating your work situation

When considering a career break, it's helpful to step back and examine your current work situation objectively. This approach helps you avoid making a rash decision.

For example, it's normal to want to hit the "eject" button, when you're exhausted or feeling frustrated with a role, project, or manager. While a break might be what you need, it's also possible that a long vacation or an honest conversation with your manager could get you back on track. On the flip side, you might be unaware of or ignoring a work situation that's sending your happiness, health, and satisfaction into decline. In both cases, an objective assessment will help you make an informed decision about your next step.

It's also possible that you really enjoy your job, your team, and your current work environment but still feel ready for a break. That's perfectly fine! You don't need to be in a toxic work situation to justify taking a break, but evaluating the situation can still be a helpful exercise because it may influence the timing of your break.

ACTIVITY

In the previous section, you rated the overall level of your current career satisfaction. Now, you'll dive deeper to get a better sense of what is and isn't working with the following activity:

1. List the things that you enjoy about your situation.

What do you like about your current work situation?

Examples: compensation, values alignment, colleagues and team members, use of your talents, engagement and interest in the work you do, work location (in office or remote)

2. List the things that you don't enjoy about your situation.

What things are contributing to your dissatisfaction?

Examples: difficult manager, lack of autonomy, values misalignment, commute, disinterested in the work you do, lack of impact

3. Determine your priorities.

As you review your lists from steps 1 and 2, circle your top priorities. Reflect on them and see what you notice.

For example, maybe the pros numerically outweigh the cons, but the cons have a bigger impact on your happiness and well-being. Review the life assessment activity in the previous section for additional help.

4. Reflect on your career goals and aspirations.

Have you achieved what you set out to do? Are you making progress? If not, be curious about why.

For example, are your interests and values pulling you toward a different path? Do you need more time to meet these goals before you'll feel ready for a break? If you've met your goals, would you feel at peace with leaving for a break?

5. **Revisit your vision of success.**

What does your current vision of success include and exclude? Does your current work situation align with that vision? Does it align with your desired lifestyle?

For example, if your vision of success includes ample time to connect with loved ones, does your current situation provide this? Review the life assessment activity in the previous section for additional help.

6. **Evaluate your current stress level and well-being.**

Does your current work situation compromise either of these? If so, explore what you would need to bring them back into balance.

For example, you might need to fully disconnect, email and all, for two weeks. Or maybe you need to block time on your calendar for a daily workout.

7. **Review your accomplishments and contributions.**

If you're an overachiever, you might tend to gloss over your achievements and roll right into your next challenge. Take time to reflect on all that you've done and contributed in your current work situation. Celebrate your wins and consider whether you're feeling ready for a change or in need of a pause.

ACTIVITY

Now that you have a more objective and comprehensive sense of your work situation, it's time to answer a few questions that will help you determine whether a break is an option. *Note:* Your answers to the following questions are just one piece of the puzzle — continue on with this chapter to collect the remaining pieces.

>> Would you be risking as much as you initially thought by taking a break? Why or why not?

>> Are there any places in your life where you see a significant upside to taking a break? If so, where?

>> Do you feel it's worth staying in your current position a while longer? If so, why?

>> Professionally speaking, what would you need to feel ready to take a break?

Clarifying your financial situation

Money is one of the biggest obstacles people face when deciding to take a break. No matter your financial situation, it's likely that having enough money to afford a break is a big concern. For example, if you've saved enough to fund a break, it can feel challenging to part with consistent income and to justify spending your nest egg. On the other hand, you might be far away from the amount of money you'd need to pay for a break and feel like this dream is out of reach. No matter where you fall, I have good news — taking a career break is more possible than you may think!

If you're thinking, "I can't afford a break," it's possible the thought is based more on fear than on reality. That's totally normal, and making a good decision requires doing the work to get clear on your financial situation. Simply put, you need to focus on the facts — that is, know your numbers.

WARNING

Each person's financial situation is unique, so it's important to consider all of the relevant factors before arriving at your final number.

Your answer will be influenced by your particular circumstances. Make sure to consider the following:

>> Are you single or partnered?

>> If you have a partner, will they contribute while you're on break? Or if you're the primary earner, what will the impact of a break be on the household?

>> Do you have children? If so, you'll need to factor in their financial needs as well.

>> Do you plan to travel? If so, will the countries be more expensive or less expensive than your current homebase on average?

>> How long do you intend to be on a break?

>> Will you have a house payment? Or will you move in with friends or family at a significantly reduced cost?

ANECDOTE

As a helpful anchor point, my clients spent an average of $3,650 USD per month while on a break. This average is based on a mix of household types, travel and non-travel breaks, and varying durations. The minimum was $1,250 per month and the maximum was $8,300 per month.

Use the following steps to collect critical pieces of information and determine if a break is a financially plausible option.

1. Examine your savings.

- How much do you currently have in your non-retirement savings? Is it enough for a break? If not, how much more do you need to save?
- Add any additional savings you would accrue if you took a break (for example, severance, PTO payout, selling belongings you'll no longer need, tax refund).

2. Review your current budget.

- Estimate your average monthly savings. To calculate: monthly post-tax income – all monthly expenses = monthly savings
- Track all of your expenses (down to the dollar) for one month. Don't change your habits, just notice where your money is currently going. You'll learn two important things: how much you would need to cover your monthly expenses while on a break and where there might be room to change your habits and save more money.
- Brainstorm ways to reduce your monthly expenses to reach your goal more quickly (for example, getting a roommate, eating out less, reducing your travel expenses).

3. Include potential income from other sources.

Consider other sources of income you might generate during your break (investment income, rental income, freelance work or consulting fees)

4. Analyze your debt situation.

Review your debt obligations to understand what you owe and your monthly requirements while on a break. Pay attention to interest rates to understand how changing your payments could affect your overall debt and consider strategies like refinancing, consolidation, deferment, or forbearance, if necessary.

5. Consider the potential impact on your long-term financial goals.

While it's possible that you can return to a great financial situation post-break (because of a raise or better benefits), it's important to consider how forgoing an income and spending money for a break could impact your long-term financial goals (for example, a reduction in retirement savings and investment opportunities or extending your debt repayment schedule).

6. Talk to a professional financial advisor.

Speaking to a professional can yield additional insight into the specifics of your situation. You don't want to outsource your decision to someone else, but a professional can provide input that helps inform your decision.

If you don't like the picture this assessment has painted, don't worry! Chapter 5's "Affording a Career Break" will help you find ways to afford your break, including how to save for a break much faster. There are many ways to improve your financial situation to afford a break. You can create better spending habits to save more each month or change your circumstances to lower your cost of living. It's possible to take a break even when you have debt. For example, I started my break with more than $42,000 in student loans and was able to pay them off in full just two years after finishing my break.

ANECDOTE

When I started saving for a break, I only had $1,500 in my bank account. I started shopping with a grocery list, buying things on sale, and eating out less to save money. I also moved into a new apartment to share my expenses with a roommate. And when I received lump sums (such as tax refunds and company bonuses), I put that money toward my career break savings. In just 18 months, I saved $40,000 and was able to quit my job and begin a 20-month career break.

ANECDOTE

One of my clients had a good job but very little savings when she began planning for a break. Realizing she needed to save more money each month to reach her goal, she made the big decision to move in with her parents. Although she was initially resistant to this idea, she realized it would help her reach her goal much more quickly. When she had to take an unexpected medical leave six months later, she was able to start her break nine months sooner than she'd planned because of this money-saving decision.

REMEMBER

Please don't feel discouraged if you don't have enough savings to take a break right now. Knowledge is power, and knowing exactly where you are and how far you have to go is very helpful for reaching your goal. And if you complete this financial assessment and realize you do have enough to take a break, I hope you'll give yourself permission to seriously consider the option.

Considering the alternatives

After reviewing your work and financial situations, you might realize that you want a change, but a break isn't the right solution. Consider other alternatives. By working through the earlier sections in this chapter to gain an objective perspective on your situation, you'll have the information you need to determine your best option.

If you're in need of some inspiration, here are a few ideas to consider. Use your creativity to adapt them to work for you and your unique situation:

>> **Review your employee handbook.** Make sure you're educated on your company-provided leave of absence options such as FMLA leave, sabbatical, and voluntary leave of absence. You may be able to take one of these shorter unpaid and company-approved breaks that will permit you to return to your job afterward.

>> **Change your work circumstances.** Consider changing whatever isn't working (apply for a new role, switch to a new company, or move to a new location). Brainstorm options that will allow you to create the change you desire (negotiate a raise, hire a career coach to help you find a new job, ask to go fully remote if you'd like to become a digital nomad).

>> **Make a pivot.** You can change careers, acquire new skills, or gain a certification to expand your career possibilities and/or increase your earnings potential. If you desire a change in lifestyle, you can consider freelancing, consulting, starting a side hustle, or going part-time for more time or location independence.

>> **Take a short break.** Consider an extended vacation or staycation to give yourself several weeks to recover or pursue a personal goal. If you need more time than your standard annual allotment allows, consider requesting unpaid time off to extend your time.

WARNING

If you've been thinking about a break for years but always default to alternative solutions without a lasting improvement, it could be time to seriously consider a break. If you decide to move forward with another alternative approach, be sure to have a plan for ensuring this time creates a better outcome.

Examining the Risks of a Career Break

There's a ton of upside to taking a career break, personally and professionally, but it would be reckless for me to write a book about career breaks and not address the potential downside, too. In this section, I share five big risks you'll need to face when you decide to take a break.

REMEMBER

Please don't feel defeated as you move through this list. Thought-fully designing your break (as Chapter 4 explains) will help you significantly minimize your risk. Instead, keep an open mind and focus on ways to mitigate the risks that concern you. They don't have to be dealbreakers, but it's important to consider the potential risks when deciding if a break is right for you. Plus, considering the risks will help you plan for them accordingly.

Many of my clients had big responsibilities when they decided to take a break. Figure 3-1 illustrates the most common respon-sibilities they faced while taking a break. Forty-four percent had at least three major responsibilities to manage when taking a break.

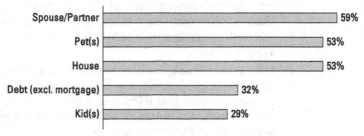

FIGURE 3-1: The most common responsibilities managed while on a break.

Falling behind financially

For many people, taking a career break will result in lost income for the length of time they're not working (exceptions include those who've received severance packages and/or unemployment benefits). But beyond the immediate loss of income, there are also longer-term risks to consider. Here I list four ways you might fall behind financially if you decide to take a break, as well as some possible solutions to help minimize the risk:

>> **Shrinking your overall savings.** The money you'll spend on a break will reduce the cash you have available for emergencies like home repairs and medical issues and for big expenses like buying a car. Although you can definitely rebuild your savings when you return to work, it's important to consider the consequences of a temporarily diminished savings account.

Pad your career break budget with a cushion for emergencies. For example, you can add an extra $5,000 to $10,000 to your budget to cover unforeseen expenses.

>> **Pausing your retirement contributions.** Whether you contribute to a 401(k), IRA, or some other retirement vehicle, taking a break will likely mean pausing your contributions. The months (or years) of missed contributions and compounding interest could mean retiring with less than you would have otherwise.

If you're afraid of falling short of your retirement goal, consider a budget that will allow for catch-up contributions to be made when you start working again.

>> **Missing out on investment opportunities.** Forgoing your income means having fewer resources to pursue investment opportunities like purchasing investment properties and investing in the stock market. During this time, you could lose out on potential gains.

If there's a big investment you'd like to make, consider whether making that investment before starting your break could yield passive income that will support your break.

>> **Lowering your compensation.** It's possible that returning to work after a break could mean receiving a smaller compensation package. While you might be fine with this, it's definitely a point to consider, especially if you have bills and other financial obligations that require a higher salary.

Use your career break as an opportunity to reduce your spending and re-evaluate your financial obligations to create a more sustainable lifestyle. Also, know that it's possible to re-enter the workforce with a pay increase and enhanced benefits; many of my clients have returned to better salaries upon ending their break.

Falling behind professionally

One of the most obvious risks of taking a break is falling behind in your career. With all the effort you've put in and the sacrifices you've made, it can feel scary to consider walking away from work, even temporarily, and possibly jeopardizing your progress. To help you think through the potential impact a break can have on your career momentum, here are five professional risks to consider:

>> **Becoming rusty at your job.** Spending a significant amount of time away from work and focused on other things can leave you feeling rusty upon your return to the office. Some of the tools you previously used with ease will feel clunky as you get back into the swing of things.

After a few weeks, you'll likely find that the ease returns. Plus, it's possible that the time away will give you a new perspective and the inspiration to create new approaches and solutions.

>> **Falling out of the loop.** As you disconnect from work and shift your attention to other things, you may fall out of the loop on significant industry news and trends that surfaced after your break began. You'll have to spend time catching up to offer thoughtful leadership.

You can use the last part of your break (the re-entry period covered in Chapter 4) to start catching up with the latest news and trends, making for a smoother transition. And because job duties aren't yet competing for your time, you may find it easier to be inspired with new ideas as they relate to this information.

>> **Becoming irrelevant.** When you're out of sight, it's possible that you'll fall out of mind, too, which could mean missing out on exciting opportunities that you're qualified for and interested in.

Being brave enough to take a break sets you apart and can make it easier to become top of mind again when you're ready to return to work. You'll come back with a fresh perspective and many great stories that you can use to snag new opportunities.

>> **Returning to a lower position.** It's possible that the timing and options available when you're ready to return to work will require you to make a lateral move or possibly even a temporary step down, when you might have otherwise been promoted or had an opportunity to step into a higher role.

When it comes to your career, you're playing the long game. Roles that might be considered below your experience and skillset are temporary and can provide a chance for you to shine and eventually leap ahead.

>> **Missing out on promotion opportunities.** If you're planning to take a sabbatical and promotions are limited in your company or industry, you may miss out on a round of promotions while away on a break. If your company has few opportunities, this could create a significant delay in your advancement.

Promotions aren't guaranteed, so delaying your break for a potential opportunity that doesn't come through can be very disappointing. It's also possible that a well-designed break can provide the edge you need to land a better opportunity once you return.

Feeling very uncomfortable

I won't sugarcoat this next one: You're going to feel very uncomfortable at certain points of your break experience. Taking a break means taking an unconventional approach to life, which will require that you embrace a lot of uncertainty.

Here are a few career break moments that might push you into feeling deeply uncomfortable:

>> Sharing your news with a loved one who doesn't approve of your decision

>> Telling a stranger that you're on a career break

>> Learning about a peer's promotion or new job while you're on a break

>> Struggling with the unease of boredom and the absence of distractions

>> Wanting to label yourself as "lazy" on a day of rest

>> Re-examining your self-identity and detaching it from the work you do

REMEMBER

At some point, you will likely doubt your decision and perhaps question your sanity. But this is actually a good thing! Comfort is not a place that leads to growth and self-improvement. On a break, you will deconstruct and replace old labels and beliefs that don't support the life you want. You will question many things — and because of this, you will find many new and incredible answers.

A career break provides an opportunity for growth, which by its very nature is often uncomfortable. But as you learn to accept the discomfort, you'll create space for a more confident, balanced, and energized you to emerge.

Losing your employer benefits

Depending on where you live, leaving your job may mean losing the benefits that came along with it. The level of risk attached to this loss will be specific to you and your unique situation. Employer-provided benefits can be a big convenience, so you'll need to be prepared to manage this loss.

If you reside in the United States, the most common benefits that you'll lose access to include the following:

>> **Health Insurance:** Your health insurance coverage will end during your final month of employment. If you need to keep your coverage to maintain certain physicians or medication, you can consider an extension of coverage with COBRA. More details about your options while on a break are covered in Chapter 8.

>> **Retirement benefits:** You'll no longer receive benefits like a 401(k) match once you leave. If you have a 401(k), also be sure to check your company's vesting rules to understand what happens if you're not fully vested when you leave.

>> **Other benefits:** Depending on the other benefits your employer provides, you might lose access to disability and life insurance benefits and other benefits like stock options and public transit passes.

If you're unwilling or unable to let go of these benefits but feel strongly that you need a break, you can pursue a company-approved leave of absence like FMLA or a sabbatical to retain your benefits during your time off.

Receiving judgment from others

Some people will judge your decision to take a break, and those disapproving few will probably be quite vocal about it. Your decision will challenge their beliefs about what's possible. If you quit your job to take a break and don't suffer because of it, you will challenge their belief that doing such a thing would be irresponsible and end in disaster for them. They might have a lot of fear around making such a decision for themselves and, thus, are unconsciously projecting those fears onto you.

This is an unavoidable part of living an authentic life. You will get pushback when you break from the status quo. But valuing others' opinions over your own results in living a life that doesn't suit you.

On the plus side, you will likely face far fewer naysayers than curious onlookers and encouraging supporters. Those around you may not fully understand the path you've chosen, but they will feel inspired by the courage you have to go after your dreams and prioritize your well-being. Your belief in this decision will influence how others perceive your break. If you believe it's an amazing opportunity — they will, too.

Acknowledging the Risks of Not Taking a Break

It's time to talk about the secret sauce to making powerful decisions: zooming out to see the whole picture. Big, important decisions can feel terrifying when you first consider them. Your brain will want to catalogue everything you could lose if you make a change, but it can easily forget the other half of the story: what you stand to gain if you do make a change.

If you've considered the risks that come with taking a break (see the "Examining the Risks of a Career Break" section earlier in this chapter), it's time complete the picture and examine the risks of *not* taking a break. Chapter 2 explores the benefits of a career break in detail to help you understand the risks of *not* taking a break, but here I give you a high-level view of them. I know that it can feel scary to imagine taking this leap, but after reflecting on the risks in this section, you might find it scarier to imagine your life without a break.

Jeopardizing your well-being

If you're burned out, physically unwell, or just exhausted and in need of restoration, continuing to push through without a significant break could jeopardize your long-term health and delay your much-needed healing. Ignoring your need for rest and time to address your physical challenges could exacerbate your condition and significantly increase your recovery time.

Beyond your physical health, it's important to support and nourish your emotional and mental health. If you're feeling overwhelmed and in need of a reset or are recovering from a deep and painful loss, taking time to heal will be critical to your overall well-being. Living in a state of chronic stress will negatively impact your health and put you at risk for developing or worsening anxiety and depression.

Even if you're not currently struggling with your health, a break provides an opportunity to reset your daily habits and create a healthier lifestyle. And if you stay consistent, you can carry this healthier lifestyle into the future, potentially adding years and quality to your life.

WARNING

Not addressing your health concerns will put you at risk for being forced into a break. It can be tempting to go for "just one more" milestone before slowing down to take care of your health, but I assure you — it's way more enjoyable to head into a break willingly and proactively than to end up there by surprise and against your will.

Missing out on new experiences and better opportunities

Life can be delightful, but sometimes we need more time and space to find this delight. A career break offers you the opportunity to do things that your annual paid time off allotment could never allow. Here are some examples:

>> **Crossing items off your bucket list and living your dreams.** Hiking Kilimanjaro, living in France, writing a novel, learning a language — you aren't going to die wondering "what if"; you'll be out there fulfilling your dreams. Your once-in-a-lifetime experiences will produce memories that belong on the highlight reel of your life.

>> **Exploring new career options and ways of working.** Whether you test out starting a business, explore your passions to create a new career opportunity, or live like a digital nomad, a break is a chance to break the mold and create a new career path that's even more aligned with your interests and values than what you're currently pursuing.

>> **Realizing your full potential and connecting with your zone of genius.** You can share your unique gifts with the world and light yourself up in the process. You can explore self-development and better align your life with your values and passions, becoming more of the person you want to be (braver, calmer, happier, and so on).

>> **Attracting opportunities that are beyond your wildest imagination.** It's hard to imagine the great things waiting for you beyond a break, because they might seem impossible right now. To help you get started, here are real-life examples of opportunities my clients and I have experienced because of taking a career break:

- Being featured in *Forbes* as a career break coach
- Becoming an author
- Starting a travel blog that inspires others
- Becoming a digital nomad and valued resource for others who want to do the same
- Landing a dream job that once felt out of reach
- Starting an animal sanctuary
- Accepting a role within an exciting startup business

ANECDOTE

After returning from my break, I paid off my remaining $42,000 of student loan debt in just two years and became a certified life coach. I launched my business as a career break coach soon after and within several months had my story featured in *Forbes*. Becoming debt-free and being in *Forbes* were two incredible accomplishments that would never have happened if I'd stayed stuck in my unfulfilling career and decided not to take a career break.

Living a life that's out of balance

REMEMBER

When overworking and a lack of balance become normalized, it's hard to see the toll they're taking on you. Like they say, "a fish doesn't know it's in water until it's out of water." It takes removing yourself from your current situation to gain the perspective you need to see what's really going on.

When you're on a break, you'll experience life on the opposite side of the spectrum: freedom and autonomy, meeting your own needs, connecting with loved ones, healthier habits, enjoying a slower pace, and the absence of urgency. Life on this side can be pretty darn delightful, and when it's time to rejoin the workforce, you won't be willing to give it all up and settle for a frazzled and unfulfilling life.

This newfound perspective will help you make better choices about how and where you invest your time. You won't want to resume the harmful habits and behaviors that led you to want a break in the first place. Not taking a break would mean never gaining the perspective necessary to improve your quality of life and skew toward a more balanced life.

Putting it all into perspective

The following activity can help you objectively examine the risks you face if you *don't* take a break. This information will help you determine if a break is your best option:

ACTIVITY

1. **List five reasons why it might be a bad idea to stay in your current situation.**

   For example, I'm feeling disengaged and might jeopardize my reputation; I'm burned out and can't sustain this pace; my body will crash, and I will be forced to take a leave of absence; I will continue to feel isolated. etc.

2. **List five positive outcomes that could occur if your break is successful.**

   For example, I will have a healthier and happier life; I will strengthen my relationship with my family; I will start a new career that feels joyful and aligns with my values. etc.

3. **List five resources you already have available to support you in taking a break.**

For example, my strong network of supporters, my MBA degree, 15 years of solid work experience and performance, a $30,000 nest egg, the support of my loved ones and family. etc.

Making a Brave Decision

When you assess your current situation, examining the risks of both taking a break and not taking a break, you discover the important aspects of determining if a career break is an option for you. Before you make the decision to start planning and mapping out a break or putting this idea on the shelf for a while, I want to share two helpful concepts that will support you in making a brave decision: examining the truth and collecting proof.

There's always an element of fear involved in making a brave decision. And while you can't eliminate it altogether (oh, the limitations of being a human), you can manage your fear to make a decision that serves your best interest.

IS FEAR DRIVING YOUR CAR?

Navigating life is like driving a car with your fears locked inside. At times, your fears might lean over from the passenger seat to grab the wheel because they're convinced you're going to crash (that is, fail). Sometimes, your big fears might even kick you out of the driver's seat altogether and completely take over.

While your fears might be well intentioned (they're just trying to keep you safe), letting them take the wheel is not how you create a life that feels miraculous, adventurous, or fulfilling. If you want to live a life that is rich and rewarding, you'll have to snatch that wheel back.

To do this, you need to gather up your fears and force them to the back. From here, they can shout directions and voice concerns when they think you're making a wrong turn. Acknowledging your fears helps you make thoughtful decisions. But buckled into the backseat, your fears will resign themselves to providing guidance but not leadership.

Ultimately, you're the one weighing all of the information and making the final decision (managing your fears). As you consider taking a break, be sure your fears are in the backseat and buckled in tight.

Examining the truth

It's normal to have fears and concerns about taking a career break. It requires living with a lot of uncertainty, which can be thrilling but also terrifying. As you consider your options and determine if a break is right for you, you'll want to examine the truth to help you make a brave and empowered decision.

Brains are tricky things. They like to default to the familiar and comfortable (they love feeling safe), and they'll flood us with fearful thoughts masquerading as facts. If you want to make a powerful decision, you'll need to examine your fears to find the truth. A thoughtful decision requires accessing the part of your brain that isn't hijacked by fear.

An example is that your brain might tell you that you'll never find another job if you take a break, and that might feel like a really likely outcome. You might work in a specialized field or have concerns about the economic forecast. Maybe you struggled to find your current job and expect the same or worse after taking a break. But when you shine the light of truth on this statement, it's highly unlikely. Now, it's possible that you might like your post-break job less than your current one. And it's also possible that it could pay less. But if you needed a job and were able to work, your chances of finding something aren't that bad. So, really, your tension point is settling for a less appealing job instead of never finding another job (which can feel very intense). You might decide this more accurate tension point is still enough reason to pass on taking a break, but you'll make that decision from a more honest place.

Here are two areas to focus on finding the truth:

>> **Knowing your numbers:** Understand what a career break might cost you and how far you currently are from that target amount (see "Assessing Your Current Situation" earlier in this chapter for help with this).

>> **Facing your fears:** Acknowledge your fears and then examine them for veracity. The following activity walks you through facing your fears so you can reveal the truth and make a thoughtful decision.

ACTIVITY

Think about taking a career break as you fill in the blank and list all of the answers that come to your mind: It would be ridiculous for me to take a break because _____.

Next, you need to separate fears from concerns so you can deal with each appropriately. For this exercise, consider your dooms-day scenarios to be fears. They're irrational (not based on facts) and predict a worst-case ending (e.g., I'll go broke; I'll never find another job; etc.). You also consider concerns, which are unan-swered questions that cause you stress (e.g.; I'm not sure what to do about my health insurance; I'm afraid it will be hard to sell my belongings; etc.).

You'll deal with your fears by asking a simple question, such as, "Do I know that this is absolutely true? Could I prove it in a court of law?" For example, you can't prove that you will go broke. In fact, if your finances took a big hit, you could always exit your break sooner than planned and settle for the first job you were offered. It's not ideal, but it's definitely a solid solution to avoid going broke. Now you've broken the spell. The truth might still feel uncomfortable, but you can make an empowered decision about this risk, knowing there are potential solutions.

To manage your concerns, you'll need to seek out information to calm your brain. In the example of worrying about what to do about your health insurance during a break (see "Evaluating your health insurance options" in Chapter 8), you can utilize resources like this book, talk with self-employed friends and family who might have helpful advice, or connect with others who've taken a break to see what solutions they've found. Concerns, like a lack of knowledge about your health insurance options don't have to be dealbreakers. You just need to do a little research to find your answers.

Collecting proof that a break is possible

Another helpful way to manage your fears and concerns is to collect evidence that a career break is possible (and not life-ending). By collecting evidence, you'll start to normalize your goal. It will seem less farfetched with every personal account you hear or read.

LEARNING TO WALK IN A WORLD OF SITTERS

Imagine that you want to learn how to walk, but you currently live in a place where everyone (every single person) can only sit or crawl. Here, it might seem impossible to imagine a life spent on two feet, not to mention having to deal with the embarrassment of falling down over and over again as you learn how to hold your balance. Learning to walk in this environment would be a long and painful process, likely filled with self-doubt.

Now imagine that close by is another place where everyone is walking. In fact, they're walking, running, skipping, and jumping! Immersing yourself in this world makes walking suddenly seem normal (maybe even inevitable). By providing yourself with more evidence that walking is possible, you've started to normalize your goal, which reduces your self-doubt and makes the experience less painful.

By normalizing your goal, you make it less likely that fear will stop you from experiencing the joys of roller skating, strolling the beaches, and so much more.

By surrounding yourself with proof, you'll find it easier to conquer your career break fears and doubts. You'll build your confidence and clear a path to make your success inevitable. When you start to surround yourself with stories and personal accounts of others who've already accomplished a similar goal, everything starts to feel more possible.

TIP

Collecting proof can also lead you down a rabbit hole of fun. Here are several places to search for your career break evidence. You can search terms like "travel," "sabbatical," "digital nomad," and "career breaks" to get started:

>> Blogs

>> Books

>> Friend (or friends of friends)

>> Podcasts

- » Online articles
- » Social media accounts
- » YouTube videos

ANECDOTE

When I took my first career break in 2013, many of these resources didn't exist. But I was desperate for a personal story and someone who could answer my big questions. I shared my goal with my friend circle and was connected to an acquaintance who had recently returned from her 13-month break. Jackpot! I invited her out for a coffee and came prepared with my list of questions. Even though our experiences had some differences (for example, she traveled with her partner, but I would be traveling solo), I found it very helpful and comforting to know someone who'd successfully taken the leap. She also gave me some great long-term travel advice that helped me better prepare for my break.

Planning Your Career Break

Lay the foundation for a successful break, including a smooth re-entry, by developing a supportive mindset and effective structure to map out your break.

See how you can afford a break. Estimate your total cost, develop a comprehensive break budget, and discover ways to save money quickly so you can take a break sooner.

Set a clear career break timeline. Determine a length for your break, choose an ideal start date, and create a simple itinerary for your break.

Chapter **4**

Creating a Career Break Plan

have some great news! There's a way to plan your break that makes the process feel doable, simple, and fun.

In this chapter, you discover this exact process to create a roadmap to a successful experience. You start by building the foundation for success and move on to the secret recipe for designing a regret-proof experience: developing a unique plan to improve your experience and results tenfold!

Understanding the Benefits of a Well-Designed Plan

Having a well-designed career break plan provides a ton of benefits. It can

>> Build your confidence and reduce stress

>> Ensure you have the best outcome possible

- ›› Generate more fun and imagination as you plan
- ›› Help you avoid getting stuck while preparing for a break
- ›› Help you manage fear when facing uncertainty
- ›› Maximize the benefits you receive from a break
- ›› Prevent you from falling into a rut while on a break
- ›› Reduce feelings of confusion and being overwhelmed
- ›› Reduce financial risk and ensure adequate support

This chapter will help you avoid one of the biggest career break planning mistakes you can make: zooming in on the details of your break before you have a solid structure in place. Life will surprise you along your break journey (in good ways and in challenging ways), so you need a sturdy structure to withstand the winds of change that blow your way.

Designing your career break plan is a blend of art and science. You're going to discover the elements you need to create a successful career break structure (the science) and learn how to personalize your plan to meet your specific needs (the art). The activities in this chapter walk you through developing your structure and plan using a straightforward approach that I've honed with dozens of clients.

TIP

Trust yourself as you connect with your vision and desires and resist the urge to overcomplicate your plan. I've distilled this process into simple steps to map out a plan for your break while minimizing the overwhelming feeling.

Setting a Foundation for Success

The most critical part of a successful plan is the structure that holds everything in place. Although many people are inclined to focus on the details when they begin planning, doing so can lead to feeling overwhelmed and a less than optimal experience. The details of your break aren't as significant as the structure itself. A well-designed structure keeps things simple and helps you weather any storms that arise before and/or during your break.

A structure provides clarity and guidance. It's like having guardrails for your break. It keeps you on track and moving in the right direction without being too restrictive or prescriptive about how you will spend your time. Having this structure is essential when life throws you a curveball and you're forced to adapt and adjust your plan (for example, a natural disaster cancels your next trip, a family member has a medical emergency, or you meet someone while traveling and decide to stick around a little longer).

Your first step toward creating the structure for your break is laying a solid foundation. In this section, I explain exactly how to do that.

Regardless of whether you decide to take a break, the structure you're about to create can serve as a north star to guide you toward the life you long to be living. If you decide to take a break, great! You'll be set up for success. And if you decide not to take a break, you'll be much clearer on what you need to adjust to get closer to the life you want.

Determining your best approach

No matter which stage you're currently in, this chapter contains essential information that will help you achieve the best outcome for your break. Make sure you've got the fundamentals down and review the following stages to discover your best approach to navigate this chapter and maximize your break.

Considering a break

If you're undecided about taking a break, this chapter arms you with useful information to help you make your decision and leaves you feeling more grounded about what to expect throughout the process. By completing the activities, you'll become clearer about what you can gain from taking a break and what your ideal break looks like. This clarity will also build excitement and motivation for your career break vision.

Planning a break

If you've made the decision to take a break and are currently in the planning stages, you're reading this at the perfect time! The activities in this chapter aid you in developing the best plan possible without becoming overwhelmed. You'll finish feeling wiser, more prepared, and even more excited about your upcoming break.

Preparing for a break

What an exciting stage! If you've already put a plan together and are currently navigating the logistics of preparing for your break, use this chapter as a checklist to make sure you haven't missed any key steps in building a regret-proof plan. And if you have — don't worry. As you skim through this chapter, you can complete the activities and fold information you glean from them into your plan so you feel more confident and prepared.

Navigating a break

If you're currently on a break — congrats, you did it! I hope you're loving your experience. Use this chapter to clarify your definition of success and alleviate any pain points you may be experiencing. I also encourage you to read the following section, "Preparing mentally for the planning process," to maximize your experience and to check out the "Setting Yourself Up for a Smooth Return to the Workforce" section later in this chapter to proactively plan your re-entry period, so that when the end is near, it'll be smooth sailing into your next chapter.

Returning from a break

If you're near the end of your break, use the information in this chapter to process and reflect on your experience. The "Honing Your Purpose to Clearly Define Success" and "Establishing Themes to Guarantee a Successful Outcome" sections will add depth to how you describe your break to others, including potential future employers. You'll be able to articulate the benefits of your break and ensure a supportive mindset as you navigate the transition. Chapter 13 provides advice for transitioning out of your break and using the re-entry period to create an easier and more successful return to the workforce. If you're already on the hunt for your next role, Chapter 14 will show you how to position your break as an asset and secure your next job.

Preparing mentally for the planning process

You may be wondering, "Can I really do this? Am I making a mistake? How will this all turn out?" Having an empowered mindset —believing in your resiliency and ability to handle challenges and embrace new opportunities — will help you navigate the waves of fear, doubt, and confusion that can arise when planning a break.

These difficult feelings are completely normal and to be expected. The key to managing them is to acknowledge their presence. When you own your feelings and accept them as part of the planning process, you won't waste energy fighting or denying them or feeling badly for having them. Plus, on the bright side, it's likely that these challenging emotions will be overshadowed by waves of excitement, joy, and an unbridled sense of freedom.

TIP

"Right now I'm feeling _____ and that's a right way to feel" is a mantra that allows you to practice acknowledging your feelings when you're experiencing difficult or confronting emotions.

ADOPTING AN EMPOWERED MINDSET FOR THE PLANNING PROCESS

An empowered mindset allows you to feel capable and confident when you're facing challenges or uncertainty, like planning for a career break.

As an example, let's say you suffer from stage fright but want to try acting. So, you sign up for a class but immediately regret your decision and consider dropping out. Your brain wants to focus on the physical discomfort you feel when you think about being on stage, the fear that everyone else will be better than you, and the panic of forgetting your lines. But you can shift into an empowered mindset to achieve your goal. To do this you can focus on

- Believing in yourself and remembering examples of when you tried something new and it went well)

- Changing your perspective (lowering the stakes by reminding yourself that you won't die or suffer physical harm through this experience)

- Giving yourself grace (allowing yourself to be a beginner, realizing that mistakes are part of the learning experience)

- Tapping into your resiliency (acknowledging the discomfort you feel and moving forward anyway)

Directing your attention and energy toward thoughts and actions to positively influence the outcome helps you feel more powerful, capable, and confident.

Your version of success is unique, so your break won't look like anyone else's. Although taking a break means welcoming a fair amount of uncertainty into your life, it also provides an unparalleled amount of freedom.

Leave room to evolve

The best career break plan leaves space for you to grow and evolve and for changes to occur without wrecking your plan. If you've embraced the right mindset, you'll be able to ride the waves of change to an even better destination than the one you'd previously envisioned, instead of allowing unmet expectations to ruin your experience.

The act of planning a break can be life-changing. Getting clear on what you truly want, deprioritizing others' perceptions of you, facing your fears, and not backing down — these actions will trigger growth that compounds. And with this ever-expanding comfort zone and opportunity to discover new strengths and interests, you'll find that your needs and desires will evolve as you move through your break, too. Having a super detailed plan means committing to an itinerary that you designed pre-break, which doesn't leave much room for growth, change, or an upgraded imagination. To experience the best break possible, don't overplan. Leave room in your itinerary so a more healed, restored, and inspired version of you can influence the plan and contribute new and previously unimagined ideas for what to do during the break.

Allow space for big life changes

Whether it's a family crisis, a health issue, an unforeseen financial burden, or just your basic "I don't like this place as much as I thought I would" experience, life will surprise you while you're on a break. Having a rigid plan may make you feel stressed and completely out of control when things change, which can jeopardize your overall experience. Having a solid structure in place means navigating any changes with grace and ease. A break isn't just another vacation. When you take this extended time off, you need to include unscheduled periods of time so you can make any necessary adjustments without ruining your entire plan.

Examining the elements of a successful career break plan

Certain elements are essential for creating a structure that can stand the test of time and help you realize your version of a successful break. They will also help you simplify your vision in moments when the details feel overwhelming so you can keep moving forward.

Unlike other big life goals (for example, finishing grad school or navigating a corporate career), there's no checklist to ensure you're doing it "right" nor a well-worn path to follow when you're planning a break. On a break, you'll be forging your own path and filling in the gaps as you go — you don't have to have it all figured out beforehand. Instead, you can set the stage for a life-changing and life-improving experience by doing the following:

>> **Create a structure and vision for your break:** Elements: purpose, themes, and re-entry period. I discuss these elements in later sections of this chapter.

>> **Have a list of possibilities and big dreams to consider:** Elements: wish list and dream bigger. I discuss these elements in later sections of this chapter.

>> **Set targets for the means to support your plan:** Elements: budget (Chapter 5) and timeline (Chapter 6).

Honing Your Purpose to Clearly Define Success

If you want to have a successful career break experience, you must define what success means to you. Taking a break without a clear understanding of what you want to achieve is like launching an arrow before the target's set up; your chances of hitting the bulls-eye are pretty slim.

To clarify your personal definition of success, you need to understand your career break purpose — your big "why" for taking this break. This structural element is critical for creating a regret-proof experience so you can design your break with the end (achieving your purpose) in mind.

To create a clear, authentic, and motivating purpose, you need to ignore what anyone else thinks success means or looks like; this includes your esteemed peers and loved ones. What matters most is that you're designing a break to meet *your* needs and fulfill *your* vision of success. Living out someone else's vision of success ultimately means failing at your own.

Understanding the power of your purpose

Creating a clear purpose helps you ensure a successful experience, but it's also a critical part of your career break structure because it keeps you motivated to stay on track right from the planning stage all the way through your break experience.

You will face doubt and obstacles on the path to creating a successful break; that's just part of the journey and the human experience in general. When these stressful moments arise, your brain will offer many reasons why you should just give up. It's wired to keep you safe and doesn't want to stray from what's familiar because it equates familiarity with safety and survival. Without a clear purpose, you're much more likely to quit your dream of taking a break or to end your break early. But when you have a clear purpose, the simple truth of why you need and want this break will serve as motivation to move through the difficult moments and overcome any obstacles. You'll be able to navigate the surprises life throws your way without jeopardizing your success.

The following are the three types of surprises (obstacles) that can arise when you're planning for a break:

The good surprises

Some surprises and changes will be positive ones, like

>> Meeting new connections who suggest exciting new ideas you hadn't considered before

>> Pursuing and incorporating a new budding relationship

>> Receiving an unexpected and exciting job opportunity

Wonderful surprises like these can entice you to alter your career break plan or scrap it altogether. In the case of an exciting job offer, do you pass on the offer and stay committed to your break or do you put your idea of taking a break on the shelf and come back to it later? When you're feeling unsure about how to proceed, your purpose helps you determine your next right step. With it, you can assess the trade-offs and reflect on the impact of your decision.

ANECDOTE

Several months into planning and saving for my break, I met a great guy who eventually became my boyfriend. Staying grounded in my purpose helped me navigate the delicate balance between embracing this unexpected development and staying connected to my meaningful mission. It helped me see where there was room to adapt my plan and where I needed to stay the course. I modified some parts to include him but maintained a lot of my solo travel plans and time at home with my family. Having a clear purpose ensured a successful career break experience when my circumstances changed.

The bad surprises

If you're planning and/or saving for a break several months or even several years in advance, it's likely that life will hand you a few unexpected challenges. When you're grounded in your purpose, you won't easily be thrown off course by this. In fact, you'll be able to double down and adapt your plan as necessary to make sure you get the break you need and fulfill your purpose. Having a clear purpose helps you stay connected to your bigger vision and not get thrown permanently off track by obstacles that arise.

ANECDOTE

During the first few months of saving for my break, the tenant in my rental property unexpectedly broke her lease. This development and the subsequent loss of income was temporarily devastating. I had to dip into my career break savings to cover the related expenses. With my big goal of taking a break in jeopardy, I felt disheartened and overwhelmed. I worried it was a sign that I should just give up on my dream. But digging deep and reconnecting to my purpose allowed me to keep going, and two months later, I was back on track and I went on to save $40,000 in less than 18 months.

The catastrophic surprises

While uncommon, it's possible that you may face a life-altering obstacle involving a significant loss (for example, job, marriage, loved one) of some kind. Your purpose will help you consider your options without losing sight of your own needs and desires. Surviving and navigating the subsequent grief that will follow the loss will require you to adapt your plan, but you don't have to let go of your career break dream altogether. You can alter it to meet your new needs and incorporate your old ones as well. This approach will help you achieve the best outcome possible — one that your future self will be incredibly grateful for.

ANECDOTE

My younger brother, Phillip, unexpectedly passed away a week before my break was set to begin. Losing him was incredibly devastating and created a lot of doubt about what to do next. The grief was overwhelming, and I felt torn between the responsibility of heading home to support my family or pushing on to take the break I'd been planning for 18 months. Because I'd done the work to define my purpose, I knew what this break meant to my future self. I could see what was really at stake. So, I made the tough decision to begin my break as planned. Some of my family didn't understand, or agree, with my decision initially, but I was willing to let others be disappointed by my actions so as to not disappoint myself. Having a clear purpose helped me honor my own needs during this difficult time.

Developing your Purpose statement

Reflection and soul searching are key in developing a clear purpose statement. Use the prompts that follow to reveal your own unique purpose for taking a break.

TIP

For the most helpful and complete answers, I recommend journaling your responses to the following prompts as a stream of consciousness. Let your words tumble out and don't edit yourself for grammar or logic. Set a timer for eight minutes and begin! You can type or write your answers — whichever feels best.

ACTIVITY

Answer the following prompts as thoughtfully and completely as possible. When you have your answers, take time to reflect on them and boil them down to a single purpose statement:

>> Why do I want this break so badly?

>> What am I risking if I don't take a break?

>> What would feel like a miracle in regard to this break?

REMEMBER

This process is quite reflective. You may need to revisit the prompts several times and continue refining your answers to arrive at your final purpose statement. You'll know you've nailed it when you read it back, think *Yes!* and feel it light you up and lift your spirits. This level of self-reflection isn't easy, but it will be invaluable in helping you achieve your goal.

Distilling your answer into a succinct purpose statement helps you feel clear about your "why" and makes it easier to articulate and explain to others. When they understand your purpose, they'll be more likely to support you and advocate for you. They'll share your joy and feel excited for the opportunity to live vicariously through you. This makes the adventure fun for everyone!

Examples of career break purpose statements

The most powerful purpose statements are simple, clear, and concise. They boil your truth down to one or two sentences that capture the significance of what a break will offer you.

To inspire you and help you solidify your own purpose statement, I've included a few examples from past clients:

>> Become a woman who lived her wildest dreams instead of letting life happen to her

>> Change the trajectory of my life

>> Discover new dimensions of myself and reconnect with the parts I've lost along the way

>> Fulfill my childhood fantasy of becoming a world-traveler

>> Maximize my quality time with loved ones as we navigate a hard season of life

>> Nourish, honor, and support myself

>> Put myself back into the center of my life

>> Reimagine my life and create a happier and more fulfilling second half

ANECDOTE

My idea to take a break was born from the desire to travel the world for a year and live an adventurous life. But as I reflected on those motivations, I realized my purpose went even deeper: I wanted to change the trajectory of my life. I didn't like nor recognize the life I'd created for myself. My corporate life wasn't a fit, but I was clueless about how to create a sustainable change. I realized a break would allow me to reevaluate my path, expose me to new experiences, and allow me to live some of my biggest and boldest dreams, ultimately helping me create a new and more aligned future for myself.

Establishing Themes to Guarantee a Successful Outcome

Themes are the second structural element that you need to create a regret-proof career break. They represent your deepest needs and desires for this time off. Your purpose is your definition of a successful experience (see the previous section for more about purpose) and your themes are how you'll achieve it. They ensure a break that will fulfill your purpose.

Your themes are the pillars of your break. By establishing and clarifying exactly what you need and want most from this time off, you'll ensure a successful outcome and a life-improving experience. Your themes pave the way for a better life post-break, personally and professionally. They help you recognize where you need to focus your time, energy, and money to get the best results. Diving into a break without them is risky; you may have some fun adventures and experience cool new things but you're likely to return to work still feeling depleted and unfulfilled.

BEWARE OF THE "SEXY CAREER BREAK" TRAP

When it's time to start planning your break, it's easy to fall into the "sexy career break" trap — that is, designing a break that looks great from the outside but doesn't actually provide what you need most.

Social media and the glamorization of international travel can make it seem like a no-brainer to spend the majority of your time and money traveling the world while on a break. It's an obvious way to fill the void of free time with epic once-in-a-lifetime experiences.

Although traveling can be (and often is) part of a successful career break experience, it's not a requirement. If you create a travel-centric break that looks enviable from the outside when you're really feeling burned out, depleted, and confused on the inside, the break isn't going to meet your needs. You'll likely enjoy your career break experience and create special memories, but you won't return feeling restored and ready to navigate your next chapter.

Designing a break concerned with how others will perceive it can lead to your career break downfall. You don't need a drool-inducing itinerary to justify a break. Any break that gives you exactly what you need will create epic results in your life.

If you want to make your break regret-proof and ensure that it's life-improving, design it to meet your deepest needs and desires so you'll return from your break feeling renewed, restored, and motivated to sustain the big changes in your life.

ANECDOTE

When Brittany began planning a sabbatical, she wanted to schedule her break around an international trip. It seemed like a waste to have a few months off and not spend at least some of it abroad. But as we uncovered her purpose and themes, it became clear that travel was a lesser priority and not something to plan her break around. Instead, through the planning process outlined in this chapter, Brittany realized that focusing on her well-being and fostering more connections were her top priorities. And while she didn't end up traveling abroad during her break, she returned to work feeling restored, inspired, and like a new person. Even without the travel, Brittany's break was a big success and a life-changing event.

Themes also help you stay on course when life tosses curveballs your way. When your life gets shaken up (see the good, bad, and catastrophic surprises in the previous section for specific examples), anchoring back into your themes helps you create alternative ways to meet your needs and fulfill your big desires. When life forces you to alter (or cancel) your original plan, it's important to know what you hoped to gain from the experience so you can create a suitable alternative.

For example, let's say you have restoration as one of your themes, and to lean into this theme, you planned a weeklong hiking and camping adventure. But weeks before your trip, you sustain an injury that makes the original plan impossible. Instead of just giving up completely, you can revisit your theme of restoration to create a new possibility. If being in nature was a big part of what felt restorative for you, you could opt to drive to a nearby lake, trail, or park and spend several hours sitting in nature while reading a book, meditating, or listening to a podcast. Whenever plans go awry, themes help you get back on track and make the most of your time.

My clients have navigated a pandemic, divorce, the death of a loved one, exciting job offers, and health crises while on a break. Because they developed clear themes for their break, they were able to pivot and adapt to the new circumstances without sacrificing their success.

Themes are a powerful tool that will help you weather storms of confusion, doubt, and complication. Having clear themes is essential for your success.

Danielle was living her dream, newly on a break and adventuring her way through New Zealand. It was during her three-week trip in 2020 that a COVID-19 lockdown began. She had just 24 hours to decide between returning to the United States and ending her break early or staying in New Zealand for an indefinite lockdown. Ultimately, she chose to return to the United States and finished the rest of her career break confined to her home city. She didn't let this unforeseen development ruin her break. Instead, she pursued experiences like enrolling in an online course on the science of well-being to embrace her theme of self-exploration.

Determining your career break themes

Themes play a crucial role in achieving your desired results. As your career break pillars, they will support your break and hold it up when things get shaky. To ensure a balance and create a sturdy foundation, I recommend setting four themes for your career break.

Whether you're planning to take a break for three months or two years, I've found four to be the magic number when it comes to creating themes (although some of my clients do quite well with just three). Having three to four themes creates a great balance for your break. It offers a diverse and holistic set of areas to address without diffusing your attention or creating a sense of being overwhelmed. It provides a healthy mix to keep you engaged without the risk of juggling too much and losing your sense of priority.

TIP

If you're struggling to reduce your themes to three or four, they might be too granular. Look for a broader commonality that links them. For example, if you have "better sleep" and "healthy eating" on your list, you could combine them into one Theme like "self-care" or "wellness."

WARNING

If you're planning to take an abbreviated break (less than three months), this guideline doesn't apply. Instead, create two or three themes to guide your break. With less time for your break, this approach helps you focus your efforts on fulfilling your purpose and avoiding being overwhelmed.

Because they play such a significant role, you'll want to achieve a balance among your themes. I see several clusters emerge among my clients:

>> Connection and community

>> Creating a new path or lifestyle

>> Exploration and learning

>> Fun, joy, and play

>> Rest, healing, and recovery

Don't forget to add the fun! If you're simultaneously feeling burned out and worried about what will come after your career break, you might overlook the importance and desire for more fun and joy during your break. Whatever your specific theme (fun, joy, adventure, lightness, play, and so on), be sure to include one that allows you to reconnect to your more creative, fun, and playful side that's likely been neglected for a long time.

TIP

A helpful rule of thumb is to keep your themes short (one- or two-word answers) so they capture the essence of your needs and wants without being too prescriptive.

ACTIVITY

This activity helps you clarify your themes and figure out what the pillars of your break are going to be. Answer all three prompts as thoughtfully and completely as possible. When you complete them, take time to reflect on your answers and summarize them into three or four unique themes. Try to keep your themes to one- or two-word answers for simplicity and clarity. No wrong answers exist when it comes to your deeper needs and wants, so please don't judge your answers!

>> What does my break need to have or do for me to feel that it was worthwhile?

What would make this experience worth the investment of your time, energy, and money? What would make you look back and say, "Yes, that was definitely worth it"?

>> What do I need to feel fulfilled and satisfied with this experience?

What would give you a sense of satisfaction and completion with this experience — like you ended on a positive note and closed the loop?

>> How would I like things to be when my break is over? Or how do I not want things to be when it's over?

Paint the picture of how you'd like things to be when your break is over. Or if it's easier, describe what you know you don't want to return to when it's over.

Examples of career break Themes

In this section I'm sharing some examples to get the gears turning as you finalize your career break themes. The following are themes my clients have used to create magical career break experiences. Each word represents the essence of an unmet desire or need that they wanted to incorporate into their experience and use as a pillar for building a successful break.

Adventure	Healing	Quality time
Allowing ease	Health reset	Reconnect
Breathe	Inspiration	Relax
Community	Joy immersion	Reset
Connection	Learning	Restoration
Creativity	Lifestyle 4.0	Savor
Detox	Next chapter	Simplification
Exploration	Nourish	Upskill
Fun	Play	Wellness

FUN AND UNIQUE THEME EXAMPLES

For your inspiration, I want to share three of the most unique and interesting career break themes I've seen:

- **Joy immersion:** Spending time consciously creating and immersing in joy. Doing things that fill you with joy intentionally and often and exploring new experiences and activities that add even more joy to your life.

- **Savor:** Creating space to savor life. Savoring sunsets, delicious meals, solitude, and time with loved ones. Slowing down to be fully present and enjoy the goodness of each experience, while letting it slowly expand and extend the present moment.

- **Dolce far niente:** Italian for the sweetness of doing nothing. Creating time to sink into the goodness of stillness and peace. Dedicating time to appreciate the sweetness of life and the simplicity and deliciousness of each moment.

ANECDOTE

My Themes during my 20-month career break were Rest, Reconnection, Exploration, and New Path. I spent time at home, resting and reconnecting with loved ones, and I also made time to reconnect with old friends during my three-month road trip. I fulfilled my travel desires as I explored and solo traveled the world, visiting places like Vietnam, Argentina, Cambodia, and France. And I forged the beginnings of a new path by talking to strangers about their own career paths, moving to Colorado, and taking community education courses on new and interesting topics like starting a life coaching business and fermenting your own vegetables. These four Themes created a life-changing experience and shifted me onto a new path that felt more aligned and fulfilling — and ultimately led me to write this book!

Bringing Your Career Break Vision to Life with a Wish List

After the introspective work to develop a solid structure for your break (see the previous sections for help creating your structure), you're ready to start fleshing out your career break plan and drafting your career break wish list. You have permission to start daydreaming!

While this is a popular starting point when creating a career break plan, beginning without a solid structure in place could jeopardize your break experience. Make sure you've got your purposes and themes solidified before shifting your focus to the activities and experiences you'll have during your break.

The pillars of your break (your themes) will help guide you as you brainstorm ideas for what to do on a break. With clarity about what your break needs to provide to be a life-changing and worthwhile experience, you can start dreaming up ways to bring your themes to life.

Let this part of the planning be fun and light! You don't need to have a detailed itinerary before starting your break. You'll have plenty of time to research and plan during your break, too. As you lean into developing your wish list, notice whether you start to feel stress or heaviness. If you do, consider it a cue to pause the planning until it feels fun again.

Beginning your wish list the right way

Each activity or experience you pursue is an investment of your time, energy, and money, so it's important to make sure your resources go toward things that will help you fulfill your career break themes and achieve your career break purpose.

Living into your themes creates a successful and rewarding experience, so as you make your wish list, note to which themes each idea applies. Some of your ideas might address more than one theme — awesome! An idea that addresses just one theme is perfectly fine, too. Some of your ideas might not map back to any of your themes; consider those ideas carefully. Anything is game for this exercise, but you'll want the majority of your ideas to relate to your career break themes.

Reflect on your themes and start brainstorming activities and experiences you can pursue to fulfill them. If you have ideas that are unrelated to your themes, you can jot them down as well. Think about the things you would love to do during this time — from the basics like daytime naps to extreme ideas like hiking Kilimanjaro. As you write down your answers, be sure to consider which theme(s) they help you connect with.

Themes are the secret to your career break success. Be sure 80 percent or more of your wish list ideas map back to at least one of your themes.

During my break, I used a three-month road trip to live into my themes of reconnection and exploration. I got to see new places (hello, Grand Canyon!) and I was able to reconnect with friends I hadn't seen in years and meet their partners and kids sometimes for the first time. I balanced spending time visiting new destinations and revisiting places I'd been before with spending quality time with friends, even if it required a significant detour. This is a great example of fulfilling two themes at the same time.

By utilizing your career break structure, you'll have a plan that can withstand any obstacles and helps you feel clear and grounded. Use this structure to develop your plan, but don't worry about creating a highly detailed itinerary right away. Ease your way into the details and give yourself time to come up with a healthy wish list before you worry about making it executable. It's also important to note that changes are likely to occur during the planning process, so your overall plan will require flexibility anyway. Diving into the details too soon can involve a lot of re-work on the backend.

Drafting your wish list creates a collection of meaningful and fun things to consider for your break. This information helps you paint a picture of your ideal career break, create an estimated cost for your break, and formalize your career break timeline. As you begin to put these amazing ideas together, you might realize you have an impractical and wildly expensive plan. If this happens, you can use the following activity to help prioritize your list.

To manage an unwieldy or expensive wish list, denote the Tier 1 activities. Tier 1 activities are the "must-do" items — the things you want to build your break around. These are worthy items that you absolutely want to include. Items that don't fit this qualification can still be considered, but they'll drop to a lower priority level. Focus on planning your Tier 1 activities and sprinkle in the others as time and money allow.

Don't get overwhelmed by creating a wish list. You can start with a few ideas and begin adding to your list as you go along. You might hear stories or listen to podcasts that inspire you. Stay open to new ideas and reflect on your Themes for inspiration. Enjoy this phase of the planning process where fun, exciting, and meaningful ideas are all welcomed.

Avoiding the most common mistake

The most common mistake future career breakers make when creating a wish list for their break is focusing on ideas that others would consider epic or envy-inducing. It's normal for your brain to offer big, over-the-top ideas when you first start putting a wish list together, but often these ideas are far from what you actually want and need.

When you do the work to develop your purpose and themes, you'll be better clued in to what you really want and need. You may face an urge to take the "go big or go home" approach to planning, but be sure to understand your true motive. Underneath the desire to "do it big" often lays a fear about needing to justify this time off. Your brain says you need to have something big and impressive to show for it all, and overlooks the simple truth that taking radically good care of yourself and upgrading your life in a lasting way is an epic act all by itself.

REMEMBER

The most important thing to focus on when creating your wish list is what *you* want and need. Your wish list can be a series of big adventures, a string of simple pleasures, or a mix of both. Don't worry about impressing others. All roads lead to a great experience when you're honoring your truth.

WARNING

Career break envy is real. If you connect with or follow others who are also taking a break, you may find yourself judging your plan. Don't! Everyone has different needs, and neglecting your themes (your desires and needs) is a recipe for disaster. Trust yourself to get what you need from your break experience and don't be distracted by others who may take a different approach.

ANECDOTE

An executive client hired me before starting a two-month break. He was about to step into the role of CEO at a new company and wanted time to recharge. Initially, he viewed his break as an extended vacation, and he wanted to include an epic capstone experience with his family. But his purpose and themes revealed a more urgent need for recovery and connecting with family and friends. He chose to honor his themes and let go of his need for an epic experience to highlight his break, and the version of him that emerged was incredibly inspired, motivated, and fully recharged.

He might have lacked a singular epic experience, but his well-designed break created an epic result that he credits with preparing him for his new role and changing the way he values his time.

Learning how to dream bigger

The activity I'm about to share with you just might change your life — or at least the way you approach it. It will help you maximize your career break experience, and you can apply it for an equally powerful impact on your life.

Dreaming bigger is about reorienting your mind from making things more practical and efficient to creating better experiences for yourself to enjoy. The working world has trained us to focus on efficiency — do more with less and do it faster. The end result is that you'll apply this same approach to your dreams and life in general.

When it comes to your wish list, your brain might want to leap into action to make things more feasible and efficient. But you don't want to "trim the fat" from your dreams because that's where things get really good. Instead of running with your initial wish list ideas, intentionally take a moment to let them be *more* — more fun, peaceful, connected, exciting, adventurous, and so on. You're going to learn how to take your great ideas and make them even better before you worry about practicalities and efficiencies. This practice isn't about going over the top; it's about expanding the goodness of every experience and creating plans and ideas that go beyond what you currently think is possible. This sets you up for an incredible break experience.

ACTIVITY

To practice dreaming bigger, start with one of your wish list ideas. It can be a big or small one. Next, ask yourself the same question three times: How can I make this even better? Write down your new answer each time you ask the question and allow your ideas to build on one another. When you've done this three times, you'll have an even juicier idea for your wish list. Practice this with as many wish list items as you'd like! When you have your better idea, you can then begin scaling it down, if necessary.

WARNING

Better doesn't necessarily mean bigger, bolder, and more expensive. You don't need to explode the budget for this activity. Better simply means that it feels better to you in some meaningful way. Your new ideas could be more creative, peaceful, enjoyable, adventurous, spacious, exciting, or connected. You can also substitute *better* with a specific word that aligns to one of your Themes.

TIP

You can apply this activity to your regular life experiences, too. Whether you're thinking about something you're dreading or something you're excited about, you can stop to explore how you can make it even a little bit better than your original idea or plan.

ANECDOTE

One of my wish list ideas was learning more about yoga. It was a simple wish that I envisioned as a short series of intermediate classes. I'd never committed to consistent practice and was interested in building a solid foundation. But after some quick research, I realized the only way to gain the type of knowledge I wanted was to take a more formal teacher training program. Initially this idea felt way outside the realm of possibility for me. But as I applied the dreaming bigger activity to it, this idea grew to become a highlight experience. I attended an all-inclusive yoga teacher training retreat in Bali. I'll admit, things escalated quickly, and that's the beauty of this activity!

Inspiring wish list examples

Through a mix of dreaming bigger and aligning their ideas with their career break themes, my clients have created an inspiring list of activities and experiences during their breaks.

Ten incredible examples

The following real-life client examples highlight the incredible opportunity a career break can offer you when you dare to dream bigger:

» Live with a host family while completing a Spanish language immersion in Guatemala.

» Hike 400 miles of the Camino de Santiago in Spain.

» Relocate to Spain for two years with your spouse and infant son.

» Move to France for a year to study abroad (in your late 30s).

» Visit Valencia, Spain, to fulfill a childhood dream and attend the world-famous Las Fallas festival.

» Witness Argentina win the World Cup while living in Buenos Aires and celebrating with locals.

- >> Become a certified diver with a non-profit that identifies and documents sunken slave shipwrecks.
- >> Start an animal sanctuary for aged animals.
- >> Pursue a dream of becoming a professional actor.
- >> Become a certified yoga instructor at a three-week retreat in Bali, Indonesia.

Ten simple, yet powerful examples

The most meaningful experiences aren't always the grandest or most expensive. To help balance out your wish list, I'm sharing 10 inspiring things that are simple yet powerful that my clients have done while on a break:

- >> Earn a diploma in Equine Healing and Communication in the United Kingdom.
- >> Connect with your biological family via an Ancestry DNA test.
- >> Travel to the West Coast for a private session with a death doula.
- >> Recover from the deep grief of losing a parent.
- >> Complete a one-month digital detox.
- >> Get a membership with your local pottery studio and discover a new talent and passion.
- >> Make friends with your neighbor and learn how to raise chickens and keep bees.
- >> Foster a child with hopes of adoption.
- >> Learn a new sport (tennis) and become a competitive player at age 42.
- >> Develop a restorative morning routine that you stick to for the first time in your life.

Setting Yourself Up for a Smooth Return to the Workforce

What will happen after your break? Will you find another job? Will it be as good as your last one, or will you have to settle? One of the biggest fears that prevents people from taking a break is the worry of what happens when their break is over. But there's a simple solution to alleviate a lot of this fear and set you up for a successful return. It's called the re-entry period.

Admittedly, taking a break requires embracing a hearty dose of uncertainty. You can't be sure what opportunities will be available when you return and how long you'll wait to start receiving an income again. For some, the risk doesn't seem worth the reward, but you aren't just anyone. You're reading this book, which tells me that you want a way forward, a way to minimize the negative impact and maximize the upside. Well, that's exactly what I explain in this section. I used this same planning tool to land five job offers in just five weeks at the end of my 20-month break.

TIP

If you're taking a sabbatical, you won't have to worry about finding a job when your break has ended. However, a re-entry period should still be included in your plan, as it allows time for you to smoothly transition back to the more demanding cadence of a full-time job.

If themes are the secret to a successful career break experience, the re-entry period is the secret to a successful return when your break is over. Adding a re-entry period into your career break plan creates space for a smoother transition back to work. With time to process your experience and adequately prepare for your next chapter, you continue the momentum of positive change. You won't slip back into the old way of doing things or settle for a job that doesn't suit you.

Understanding why you need a re-entry period

No matter how you envision your post-break version of success, a re-entry period can help you create those results faster and easier. With it you can

>> Become a digital nomad

>> Change your career

>> Consult or freelance

>> Find a new job, role, and/or company

>> Relocate

>> Retire

>> Semi-retire

>> Start your own business

The re-entry period is a dedicated period of time at the end of your break that gives you adequate time to process your experience and prepare for your next move. Specifically, it provides the following invaluable benefits that will help you maximize and enhance your career break experience. Having a re-entry period also saves you tons of stress and worry. With it, you can thoughtfully approach your next right step and be sure you'll show up as the best version of yourself.

Increasing enjoyment of your break

Worrying about an unknown future can easily derail a great career break experience. With a re-entry period, you're proactively setting aside time to solve problems, like figuring out what comes next. And with this approach, you'll be able to postpone and redirect the waves of fear that want to wash over you and drown out your good time.

Even if you're sure that taking a break was the right decision, your brain will sneak in fearful thoughts and run worst-case scenarios, It's just worried you might drop the ball and forget that you'll eventually need to work again. But you can gently remind your brain that now is not the time to solve such problems because you can give it your full attention during the re-entry period. It will be easier to ride the waves of fear and uncertainty without drowning, because you'll have a fully-funded period of time to take action and create solutions. Banishing your worries into the future makes it easier to convince your brain it's safe to fully enjoy your career break experience, and that makes for a more delightful result.

Processing your career break experience

Coming back from a career break will be messy. After months (or years) of freedom and autonomy, it can be hard to switch back to a full-time work schedule. If your experience included international travel, you'll likely need time to process your reverse culture shock as you readjust to life in your home country. You might feel ready to go back to work but simultaneously resistant to the idea.

I won't sugarcoat this: You're going to have a jumbled mix of feelings when it's time to transition to a post-break life, and parts of it won't be pretty. Reflecting on what this amazing experience meant to you and all the ways it's changed you is critical to maximizing the benefit of your break. It allows you to show up as an even better version of yourself for your next chapter. Maybe you return with new boundaries and priorities or a better sense of balance. Maybe you'll feel incredibly inspired and motivated to try something new and take on a big challenge. No matter the specifics of your experience, you'll want time to get the messy feelings out and cement the new version of you that's emerging from your career break cocoon.

Creating your next opportunity faster

One of the worst things you can do at the end of your break is desperately hunt for your next opportunity. The panic can be a big turnoff to potential employers and can create a strong desire to settle for the next opportunity. If you want to attract a great opportunity and do it quickly, you need time to prepare and do things like network, consider your options, search for a job, update your resume, or launch your new business idea. Whatever your next step is, it will be best served by creating space to adequately prepare and embracing an inspired and excited energy versus a desperate and panicked one.

ANECDOTE

I had an extended re-entry period because my last theme was around creating a more aligned next chapter. The first part of my re-entry period was to explore my options, move to a new city, and consider new careers. I took classes at the local community education center, had a ton of informal coffee chats, and attended meetups with interesting topics. I also used my re-entry period to process my bad attitude and messy feelings about ending my travels. Coming in hot off the heels of four months in Southeast Asia, I was also suffering from reverse culture shock. It took several weeks for me to return to normal and stop lamenting the nearing end of my break. When I realized that my next big goal was to be debt-free, I decided to return to my corporate career and pay off my student loans as quickly as possible. My re-entry period gave me time to get clear on this goal and prepare for the job search. I launched my updated resume, and just five weeks later I'd landed five exciting job offers.

Incorporating a re-entry period into your plan

To have a successful re-entry, you'll need to proactively dedicate time and money for this period and incorporate it into your career break plan. Setting aside resources and budgeting for your re-entry period in advance ensures you have time to figure out your next step and process your career break experience as your break is winding down.

In this section, you determine how much money and time to dedicate to your re-entry period so you can fold it into your overall plan and budget. When you're nearing the end of your break and ready to return, Chapter 13 guides you through creating a more detailed re-entry plan and successfully navigating your re-entry period.

It's important to consider actions you may want to take during your re-entry period as you begin estimating the resources you'll need to set aside. They influence the amount of time and money you'll need for your re-entry period. Here's a list of examples to help you get started:

>> Recovering from your travels and reconnecting with loved ones before hopping back into a demanding work environment

>> Networking, updating your resume, hiring a career coach, and searching for your next role

>> Signing up for an online course to teach you all the things you need to know, like how to set up a limited liability company (LLC) and build a website

>> Spending quality time with your family to enjoy the last few weeks of your break and help ease them through the transition as well

>> Spending two weeks alone in a vacation rental home to flesh out your business idea

>> Taking an online course or program to learn new skills and prepare to re-enter the job market at a higher level

Dedicating adequate time

When you have a rough idea of what actions you may take during your re-entry, you can estimate the amount of time you'll need for your re-entry period. If you're unsure of what you'll focus on during your re-entry period, use the following tip to create your estimate. It's okay if your estimate changes; at least you'll know you have time budgeted for this experience before your break begins. You can refer back to this estimate when you move on to develop your break timeline in Chapter 6.

TIP

To help you estimate how much time to dedicate to your re-entry period, use the 1 for 6 Rule: For every six weeks of a career break, dedicate *at least* one week to your re-entry period, with no less than one month regardless of the length of your break. If you're planning a four-month break, you would calculate about three weeks for re-entry (4 months × 4 weeks = 16 weeks ÷ 6 weeks = 2.7 weeks). But because this length falls below the one-month minimum, you would bump it up to at least a one-month re-entry period. This helps you avoid skidding in on the hot mess express. You should plan for significantly more time if one of your themes deals with exploring or creating a new career path.

Budgeting for your transition

After you've estimated a length of time for your break, you can estimate how much money to set aside to cover your expenses and invest in preparing for your next step (for example, hiring a resume writer or career coach, traveling to conferences, taking an online class to upskill, starting a business, etc.). This number is only an estimate, but it ensures that you have something set aside to help ease your transition. Include this estimate when you calculate the overall cost of your break in Chapter 5, so you can return with ease, carry forward all of the good things you've worked hard to create, and continue your momentum into your next chapter.

Chapter 5

Figuring Out Your Finances

f you're not sure how you can afford to take a break, you're not alone. This is an obstacle many people face and one you'll resolve in this chapter by creating a financial plan for your break. To adequately prepare for a break, you'll need to make the math work. By showing you how to estimate the cost of your break and how to create a budget for this time off, I explain how to sort out your finances before taking the leap.

If you already have the money set aside, congrats! This chapter can help you make smart decisions to ensure you put your money to good use and don't run out of it prematurely. If you're still saving for a break, this chapter helps you set a clear financial goal. It also breaks down the process I used to save $40,000 in 18 months to fund my break. You can use the same process to reach your savings goal quickly.

REMEMBER

As you navigate this chapter, think of your break as an investment in your well-being and in a better future, and not just as a big expense.

Determining the Cost of Your Break

Clarifying the overall cost of your break is important for creating a successful experience. Here are five great reasons to know your number:

>> **It heavily influences your start date.** If you're saving for a break and/or putting your financial plan together, understanding exactly how much you'll need to have in the bank informs when you can leave your job and begin your break.

>> **It builds confidence.** Working through the process to develop a target number can create a sense of safety. You'll know how much you need to cover your expenses and understand the implications of your plan.

>> **It helps prevent an early exit.** No one wants to run out of money in the middle of their break but it happens. If you want to follow through on the amazing plan you've developed, it's important to understand the true cost so you're adequately prepared.

>> **It helps to appropriately allocate your career break money.** When you're ready to draft a career break budget, knowing the overall cost helps you allocate an adequate amount of money to each phase of your break, including your re-entry period.

>> **You'll reach your savings goal much faster.** Knowing your number allows you to track your progress and stay motivated while you save and plan. It also helps you make informed financial decisions on the way to reaching your savings goal.

This section helps you create an inclusive number that accounts for your unique career break plan and the various unknowns you'll face. I also share real-life numbers to help you gauge your estimate. You can approach this section in two main ways:

>> **Design your ideal break first and then estimate the cost of bringing this idea to life.**

If you're like me and want to begin with your ideal break in mind, the remainder of this section shows you how to start with your ideal break to develop a budget and then calculate an overall cost.

>> **Start with a fixed number and retrofit your activities and experiences to stay within budget.**

If you're starting with a fixed number, you've already determined the upper limit cost for your break. You can use the remainder of this section to draft a break budget, ensure you've included hidden costs associated with a break, and adopt a supportive mindset for this investment.

Creating a budget for your break

Drafting a budget does two important things: It shows you how much money you'll need for a break and helps you avoid running out of money prematurely during your break. A budget can reduce your money stress and pave the way for a better experience. See Chapter 11 for tips on managing your budget when you're on a break.

TIP

If you manage your budget well, you may be able to extend your break. I was able to turn a 12-month break into a 20-month break — and 30 percent of my clients have extended their breaks, too!

Decide what you'll do during your break

First, create a list of things you'd like to do on your break. Let this be a fun part of the process. Don't get bogged down in the details; a simple list will do. Start with what you know and build from there as you work your way through this chapter.

TIP

If you created your themes and wish list in Chapter 4, you already have this information. Revisit your answers as you build your budget.

ANECDOTE

When I started mapping out my break, I didn't have a lot of specifics, but I knew this was an important step in understanding the overall cost. So, I created a short list of things I wanted to do, based on my career break themes (see Chapter 4 to develop your own). Here is my list, which may give you inspiration for yours:

>> Explore new paths and career options
>> Get into better shape
>> Learn more yoga
>> Live in Buenos Aires

- >> Relocate from Minnesota
- >> Road trip the United States and visit friends
- >> See the Grand Canyon
- >> Spend time at home with family over Christmas
- >> Visit Southeast Asia

Organize your ideas

If you have a big list, pricing each idea individually can become tedious and overwhelming — so many details to research! Instead of jumping immediately to pricing, create an outline of your big ideas and key experiences. As you move forward in the planning process, you can break your plan into smaller pieces to get a more accurate estimate.

TIP

This step is meant to simplify your budgeting process but feel free to skip the outline method and dive into as much detail as you feel comfortable with.

Figure 5-1 shows the original outline of my 12-month break. I started with four big ideas and several supporting experiences for each. I also included an estimated length of time for each idea.

TIP

If you already have a specific overall cost in mind, outlining your ideas will help you understand which combination of activities will and won't fit into your budget.

WHEN YOUR BREAK INVOLVES TRAVEL

If you plan to travel during your break, I have two tricks to make your estimation process easier and more accurate.

For greater accuracy, separate your slow-travel expenses from your fast-travel expenses.

- Slow travel involves spending a month or more in a new location and establishing a temporary homebase. This style of travel often helps keep costs down and allows you to experience your destination more like a local. To calculate these expenses, focus on the cost of living for your destinations.

- Fast travel involves changing locations every few days or weeks. With this approach, you'll experience more destinations but also eat out more often, participate in more tours and activities, and stay in more expensive accommodations (like hotels). This adds up to a notably higher cost. To estimate these expenses, focus on the daily or weekly cost of travel.

For more ease, start by grouping locations with a similar cost of living or daily/weekly cost of travel in your budget.

For example, instead of trying to create a precise itinerary for hopping around Italy, France, and Spain, you can create one estimate for two months in Western Europe. Because the daily/weekly cost of travel doesn't vary wildly for a tourist traveling in those countries, you can set an average that's in the ballpark of all three and save time and energy in the early planning and budgeting stages.

If, however, you plan to spend a month in Spain and then a month in Thailand, you'll likely want to estimate these separately because the cost of living is notably different. In Figure 5-1, you'll see that I listed Buenos Aires, the EU, and Southeast Asia are listed as separate ideas for this very reason.

ANECDOTE

Planning a three-month road trip was challenging. My plans and route were constantly changing. It was hard to coordinate exact dates with friends several months in advance, and I was frequently adding new stops to the list. Pricing each stop felt impossible, so I rolled everything into one big idea and used an average daily cost to estimate my expenses.

Draft your budget

When you've got an outline for what you'd like to do during your break and an idea of how long you'd like to be doing it, it's time to draft your budget (see the earlier section "Organize your ideas" for tips on creating your outline).

Think of your budget as a set of spending guidelines. It isn't meant to hold you prisoner or overwhelm you. Instead, it helps you make clear decisions and trade-offs. For this next step, you estimate the cost of the ideas in your outline. If this level of detail is too much, you can take a break and revisit when you feel ready.

MY CAREER BREAK OUTLINE

Road trip through the United States [3 months]

- Visit friends and family
- See the Grand Canyon
- Drive up the West Coast on Highway 1
- Visit New Orleans and eat a lot of great food

Visit family in West Virginia [2 months]

- Spend 1-2 months at home with family over the Christmas holiday
- Reconnect with friends and family
- Lean into rest and restoration

Travel abroad [4 months]

- Visit Southeast Asia
- Visit Buenos Aires
- Explore the EU: Spain, France, Italy
- Take several food tours and learn more about other cultures

Explore new career paths and ideas [3 months]

- Take community education classes to explore new career paths
- Relocate to a new state
- Explore new hobbies and interests

FIGURE 5-1: My original 12-month career break outline.

ACTIVITY

Using your outline (or list of ideas), research and estimate the associated costs for each item or big idea. Some items will have a straightforward cost (for example, a three-week yoga teacher training), whereas others will be a combination of expenses (such as a 10-day trip through Colombia). If your break involves travel, check out the "When your break involves travel" sidebar for guidance on estimating your travel expenses.

To help you get started, consider the following common types of expenses as you draft your budget:

» **Development:** Upskilling courses, in-person workshops, community ed classes, books, coaching programs, equipment for hobbies and interests.

» **Events:** Travel, food, admission fees, upgrades for more personal experience or better accommodations, necessary supplies

>> **Road trips:** Accommodations, food, gas, car maintenance, activities and entertainment, tolls, parking, thank-you gifts if staying with friends

>> **Support:** Help for services like child care, pet or house sitting, home maintenance, and outsourced tasks

>> **Time at home:** Rent/mortgage, utilities, gas, food, fitness and other health-related activities, public transit

>> **Travel:** Accommodations, food, gas, transit (public transit, flights, buses, trains, car rentals), activities and entertainment

- You'll spend significantly less when traveling slowly and living more like a local (establishing a homebase) versus when you're hopping around to new destinations and traveling as a tourist. For this reason, calculate your slow-travel expenses separately from your fast-travel expenses for a more accurate estimate. See "When your break involves travel" for more information.

- Don't forget to account for the impact of currency conversions. This can greatly impact the overall cost of your travels.

TIP

Always include a "miscellaneous" or "other" category when estimating costs. This helps buffer for unexpected expenses, like purchasing medicine if you get sick.

ANECDOTE

My 21 days in Thailand averaged $55 per day, whereas two weeks in the South of France rang in at $140 per day. The significant difference was partly due to the variation in the cost of travel and partly due to the currency conversion.

Don't get overwhelmed by the details. Your plans will continue to evolve, even after your break begins. Just start with what you know and include averages and best guesses for what you don't.

For simplicity's sake, I recommend starting with a daily, weekly, or monthly average for your travels (depending on the length of your stay) and multiplying it by your estimated time spent in that country. After you start traveling, you can adjust your expenses as you go to stay within budget.

TIP

Want help estimating the average cost of new locations? If you're planning to spend at least one month in a new location (slow travel), check out online cost-of-living calculators like Nomad List, Numbeo, and The Earth Awaits. If you plan to change locations more frequently, use a cost of travel calculator like the one at www.budgetyourtrip.com/ or browse destination-specific travel guidebooks and blogs to better estimate your daily or weekly travel costs.

TIP

My favorite way to estimate the average cost of my accommodations is to do a quick search online using my tentative dates and location. I'll compare prices on Airbnb (for home rentals), an OTA (online travel agency) like Booking.com (for hotels), and Hostelworld (for hostels) to get a sense of pricing and create a more accurate estimate. Because seasonality can drastically affect travel costs, it also helps me create a more accurate estimate based on my preferred travel dates.

Set your priorities

If you start drafting your budget and realize you have too many ideas competing for your time and money, first celebrate your imagination! Many of my clients initially struggle to dream big and come up with juicy ideas for what to do on their break.

Then, on a practical level, you can resolve this issue by clarifying your priorities. This means elevating those ideas and/or experiences that are a high priority (must-do items) and allocating your remaining time and money to lower-level priorities (would-be-nice items) that fit your itinerary and add value to your break. Reflect on your themes and wish list from Chapter 4 to make sure your high-priority items align with your personal definition of success.

ACTIVITY

To establish your priorities, start with the outline or list of ideas (see the "Decide what you'll do during your break" section earlier in this chapter if you don't have one) and bold or asterisk those ideas that you simply must do to have the break you want and need. Start with these items as you create your budget to get an idea of the total cost. If you can afford it, sprinkle in some lower-priority items that also align with the purpose and themes of your break.

Calculating the grand total

To calculate the overall cost for your break, sum up the items in your budget and add a line item for a few additional expenses. In this section, I share common career break expenses you may want to include in your grand total.

Account for your ongoing expenses

Even though your life changes considerably during a career break, some expenses in your regular life remain. (Oh, the joys of adulting!) The following are ongoing expenses and expenditures that you'll want to account for as you budget for a break:

>> Beauty regimen (hair, skin, nails)

>> Car insurance and maintenance (oil change, repairs, tires)

>> Caretaking (pet sitters, child care, etc.)

>> Cellphone coverage

>> Gifts (birthday, wedding, holiday, thank you)

>> Health insurance (see Chapter 8 for details)

>> Healthcare (prescriptions, fitness, massages)

>> Life insurance

>> Monthly and annual fees (credit cards, memberships)

>> Storage (car, household items)

>> Travel insurance

WARNING

Gifts and presents can be budget killers. While you may not want to avoid them completely, consider leaning into your creativity to give meaningful and budget-friendly gifts. As you calculate your overall cost, be sure to pick a target for this line item and do your best to stick to it.

Include ad-hoc items

In addition to ongoing expenses and maintenance, you might also incur one-time expenses before beginning your break, especially if travel is involved. Here's a list to get started:

>> Car tuneup

>> Final appointments (dentist, annual physical, beautician, esthetician)

- » Lease-breaking fees
- » Legal documents
- » Medicine (to stock up)
- » Moving expenses
- » Travel gear (luggage, electronics)
- » Travel guides
- » Vaccinations
- » Visas and passport fees

Add a buffer for emergencies

If you want to make sure you won't run out of money mid-break or have an unexpected expense derail your break, you need to include a buffer for emergencies. This better prepares you to weather any storms or surprises that arise.

TIP

You need to determine what amount feels right to you, but as a rule of thumb, I recommend setting aside an extra 15 to 20 percent of your estimated cost for emergencies. So, if you anticipate your break costing $25k, I'd add another $5k (20%) as your buffer.

ANECDOTE

When I was saving for a break, I owned a rental property that wasn't producing a profit at the time. I worried about unforeseen expenses that could arise during my unemployment and wanted easy access to funds that could cover these costs. I also needed money for personal emergencies. Therefore, I added a $10k buffer (35%) to my total break cost to account for potential rental property issues plus personal emergencies.

Add a buffer for your re-entry period

No total is complete without money set aside for your re-entry period. This critical stage of your break is essential for successfully transitioning out of your break and into your next chapter. Depending on your situation, this stage may cost less than the majority of your break, but it could still require significant savings.

TIP

For details on the importance of the re-entry period and guidance on creating a more accurate re-entry period estimate, see Chapter 4.

Compare with real-life examples

As you prepare to calculate your career break total, I want to share a few data points to help you finalize your estimate.

Many factors will influence the cost of your break:

>> Being the primary (or only) earner in your family

>> Caretaking others (children, pets, parents, etc.)

>> Having a mortgage and/or other large expenses to maintain your previous lifestyle

>> Having a spouse or partner cover the household expenses while you're on a break

>> Living with family or friends during your break (for example, free or low-cost accommodations)

>> Starting or investing in a business during the re-entry period of your break

>> The length of your break

>> Traveling internationally versus staying at home

>> Using points and miles for free travel

>> Your country of residence, currency, and cost of living

Each person's situation is unique, but the following reference points from my past clients (most from the United States) may help you:

>> $3,650 USD is the average monthly cost while on a break (includes a mix of factors previously mentioned).

>> 50 percent of respondents spent between $2,000 and $4,500 USD per month while on their break.

>> For some, the cost was $0 (not including lost wages) because they stayed at home and had a partner to cover the monthly expenses.

REMEMBER

There's no "right amount" to spend on your break. To illustrate this point, I'm sharing three career breaks with very different price points. I hope this gives you permission to create the break you desire.

My break was a lower-budget break. I'm a huge fan of budget travel and a bit of a minimalist, so I enjoyed keeping my costs low. Table 5-1 gives a breakdown of my 20-month break, which included a U.S. road trip, international travels, time at home with family, and a lengthy re-entry period to explore new career paths.

TABLE 5-1 Lower-Budget Break Cost

Expense	Duration	Cost
U.S. road trip	3 months	$5,200
Home w/family	3 months	$1,800
Southeast Asia	3 months	$4,900
Yoga training	3 weeks	$3,100
South America	2 months	$2,800
Western Europe	1 month	$5,200
Re-entry period	4 months	$4,000
All other (incl. buffer)		$11,000
Total		**$38,000**

The next example is a mid-budget break. My client took a break focused on health and exploring new career options. They lived with family during their break and focused on restoring their health and exploring new career paths. The breakdown in Table 5-2 shows how they spent $65,000 over a 16-month break.

TABLE 5-2 Mid-Budget Break Cost

Expense	Duration	Cost
Health and healing expenses	16 months	$30,000
Professional exploration	10 months	$20,000
All other expenses		$15,000
Total		**$65,000**

The last example is a higher-budget break. For some clients, the break is a once-in-a-lifetime experience they don't want to compromise on. This client graciously shared the cost of their 15-month break (see Table 5-3), which included international travel and maintaining a U.S. homebase.

TABLE 5-3 Higher-Budget Break Cost

Expense	Duration	Cost
Europe trip #1	3 months	$22,000
Europe trip #2	1 month	$8,000
South America	2 weeks	$4,000
U.S. travels	20 days	$4,000
Bills/home expenses	15 months	$24,000
Personal development	15 months	$12,000
All other expenses		$18,500
Total		**$92,500**

Sum everything up for the overall cost

It's time to calculate the grand total. For this last step, add up the following numbers to determine your career break cost:

» Ad-hoc expenses and one-time expenditures

» Buffer for emergencies

» Estimate for your re-entry period

» Ongoing expenses and maintenance costs

» Preparation expenses and fees

TIP

As your plans and ideas evolve, revisit this estimate and your break budget and update as necessary.

Affording a Career Break

As you explore the monetary cost of taking a break, it's likely you'll question whether you can really afford to do it. You may be tempted to delay the decision and revisit in a year's time or dismiss the idea altogether in hopes that a long vacation will do the trick. But this could be a mistake. In the previous section, you see exactly what a break would cost you, but there's also a cost to postponing or denying your desire or need for a break (covered in Chapter 3).

In this section, I walk you through how to determine whether you can afford a break and suggest ways you can save money more quickly, if necessary.

Feeling empowered to invest in a break

Investing in a break requires an empowered mindset — one that doesn't let fear call the shots. To adopt this type of thinking, you need to zoom out to see things clearly and escape any fear-induced haze. In this section, I explain why you should give yourself permission to consider this investment and teach you how to embrace the flexibility it will require.

Give yourself permission to make this investment

If you want to take a break, you need to give yourself permission to make the investment. This requires that you recognize the power of this investment and acknowledge that you're worth it.

Seeing your balance increase paycheck after paycheck can feel quite comforting. It might seem reckless to deplete your financial safety net for a break. But equally as important as saving for a rainy day is understanding why you work hard to save this money in the first place — to invest in yourself and your well-being. It can be easy to devalue this kind of investment, but being wise with your money doesn't mean saving as much as humanly possible no matter the toll it takes on you. It means knowing when to hold on and when to let go. Your quality of life is worth investing in, and doing so can pay off in ways that money can't measure.

One client wasn't sure when to start his career break. He already had his next job lined up, so each week he stayed on with his current employer meant one less week for his break. But there was additional money involved if he stayed on for a few more weeks. While it seemed crazy to leave this money "on the table," I asked him to consider what he would be leaving on the table in exchange: his precious time. He considered this and ultimately made the decision to leave sooner rather than later, giving himself and his family more time for the break. He did not regret his decision. In fact, it provided a powerful lesson: He was worth the investment. Sometimes it's not simple math — your time is invaluable, and more money isn't always worth the sacrifice.

If you're using this book to create a thoughtful plan for your break, you're setting yourself up for an amazing experience with a life-changing outcome. Your break is a gift — one that you can give yourself permission to receive.

Embrace flexibility to make it work

If you feel uncomfortable with the estimated cost of your break, remember that you can always adjust the parameters to make it work for you. For example, you can

>> Reduce your current cost of living to save more money
>> Change your travel plans to reduce your expenses
- Switch to more affordable destinations
- Slow down your travels and establish an affordable temporary homebase
>> Find creative ways to save or make more money
>> Shorten the length of your break

If you're already on a break when financial complications arise, you can

>> Pursue a new source of income (i.e., side hustle)
>> Adapt your plans to reduce the cost
>> Consider ending your break early to return to work

You can always pick up a side hustle or alternative sources of income, if necessary. More than 60 percent of my clients collected some form of income during the later part of their break.

When considering whether you can afford to take a break, know that you can be flexible with your plan to accommodate your ever-evolving circumstances. A career break isn't an irreversible decision. You can always return to work when you need or want to.

Funding your career break

When you know your career break cost (as calculated in the preceding section), a critical part of affording a career break will be acquiring the money needed to cover it and making sure you manage that money well.

The most common approach to funding a break is saving for it (or using pre-existing savings to pay for it). That said, some of my clients have funded their break through alternative means, such as these examples:

>> Collect passive income to reduce or offset the cost (for example, rental income, interest on investments, etc.)

>> Have a partner absorb your expenses while on a break

>> Receive a severance package

>> Receive an inheritance

>> Relocate somewhere significantly more affordable

>> Sell a home

No matter how you plan to cover the cost of your break, it's important to consider the management of your career break funds to ensure that you reach your goal and minimize the financial impact of taking a break. Two steps can help you with this: seeking expert guidance and setting up a dedicated account for your career break money.

If you're struggling to finance a break, you can also consider applying for a paid professional fellowship. This approach allows you to access new opportunities, learn new skills, contribute in a meaningful way, and travel to new places. However, it won't provide the full benefits of a break.

TIP

If you're still saving for a break, make sure you check out the five steps to save money more quickly in the "Saving money more quickly and easily" section.

Seek financial guidance to inform your plan

No matter how you plan to arrive at the funds needed for your break, it's helpful to seek professional guidance for your finances. A professional perspective can help you consider the broader implications and make informed decisions about your approach. This can make your break more affordable and minimize potential consequences you may face down the road.

The guidance of financial advisors and planners, accountants, and online tools like retirement calculators can help you assess things like

>> Debt management and solutions to minimize interest payments while on a break

>> Financial vehicles that can yield interest payments on your savings while on a break

>> Investment portfolio distributions for current investments

>> Long-term impact on your retirement

>> Potential impact on your financial goals (such as buying a home)

>> Tax implications and strategies for the upcoming change in income and employment status (see the "Potential tax benefits of taking a break" sidebar)

A few of my clients have considered using a portion of their retirement savings to help fund their break. This controversial approach could have a big impact on your financial future, so it's a great example of something to discuss with an expert before making a final decision.

REMEMBER

You're going to the experts and tools for input and perspective, but you get to make the final decision. Everyone has different risk tolerance and values, so you'll have to account for this when receiving advice, even from professionals. They may provide valuable information, but ultimately you understand your situation and values best and will have to do what's right for you.

POTENTIAL TAX BENEFITS OF TAKING A BREAK

You may benefit from several tax-related benefits during your break. Leaving your job or embarking on an unpaid sabbatical lowers your income and, thus, your tax bracket, which means you may receive a (larger) refund at tax time. If you have long-term investments that have increased in value, you can consider selling them during your break to take advantage of lower capital gains tax rates. You may also be able to deduct some of your re-entry expenses such as career coaching or professional development. All of these are potential ways to save during your break and make for great topics to discuss with an expert.

ANECDOTE

When saving for my break, I had more than $40k in student loan debt and a rental property that was only breaking even in the best months (and costing me money in the worst). My financial advisor suggested I use my savings to first pay off my debt and then consider saving additional money for my break. But I knew I couldn't wait another two years to take a break, so I chose to put my loans into deferment and forbearance and left for my break. I was grateful to feel informed and prepared for the consequences of my actions, but ultimately, I decided to go, which turned out to be a great decision because I became debt-free just 21 months after my break ended.

Create a separate career break account

Creating a separate account for your career break funds can be immensely helpful, both before and during your break.

Before your break, creating a separate account has the following benefits:

>> **Helps you reach your savings goal more quickly:** Having a separate account can help you manage the urge to spend your savings on non-break related things. This lets your money accumulate faster than it otherwise would.

>> **Keeps you motivated and on track:** A separate account helps you see your financial progress clearly. When it starts growing, you'll realize that your hard work is paying off, which will motivate you to keep going.

>> **Gives you permission to start your break:** Putting your money into a separate account gives it a purpose. When you hit your target, it will be easier to give yourself permission to leave your job and start your break.

TIP

If you need extra help not touching your career break savings, consider setting up direct deposits or automatic transfers from your primary bank account. This will allow you to "set it and forget it," reducing the temptation to spend it as it grows.

When you're on a break, the two big benefits of having a separate career break account are the following:

>> **Provides clarity around your finances:** This keeps a clear separation between money meant for your break and money meant for other things (for example, unforeseen emergencies, home repairs, investments, and so on), which leaves you better informed to make financial decisions while on your break.

>> **Keeps you out of the danger zone:** Having a separate account allows you to monitor your spending and understand if you're staying on budget. If adjustments need to be made, you'll see this much sooner and before it's too late.

WATCH YOUR DOLLARS ADD UP IN A HIGH-YIELD ACCOUNT

When it's time to set up your career break fund, consider opening a high-yield checking or savings account. This type of account allows you to earn interest on your savings and potentially grow them more quickly so you can reach your goal sooner. You'll want to consider factors such as interest rates, fees, and minimum balance requirements to find your best option.

If your break involves travel and you're a U.S. citizen or resident, the Charles Schwab High Yield Investor Checking account is a great option to consider. It includes benefits like no minimums, monthly fees, or foreign transaction fees, plus a big money-saving benefit of unlimited ATM fee reimbursements. You can withdraw money from anywhere in the world using your Charles Schwab ATM card, and they'll reimburse you for any fees incurred from the local bank (which means more money for your break!).

Saving money more quickly and easily

After calculating the cost of my ideal break, I realized there was a huge gap between how much money I had and how much money I needed. I wanted to close the gap, so I thought about ways I could save money more quickly. If you're currently saving for a break and feel far away from your goal, use the five steps in this section to help you.

ANECDOTE

These five steps are how I saved $40,000 in 18 months while still enjoying my life in the process. In tracking my consistent progress, I knew when I was eight months away from reaching my $38k goal and gave my company ample notice that I was leaving.

REMEMBER

The approach I'm about to share isn't about depriving yourself. It's about prioritizing your goals and desires. You can (and should) enjoy your life while also saving for your break. It's likely you'll need to deflate your cost of living to reach your goal, but you can still invest in things that are important to you.

ANECDOTE

While saving for a break, I managed rental property repairs, continued my monthly $700 loan payment, and invested $3,000 in an orthodontic treatment and another $2,500 in laser hair removal (I mean, who wants to worry about waxing and shaving when you're traveling the world?). You don't have to deny yourself when saving for a break; just be very intentional about how you're spending your money.

Know exactly where your money is going

To save a lot of money in a reasonable amount of time, you need to fully understand your financial situation, which means you need to know exactly where your money goes. I recommend tracking what you spend (down to the penny) for one to two months. This information is powerful and critical to your success because it accomplishes several things:

>> **Helps you make better decisions:** When you can see where your money is really going, you'll understand the trade-offs you're making and collect helpful information to make powerful decisions about how to proceed.

>> **Informs you of the time required to reach your goal:** When you know how much you're actually saving each month, you can do the simple math to figure out how many months or years you'll need to reach your goal.

»» Prepares you to live on a budget during your break: After your break begins, it will be important to stick to your overall budget, and tracking what you spend can help you understand the spending habits you'll want or need to change when you're on a break.

»» Shows you what to change to reach your goal more quickly: If you want to speed up the process so you can take your break sooner, you'll understand what levers you can pull or adjust to save more money each month.

We're always making choices with our money, but if we're not keeping track, most of them are unconscious. Tracking your spending and setting a budget are ways to make these choices consciously and ensure they serve your best interest.

ANECDOTE

When I did this activity, I was surprised to learn that I was saving about $200/month with my $95,000 annual salary. My spending was out of control in ways I hadn't realized (like spending $700/month at the grocery store). I also realized that, at this rate, it would take more than 10 years for me to reach my savings goal of $38k. But I couldn't wait that long, so I moved on to the next step I'm about to share with you.

ACTIVITY

Brainstorm a list of categories where you currently spend your money (for example, groceries, dining out, rent/mortgage, utilities, car expenses, debt payments, entertainment, clothing, beauty, fitness, health, miscellaneous). Next, start tracking how much you spend in each category over the course of one or two months. Count every penny — no guessing or estimating!

ANECDOTE

One of my clients was *very* resistant to the idea of tracking and setting a budget. But as her break began, her lack of income necessitated a change in her spending habits. So, she tracked her expenses for one month and was surprised at how high they were. She discovered some places where her spending didn't align with her priorities, and one month later, she dropped her monthly spend by 40 percent without a tight budget. After she knew what was really happening, she was able to make better choices with her money.

TIP

If you like spreadsheets, you can build one to track your monthly expenses, like I did. Otherwise, you can try a budgeting app like Mint or You Need a Budget that will connect with your bank(s) and make tracking in real-time easier. If your bank tracks and categorizes your expenses for you, you can look back at your recent history to analyze your spending.

Develop a realistic budget

A budget is a map that shows where you want your money to go. It doesn't have to be restrictive; it just needs to reflect your priorities and values. After you've tracked your spending for a month or two, you will likely see places to realign your spending (places you want to spend less), and some might even be easy wins, like my grocery spending. If your bank is already tracking and categorizing your expenses, you can gather this information more quickly by looking at your most recent months of spending history.

ANECDOTE

With my $700/month grocery spend, I was mainly shopping at a high-end grocery store and the local co-op. This actually did align with my values; I just didn't feel great about how much I was spending. So, I changed my shopping habits and began shopping with a grocery list, stocking up when my favorite items were on sale, and substituting ingredients for cheaper alternatives. These changes immediately dropped my groceries expenses down to $350/month.

ACTIVITY

To set a simple and realistic budget, refer to the categories you developed while tracking your expenses (in the previous section). Examine the categories and what you spent for each; then decide how much you would like to spend in the next month. Start with what feels good and doable over the next month. You can always adjust your budget later, as you get better at saving.

REMEMBER

To create a budget you'll actually stick to, make sure it's realistic rather than aspirational. Saving for a break is a marathon, not a sprint, so you have to set a pace you can maintain. Otherwise you'll burn out, feel super deprived, and give up.

TIP

To make sure you don't feel deprived, I recommend adding a category to your budget for fun and/or exploration. Essentially, you want to set aside money each month (that you're required to spend) to keep enjoying life and experience new and interesting things. This is the secret to living well while also working hard to save a lot of money.

ANECDOTE

I named my category the Exploration Fund and set aside $200 each month. I was required to spend this money on things that stoked my sense of curiosity and adventure. It kept me learning, growing, and having fun, which kept me on track and helped me reach my savings goal in just 18 months. If all you do is cut things out without adding anything back in, you'll quickly want to give up on your goal.

Don't be discouraged if saving money is hard at first. You're learning new habits and will get better at it over time. Starting can be messy and imperfect, but to create the results you want, you have to start somewhere. Welcome to your new start!

I had just $1,500 in my bank account and $50k in student loan debt when I decided to start saving for a career break. My first few months, I could save only $200 a month. But by sticking with it, I got much better at making money decisions and eventually ramped up to saving $1,200/month.

Save your lump sums

This step was one of the biggest contributors to my success and really sped up my results. I saved the lump sums of money I received.

When you're working hard to save, it can be tempting to splurge on a treat when you receive a lump sum of money, especially if it's unexpected. But immediately diverting these lump sums into your career break account can turbo charge your savings and drastically reduce the time needed to reach your goal.

While budgeting helped me reach my goal, almost half of my $40,000 came from saving my lump sums, including tax refunds, corporate bonuses, birthday money, holiday gifts, and an unexpected refund check from my escrow account. Not saving my lump sums would have meant an extra year of working and saving to reach my goal of taking a break.

Spend your money wisely

Budgeting well doesn't require living super frugally. Achieving your financial goal is really about making thoughtful choices and living in alignment with your values. So, instead of working hard to afford things you "kind of" want but that will go unused, unworn, uneaten, and so on, or the things that you think will impress others and ooze success, invest in things you truly value and that provide meaning.

REMEMBER

Don't be afraid to reduce your cost of living. It's a short-term sacrifice that can lead to a massive long-term gain. Six months into saving for my break, I decided to get a roommate. My new apartment was still nice (and spacious) and this move enabled me to save an extra $800 each month, which helped me reach my goal a lot sooner.

Celebrate your progress along the way

Sometimes saving for a break can feel like a slog, especially when your goal is far away. So, it's critical to your success that you celebrate the smaller milestones along the way. Taking a moment to acknowledge your progress and dedication will work wonders to keep you motivated, in high spirits, and excited for your break. If you need some inspiration, here are a few ideas:

>> Call a friend to cheer you on and celebrate every time you reach another $1,000 in savings.

>> Reward yourself with an hour of free time to do something fun (binge watch a show, visit a nearby park, go for a walk around the lake, have coffee with a friend, and so on).

>> Grab your favorite beverage (cappuccino, wine, kombucha, and so on) for a small celebratory splurge.

>> Create a celebratory music playlist and dance it out for 10 minutes every time you hit another $1,000 in savings.

Applying for a fellowship

If your desire to take a break is centered on learning, growth, and new experiences, you can consider a professional fellowship to fund your experience. Social impact organizations provide fellowships to professionals who can support and advance their mission via project-based work. Projects can last weeks or months and take place all over the globe. Here are four fellowship examples for mid-career professionals:

>> **AsiaGlobal Fellows Program:** Leaders and experts collaborate on global issues related to Asia.

>> **Eisenhower Fellowships Global Program:** Professional and personal development opportunities for leaders from a diverse mix of sectors.

>> **Fulbright Specialist Program:** Connects U.S. professionals with international host institutions for short project-based exchanges.

>> **Peace Corps Response Program:** Short-term, high-impact projects to support urgent needs across the world.

TIP

To discover more options, you can access a comprehensive fellowship database at ProFellow.com and/or perform online research to learn about fellowships within your industry.

WARNING

Fellowships are structured professional experiences. They're not intended for rest, recovery, enjoying free time, or unstructured exploration. If you're in need of a break from professional expectations and/or a highly structured life, a fellowship will not be a suitable replacement. It can, however, be a meaningful addition to your overall break experience that helps you explore new interests and further develop your professional experience while also expanding your network.

ANECDOTE

Stephen took a 15-month career break to rest and recover from burnout, pursue hobbies and interests, and to figure out his next career step. During his break, Stephen was able to recharge, spend time with loved ones, and travel abroad. Near the end of his break, he received a three-month clean energy–focused fellowship. While the majority of Stephen's break focused on his personal goals for this time off, he was able to add a fellowship experience to inform his future career path, explore new options, build friendships, and expand his peer network.

Chapter **6**

Establishing a Timeline for Your Break

The final aspect of putting together a solid career break or sabbatical plan is developing a timeline for your break. In this chapter, I share how you can determine the best time to start your break and estimate how long it will last. I also explain how to lay out a timeline of your break activities to see how it all comes together.

As you move through this chapter and begin developing your timeline, your plans may change. That's totally OK! Even if things change, creating a tentative timeline helps you build momentum, makes your break feel more real, and keeps you grounded in the planning process. The sooner you start planning your timeline, the sooner your break can begin!

Determining the Length of Your Break

The length of your break will heavily influence your timeline and budget. It can also impact the timing of travel plans (if your break includes travel). So, as you begin developing your break timeline, it's important to consider the length and make an informed estimate as to how long your break will last. There are several ways to approach estimating the length of your break. In this section, I walk you through how to use each one.

No matter how you approach it, some key factors influence the length. Following are several common factors; note the ones that are relevant for you and consider them as you determine your break length:

>> **Break themes and goals:** Does your estimate allow enough time to address and achieve them?

   While you might not be able to do everything on your wish list, it's important to fulfill your themes/needs (as explained in Chapter 4) so you'll get what you need most out of this experience.

>> **Burnout level:** How much time will you need to recover and prepare yourself to re-enter the workplace?

   In my experience, it can take an average of three months to fully decompress from work, so consider this as you plan your break's length.

>> **Finances:** How long can you afford to be on a break, and how much are you willing to invest in this experience?

   If you need help answering these questions, see Chapter 3 to help clarify your financial situation and Chapter 5 for steps to determine what you can afford.

>> **Responsibilities:** Do you have a partner, children, and/or other responsibilities and commitments?

   You'll want to consider the impact the length of your break may have. Your needs are important, but creating the best estimate requires consideration of all inputs.

REMEMBER

A break's length is fluid. As it unfolds, the length may change. You can end your break early or extend it. Thirty percent of my clients reported that their break lasted longer than they'd originally predicted, and almost half reported that their original guess was accurate (within a month).

Your goal is to set a break length that works well for you and allows you to meet your break goals. If you have an impending obligation, like a start date for a new job or a new school year (for your kids), or if you've taken an approved leave of absence like a sabbatical, your length is predetermined. Move ahead to the "Choosing Your Start Date" section to find out how to set your start date.

Deciding how much you want to spend

One way you can determine the length of your break is to decide how much you want to invest in a break and then back into how long that amount would last. You can do this in four simple steps:

1. **Determine the total cost (investment) for your break.**

How much do you want to spend on your overall break experience?

2. **Adjust your number to account for ad-hoc expenses and add an adequate buffer for emergencies.**

Refine your cost to factor in things beyond monthly expenses (see Chapter 5 for suggestions and guidelines).

3. **Estimate average monthly expenses for the break.**

What's the average amount you plan to spend to live each month while on a break? (Visit Chapter 5 for help answering this question.)

4. **Determine the number of months your adjusted investment would last.**

Use this equation:

total investment / monthly cost of living = # months on a break (including time for re-entry)

Figure 6-1 provides an example of how to estimate the length of your break when starting with an overall cost. Note that this includes your re-entry period and assumes that your re-entry period expenses will be roughly the same as your overall monthly average. If you plan to spend significantly less during your re-entry period, you may extend the length of your break.

1. Set the overall cost/investment of your break:
$30,000

2. Adjust for ad-hoc expenses and a buffer for emergencies:

Ad hoc expenses	$1,500
Buffer	$4,500 (15% of $30,000 investment)
Total	$6,000

Adjusted amount to spend on break $24,000

3. Estimate your average monthly expenses:

Food	$500
Accommodations	$1,200
Entertainment	$300
Ongoing expenses	$300
Miscellaneous/other	$200
Total	$3,000

4. Determine number of months your adjusted investment will last:
Adjusted amount to spend ÷ average monthly cost = # months on break
$24,000 ÷ $3,000 = 8 months

⟶ **Start planning for an 8-month break!**

FIGURE 6-1: The four steps to determine the length of your break when starting with an overall cost.

Creating your ideal break first

With this approach, you start by outlining your ideal break experience. What are the highlights of your plan — the "must-do" items that are a high priority and will help you fulfill your goals? If you created your themes, wish list, and re-entry period in Chapter 4 or your break budget in Chapter 5, you've set your outline. (If you haven't, read those chapters now to help with this exercise.)

When you have an outline of the important things you want your break to include, review your list and begin estimating the length of time needed for each one.

TIP

For simplicity, group overlapping ideas together when estimating the length of time.

As an example, let's say your ideal break includes downtime at home, a six-week cooking class, and short road trips to visit friends. If you plan for these to happen around the same time and expect some overlap, you could group them together and estimate three months for this phase. If you're planning a visit to Thailand and want to take a three-week yoga training class while you're there, you could lump these together and dedicate two months to this phase. You'd then add these two phases together plus one additional month for your re-entry period (per the 1 for 6 Rule in Chapter 4) and plan for a six-month break.

Picking a number that feels good

You may have a length in mind. Choosing the length of your break can be as simple as deciding how much time you'd like to be away from work. Your inner wisdom might be telling you that you need a six-month break, or you might receive a six-month severance package and decide you'll use it to take a four-month break. This is a completely fine way to arrive at your estimated length of time.

Here is some information that may be a helpful anchor point: The average break length among my clients is 12 months, with 32 percent taking a break that lasts between 11 and 12 months. Collectively, their breaks ranged anywhere from 2 months to 2 years.

Taking a hybrid approach

You can use any combination of the previously mentioned approaches to estimate the length of your break. You can also apply multiple approaches to validate and refine your number.

REMEMBER

Regardless of how you approach determining the length of your break, stop when you land on a number that feels good to you, and remember it can be changed.

ANECDOTE

To estimate the length of my break, I started with a number that felt right at the time: 6 months. That length actually seemed extravagant, and I could barely imagine how I would pay for a break that lasted that long. But as I moved forward in the planning process and developed my themes (as explained in Chapter 4), I realized I would need more time to accomplish my goals. So I bumped my break up to 12 months and used the steps in Chapter 5 to estimate the total cost. After my break was underway, I realized I was spending a lot less than I'd anticipated, and I ultimately extended it to 20 months, including my re-entry period.

Choosing Your Start Date

It can feel hard to nail down a date to start your career break. With so many factors and options to consider, it's normal to feel a bit overwhelmed. Add in the realization that you'll eventually be parting with a steady paycheck, and you might be tempted to delay this critical piece of the planning puzzle. But setting a date unlocks benefits you don't want to miss! In this section, I help you determine your best start date to create accountability and provide a list of factors to consider as you set your ideal date.

REMEMBER

There will be pros and cons to any date you choose. Your goal isn't to find the perfect date, it's to find a good date that supports you, your well-being, and your career break goals.

Your start date serves as an anchor point for your break. From here, things will start coming together and move you into action. For example, setting a start date will

>> Create clarity for coordinating with friends (visits, travels, etc.)

>> Create focus for saving money for your break

>> Inform when you give your notice or leave your job

>> Make your break feel more real and create momentum

>> Move you forward in the planning process, including managing logistics (what to do with your belongings, insurance, visas, signing up for courses, etc.)

>> Provide clarity and guidance for your travel plans, such as understanding the impact seasonality may have on your timeline

ANECDOTE

Originally, I planned to start my break in October (right before my birthday). But as I moved forward with the planning process, I realized I'd need to start sooner to avoid driving through the Northern Plains during a winter blizzard on my three-month road trip. So I moved up my start date to early September (for the Labor Day holiday). As my savings began to accumulate, I realized I would reach my $38,000 savings goal sooner than I'd thought. So I bumped up my start date again and gave my company eight months' notice that I would be leaving to take a career break in early August.

It's normal to feel "scared-cited" (a combination of fear and excitement) as you set your start date. It can feel terrifying to make this commitment and exhilarating to envision starting your break. If you're feeling this emotion, please know that nothing has gone wrong. It's actually a sign that you're heading in the right direction!

Discovering how soon you can begin

Before you set your ideal start date, it's helpful to know how soon you can begin. You can definitely start after the earliest possible date, but establishing this anchor point leaves you better prepared to navigate surprises that arise, like

>> A serious health-related issue

>> Losing a loved one

>> Losing your job

>> Being offered a voluntary severance package

If you already have the money necessary for your break, you could likely begin right away. This doesn't mean this is the best option (see the next section for other factors you need to consider), but it's a helpful data point to have.

If you're still saving for a break, understanding how soon you could start your break requires an assessment of your financial situation and calculating how long it would take to reach your savings goal to pay for the break (as covered in Chapter 5).

When Karin's health unexpectedly declined, she was forced to begin her break eight months before her planned start date. Luckily, she'd already been preparing and saving for her break for several months. With her tentative career break plan and an acute awareness of her financial situation, Karin was able to make adjustments and successfully navigate the unexpected early start.

Considering your constraints and finances

Determining your earliest possible start date is a big piece of the timeline puzzle, but you'll also want to think through your obligations, constraints, and the financial implications of starting your break.

Plotting your ideal start date requires looking at the bigger picture. You might decide it's best to wait, even when you have the money. Ultimately, you want to choose a date that prioritizes your dreams, desires, and well-being without putting yourself into a logistical or financial pickle.

Here are common considerations to help you set an ideal date:

>> Career break considerations

- Seasonality for travel destinations (affects crowd size, cost, and availability of transport and activities)
- Weather (especially for travel, such as to avoid hurricane, monsoon, or tornado season)
- Wish list activities with fixed dates or timeframes (festivals, tours, courses, unique experiences like whale watching)

>> Financial considerations

- Annual income (tax impact, increased refund, etc.)
- Apartment lease end date
- Employee bonuses
- High season versus low season for travel costs
- Home updates or repairs necessary to list it for rent
- Sizeable upcoming expenses (home or car repairs, healthcare, etc.)
- Rental unit demand (if renting out your home – high versus low season)
- Savings goal (time needed to reach your target)
- Vesting schedule for company-provided benefits

>> Personal considerations

- Health insurance (health issues and/or medications that require your current health insurance)
- Personal preferences (choosing a date that feels good to you)

- Prior commitments and obligations (weddings, family vacations, reunions etc.)
- School calendars (for yourself or children)
- Your well-being (not sacrificing your mental or physical health)

>> **Professional considerations**

- Project(s) you want to complete
- Staff transitions (rotations, hiring seasons, staff changes, etc.)
- Upcoming promotion

TIP

Have a calendar handy as you reflect on your considerations. Marking them down and visually tracking their impact on your timeline will help you determine your ideal start date.

WARNING

Don't let finances alone determine your ideal start date. It can be tempting to maximize your savings, but there will always be a financial benefit to waiting. Choose a date that also honors your goals and factors in your well-being.

Putting it on the calendar

After you've considered the influencing factors and determined your ideal start date, it's time to claim your date by putting it on the calendar. Owning your tentative start date in this way makes your break more real and moves you forward in the planning process. It also helps you determine your resignation date. Chapter 7 provides great advice for determining the optimal date to give your notice and how to approach things with your manager.

ACTIVITY

For bonus points, share your date with a friend or loved one after you've put it on the calendar. This step helps build momentum and make your break feel more real.

REMEMBER

Your start date is tentative. While it's important to own your ideal start date to get the ball rolling, you can always revise your date, if necessary (as I shared in the earlier anecdote for choosing your start date).

Planning the Timeline of Your Break Experience

As you continue developing your career break plan, it will be helpful to have a general sense of how your break will flow. For several reasons, I don't recommend attempting to plan all the details upfront or developing a complete itinerary:

>> With an endless array of possibilities, trying to plan the details of a 6- to 12-month break can quickly become overwhelming and leave you stuck in analysis paralysis.

>> You can work out many of the details during your break, when you have more free time and energy to plan (which makes the whole experience more enjoyable).

>> Your break will continue to evolve as you plan and later begin your break. Attempting to plan all of the details upfront can create a lot of wasted time and rework.

Although you don't need to plan all the details upfront, mapping out a high-level timeline of events is a helpful first step. You'll uncover trouble spots that might jeopardize your break experience. This section outlines an approach that simplifies the process of developing a timeline and itinerary and that helps you avoid jeopardizing your break.

Drafting a monthly overview of your break timeline

To ease into the process of planning your timeline and itinerary, start by creating a monthly overview of your break timeline. This approach keeps things high level, reduces feelings of being overwhelmed, and lets you visualize your break to easily catch the two big trouble spots:

>> **Overload:** You can easily see where you're overloading your break (i.e., being too ambitious with your time) so you can make adjustments to bring it back in balance.

>> **Solution:** Reschedule or remove activities and events to create balance and a more even distribution.

>> **Neglecting your themes/needs:** You quickly realize if you're neglecting your break themes and needs, so you can create more space to include them.

Solution: Add more theme-based activities and/or remove those that don't align to your themes.

Don't overload your timeline! If you succumb to FOMO (fear of missing out) or the desire to impress others as you develop your itinerary, you'll end up with an inauthentic and exhausting break. Don't fall into these traps — stay connected to *your* purpose and goals for this break to ensure a restorative, meaningful, and fulfilling experience.

Fulfilling your themes (as discussed in Chapter 4) is what creates your most successful break experience, so make sure to heavily include activities that align with them in your timeline and itinerary.

Don't forget to include a re-entry period in your career break timeline. If you need help estimating the length of your re-entry period, check out Chapter 4.

Creating a monthly overview of your break timeline shows you how your potential activities will flow together and where you might be overloading your break and helps you ensure that you haven't underprioritized your break themes.

To create a monthly overview of your break timeline, write down the month you want your break to start and then list the remaining months until you've reached the length of your break (as developed in the earlier section). Next, write down your planned events and activities for each month, listing the higher-priority ideas above each month and the lower-priority below. As an example, Figure 6-2 provides a three-month snippet of a monthly break timeline.

Upon drafting a monthly overview, you'll see your timeline in a new light and be able to review it for potential gaps or trouble spots. If I were reviewing Figure 6-2 for a client, I would point out the following concerns:

>> If their break starts in June or July and one of their themes involved rest/recovery, I would point out that July seems very busy for the beginning of a break. I would encourage them to shift most of these activities into the later part of their break and proactively include experiences and activities that fulfill their rest/recovery theme, especially toward the beginning of their break.

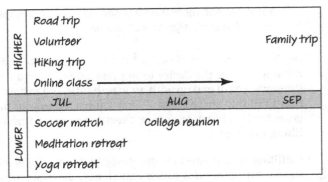

FIGURE 6-2: A three-month excerpt of a monthly career break overview (July through September).

>> July appears quite busy and could lead to feelings of being overwhelmed. I would ask if any of these activities can be moved to a different month or removed altogether. If this were challenging for them, I would emphasize removing or rescheduling the lower-priority activities first (i.e., the soccer match, meditation retreat, or yoga retreat).

>> August and September appear much lighter. Lighter, unscheduled months are great to have on a break, so I would support this while encouraging them to stay connected to their themes during these months. However, if they were struggling with a heavy July and wanted to keep most of their activities, I would suggest rescheduling an activity or two for August or September, which appear to have more room.

>> I would also review their themes to ensure that over the entire timeline of their break, they're creating adequate time and space to address and fulfill them.

REMEMBER

Don't forget to have fun! You have time to figure this out, and there's no "right" way to do it. Just keep your themes in mind and adjust your timeline as necessary.

Accounting for factors that impact your timeline

As you lay out a proposed timeline for your break, you want to incorporate key factors that can heavily influence the optimal order and distribution of your break activities. This is especially true if your break involves travel.

Here's a list for you to consider:

>> Appointments: Be sure to account for any appointments you or your loved ones expect to occur during your break (surgeries, anniversaries, reunions, etc.)

>> Big events: It's important to account for big events you'd like to attend (summer break, weddings, birthday parties, etc.) in addition to those you'd like to avoid (due to the impact on cost and availability at your chosen destinations).

>> Holidays: Similar to big events, it's important to account for those you'd like to celebrate during a specific time and place, in addition to those you'd like to avoid for convenience, cost, or personal reasons.

>> Seasonality (high versus low): If you plan to travel during your break, this is a big one. High season is the most popular, and with it usually comes ideal weather, tons of activities, higher costs, and lower availability — think Europe in the summer. You'll have to decide what matters most to you, but if you're traveling on a budget, shoulder season (which occurs between the high and low seasons) can be a great option as there are smaller crowds and lower costs, but you'll generally benefit from good weather and availability. If you decide to travel during high season, be sure to account for the higher costs in your break budget.

>> Weather: This can have a major impact on your timeline. It can affect your mood, the road conditions, accessibility, and the cost.

- If you plan to ski the Rocky Mountains, you'll want to make sure you get there before the snow melts.

- If you struggle with the wintertime blues, winter might be the best time to travel.

- If you want to visit the Greek Isles, you'll need to account for a higher cost during the warmest months.

- If you want to visit Malaysia and walk around and explore, it's likely you'll want to avoid the rainy monsoon season.

- If you're planning a road trip, understanding the possible road conditions you'll face is critical so you don't get caught in bad weather.

To help you plan for specific destinations, seek out helpful resources to aid you: travel guides, websites, blogs, vlogs, You-Tube channels, and social media accounts.

After I'd decided I would visit Southeast Asia, I referenced travel guidebooks and several travel blogs to determine the optimal timing. When I confirmed I would be traveling in early fall, I researched the weather patterns to finalize my route across six countries and avoid the heavy rains as much as possible.

Building your break itinerary

When you've got a draft of your break timeline, you can begin diving into the details and putting together your break itinerary (i.e., your more detailed plan).

If you don't have any travels planned for your break, your itinerary will likely be a collection of commitments, appointments, and activities you hope to experience during your break. If you do plan to travel, you'll need to plan things out a bit more. Either way, I recommend using a calendar to keep track of things and make sure the pieces fit together.

Figure 6-3 is a simple calendar format you can use to plan out your days and ensure that you'll have adequate time in your chosen destinations as well as account for the time spent traveling between them.

FIGURE 6-3: A calendar format to help you keep track of your travel schedule that includes your daily destination(s) and key events and activities.

Gearing Up for
Your Break

Discover how to share your news with others and resign from your job with fantastic results.

Get ready and feel prepared for your break. Discover the key details and specific action steps that will help you navigate the logistics and practicalities of taking a break.

Create an easier travel planning experience and discover invaluable travel resources to ensure a great experience while globetrotting on your break.

Chapter **7**

Sharing News of Your Career Break

S preading the news that you'll be taking a break is a really important step in your career break journey. Somewhere between making your decision and leaving your job, you'll need to start informing people of your plans. In this chapter, you find out how to bravely put yourself out there and share your news with fantastic results.

I explain how to communicate your decision simply and confidently to those around you, including friends, family, colleagues, and strangers. Mastering this approach will create a groundswell of support that follows you into your break and allows you to leave your job on great terms. It will also pave the way for a braver you to emerge. Sharing your news is one of the ways that the act of planning a break can change your life. If you want to transition into your break feeling empowered and confident and having tons of support, this chapter explains exactly how do it!

Building Your Confidence

How will you explain your career break to others in your life? The first step to creating great results actually happens before you start sharing your news: building up your confidence and belief. Garnering support will be much easier when you're feeling clear and confident about your decision.

In this section, you establish a healthy dose of confidence by understanding the benefits that sharing your news will provide and discovering an empowering way to reframe your break that makes telling others an easier and more fruitful experience. If you're lacking confidence or want to amplify what you already have, this section gives you a big boost as you prepare to share your news!

TIP

Normalizing your goal of taking a break can help you build confidence. Immerse yourself in podcasts, vlogs, articles, and stories of others who've walked a similar path. Give your brain ample evidence that taking a break won't ruin your life and can actually change it for the better.

Realizing the benefits of sharing your news

Telling people that you're taking a break can feel like a difficult and vulnerable step — to put yourself out there as you go against the status quo — but it's also an exciting opportunity to inspire others and invite support for your break. You receive several great benefits when you start telling people about your break. Delaying this step in the process can actually hinder your progress and be a detriment to your career break. As challenging as this step might feel, I promise you it's worth taking. So many good things are waiting for you on the other side of sharing your news!

Setting a new tone for your life

It's not an exaggeration to say that the practice of sharing your news can set a new tone for your life. It's one of the simple yet powerful ways that the act of planning a break can change your life.

Telling people around you that you're tired of following "the rules" and are planning a courageous leap into the unknown is not easy. But the act of speaking your truth and being willing to sit in the discomfort of others who potentially don't approve of your choices is a huge growth opportunity. When you're able to be vulnerably honest and real about what you want for yourself and your life, you'll access a new level of personal freedom and draw in people who want to support you on this journey.

Some people may not respond well to your surprising news, but the vast majority of people will feel a mixture of excitement, envy, and curiosity. As you practice sharing your truth with others, you'll likely notice that many of those whose reactions and judgment you feared respond more positively than you'd imagined. And for those who respond negatively, you can find advice on how to handle them in the "Handling the naysayers" section later in this chapter.

Making it feel more real

Planning a career break can be an intimidating feat, and after you've made the decision to take one, there's likely to be a part of you that still doesn't believe it's real. You may even find yourself waffling back and forth on your decision.

Sharing your news can remedy this and help make your break feel like more of a reality. Sharing your intention with another person triggers your brain to start creating more certainty and confidence around your break. By speaking it out loud, you're claiming your goal and owning your dream. This is a powerful step that will increase your commitment to achieving your goal. The more you practice saying it, the more deeply your brain will accept it as a fact, which helps you move forward with the planning process.

Creating accountability

Telling people that you're planning to take a break will help you create an external source of accountability. This can significantly increase your likelihood of taking a break. When sharing your news with others, their excitement and curiosity prompts them to check on you and your progress. They'll be interested and invested and want to know how things are going with details about your savings goal, your itinerary planning, and giving your notice. This supportive social pressure will help motivate you to follow through on your commitment to yourself and your break, even during hard moments. This creates another layer of account-ability to continue taking the smaller steps along the way that will lead to realizing your career break dream.

Receiving support and assistance

This is one of the biggest benefits and reasons why you should share your news with others — so they can support you, advocate for you, and cheer you on along the way! You open yourself up to an immense amount of support when you start telling people about your plan to take a break. People will want to help you. You just have to give them the opportunity.

ANECDOTE

Sharing the news with my colleagues brought a lot of fun sur-prises into my life. Coworkers treated me to dinner to support my savings goal and to have fun conversations about my travel plans. We had happy hours to celebrate my big news, and one col-league connected me to a mutual friend who'd recently returned from a break and could offer me helpful advice. One of the best surprises came through a coworker I'd met only twice. He offered up a connection with his friends and family in Colombia for when I passed through. I took him up on the offer and stayed with his cousin's family in Bogota and spent several days with his best friend's family in Medellin. These were some of my fondest career break memories.

People may help you and support your break in many ways. When you share your news, you lean into the belief that others want to delight in this goodness with you. And that attracts even more opportunities for fun, connection, and support like the following:

>> Checking in and offering words of encouragement to keep you motivated and on track

>> Connecting you with people in their circle who've taken a break and can offer advice

>> Introducing new ideas and destinations for you to consider while planning your break

>> Putting you in touch with friends and family in other places so you'll have tour guides and trusted sources along your travels

>> Treating you to dinner or other social outings to help you reach your savings goal and celebrate your big news

Reframing your break for a better outcome

When it's time to share your news, you might worry that others are going to see your choice as self-indulgent, irresponsible, and maybe even reckless. How do you explain it in a way that makes your friends, family, and colleagues understand and want to support you? You frame it in a positive light and invite them to join you on this exciting journey.

You might feel powerless to shape how others view your decision to take a break, but you actually have a lot of control here. Your thoughts and energy around your break will set the tone for others. By taking a break, you're charging off in a new direction that many have never considered, and some aren't brave enough to follow. Because this is unchartered territory for most people, they'll be unsure of how to react to your news and will look to you for clues. This presents an amazing opportunity for you to frame the narrative and gain their support! If you feel confident about your decision and believe taking a break is ultimately a good thing, most will follow your lead and assume that to be true. But if you seem doubtful when you share your news and seem to believe your decision is irresponsible, they're likely to follow you down that slippery slope. So first, you have to be sure that you're sold on your decision to take a break. Often, the negative feedback we receive hurts because it reflects our own fears. If you need help working through your career break fears, check out Chapter 3.

Before you share your news, frame your break in a positive light in your own mind so you can feel more certain and confident about your decision. You aren't responsible for changing people's beliefs, but you are responsible for carefully choosing your own. Before you share your news, make sure you believe in your break so you can help others believe in it as well. Following are a few of my viewpoints on taking a break. Consider this a pep talk delivered via bullet points!

>> A break demonstrates your courage and commitment to your well-being and happiness.

>> Even if you don't have it all figured out just yet, you're dedicating time to restoring, recharging, and eventually upleveling your entire life.

- » It's an exciting chapter of creation and one that will unlock new possibilities, personally and professionally.

- » You're being a good shepherd of your one precious life and ensuring that you don't waste it.

- » You're brave to go on this thrilling journey and not let a fear of the unknown stop you. The world needs more brave people.

- » You are valuing a life that feels good to live instead of one that only looks good from the outside.

ACTIVITY

Spend 15 to 20 minutes thoughtfully considering reasons why your break should be celebrated. You can find an extensive overview of career break benefits for inspiration in Chapter 2.

Think of sharing your news as a special invitation for others to join you in spirit and share in your excitement as you embark on this spectacular journey. Many people who care about you will be thrilled to accept that invitation.

Gaining Support from Others

It can feel overwhelming to start sharing your news, but with a little effort, you can open the floodgates to receive support that will keep you moving forward (and it will make your break a lot more fun!). As you prepare to start telling others about your break, use this section to help you strategize your message and assess the optimal time to start spreading your big news.

Breaking your news to others

How do you tell someone you're taking a career break? How much information do you share? How much information is too much? The simple answer is: Share your truth.

If you have developed your purpose statement and themes (see Chapter 4), you already have everything you need to do this. Being able to clearly express your why (your purpose) makes a compelling case for people to want to support you. And knowing the pillars of your break (your themes) helps you explain, at a high level, how you intend to spend your time, even when the details are still in development. Having these critical pieces of your career break structure will help you articulate your reason for doing something so unconventional and unfamiliar and help you share your career break vision with others.

TIP

You get to set the tone for this conversation. An easy way to open it is with a simple, "I have some exciting news" or "I have some big news to share." In both of these examples, you're communicating a positive and upbeat tone about the news you're going to share.

When it comes to what to actually say when you break the news, I recommend starting with your purpose and thinking of it as your "nugget of truth." You don't need a long explanation or justification. Keep it simple and heartfelt. Sharing in this way can have powerful results. It invites others into your world and gives them an opportunity to connect with you and your mission. Reflect on your "big why" for this break and what you hope to gain from it and then share your answer.

Here are a few examples for inspiration:

» I'm tired of feeling like I'm watching my life from the sidelines. I'm ready to be the person who goes for their dreams and actively pursues the life they want.

» I've achieved some great goals in my life, but I feel ready to change my trajectory, and I want time to explore what that could look like.

» I'm exhausted and honestly feeling a bit lost as to what I want for my next chapter. I'm excited to take some time to thoughtfully figure that out.

» I decided it was finally time to live my dream and travel around the world! My annual PTO allotment wasn't cutting it, so I'm taking a break instead.

» I realized life is short and I really want to spend some quality time with the people I love most and support them as we navigate this next season of life.

» I need a time out to nourish myself, my spirit, and my body. I'm building a foundation for an amazing second half of my life.

» I'm learning how to put myself back into the center of my life and make choices that feel really good to my soul.

>> I'm taking time to reimagine my life and explore exciting new possibilities for what comes next!

After expressing your nugget of truth, you can ease into more detail by sharing your themes. When someone asks, "What are you going to do on your break?" this is what they want to know. You can share your break pillars (themes) and say, "I plan to recharge my batteries, spend time connecting with my loved ones, explore new countries, and eventually start my own business." This will be enough to get most people onboard and excited to support your break.

TIP

Let the conversation flow organically. Start with your purpose, and if it receives a warm (or curious) reception, move into sharing your themes and more details about your break. Some people may have a ton of questions and concerns. This is natural. Try to view this as curiosity more than judgment — this will help you feel less tense.

WARNING

Try not to get defensive when people ask questions. Your brain might tell you that you're being put on trial, but the truth is that most people are just genuinely curious (and probably a bit confused), so their questions are well-intentioned and just a bid for more information. If you don't have answers that you're ready to share, it's totally fine to say, "I don't know. I'm still figuring it out" or "That's all I know for sure. It's still unfolding."

Handling the naysayers

Generally, you'll find most people to be either supportive or indifferent to your decision. But you're likely to encounter a naysayer or two along the way. When you do, know that they're likely doing one of a few things:

>> **Worrying about your safety:** If they haven't been privy to your thoughtful planning, they may worry that you'll be professionally penalized or go broke in the process of taking a break. They don't see all that you stand to gain and instead are focused on what you could lose (steady paycheck, good job, social acceptance).

>> **Projecting their limiting beliefs:** If they live in a reality where breaks aren't possible, you are blowing their mind and stretching beyond their imagination. Their lack of belief

isn't personal. They're simply giving you a glimpse into the fears and limiting beliefs they have about themselves and life in general.

>> **Reflecting your own fears and insecurities:** If you aren't sold on your idea of taking a break, they may subconsciously pick up on your doubt and insecurity and reflect it back to you. If you don't fully believe in your vision, they may sense that and join you in your worry.

If the naysayer is a loved one, you might want to invite them into an open conversation to share their concerns. It's possible that understanding more about your decision and the planning you've done will calm their fears. But please remember you're not responsible for how others feel about your decision, and you don't have to convince them that it's a great idea. Your plan to take a break may be something they've never heard of or considered. Their reaction is about their beliefs of what is possible; it's not about you. No one can know how to live your life better than you do, so be willing to have a few naysayers and lean in to celebrate with your cheerleaders.

REMEMBER

Sharing your news provides an opportunity to practice detaching yourself from other people's opinions about your life and your choices. Needing acceptance and approval will always create more of what you currently have. If you want something different, you'll have to make some brave choices and be willing to do things differently.

ANECDOTE

Two of my clients struggled with a loved one who vocally disagreed with their decision to take a break: one a spouse and the other a parent. In both circumstances, the negative comments hurt because they mirrored the fears and worries my clients had themselves. However, they each focused on the positive aspects of their break and those who supported them as they moved forward with their plan. Over time, both clients experienced a softening in their loved ones who saw them thriving while on their break. In the end, their loved ones came around to see the benefit of the experience and ultimately supported their decision.

Sharing your news sooner is better

There's no perfect time to share your news but sooner is often better than later (with two caveats that I mention in the next Warning). It can feel safer to hold your cards close and not show your hand until your plan has been set. A fear of judgment and unsolicited advice are usually to blame for this approach. While it's true that you'll potentially avoid judgment from the occasional naysayer, you're also missing out on receiving a ton of support in the process.

When it comes to sharing your news, pick a safe person for your first declaration and consider it a practice run. A "safe" person is someone who can listen with an unbiased ear. They won't project their own fears and concerns onto you. They're able to be neutral and listen with an open mind. Sometimes this safe person can be a complete stranger; other times it may be a confidante. Whoever they are, they don't need to share your dream of taking a break. They just need to allow you a space to openly share yours.

TIP

You don't have to tell everyone all at once. After practicing with your safe person, you can slowly start to tell more people about your big decision. I encourage you to keep sharing your news, as you feel ready, and welcoming in the support.

As you weigh out the best time to start sharing your news, I recommend beginning soon after you've made your decision (if you haven't already shared your idea with others while considering the option). As covered in the previous section, sharing your plan to take a break offers a lot of benefits, and I don't want you to miss out on receiving them. Supporters can brainstorm solutions when you feel stuck and offer encouragement when you're struggling with doubt. This isn't a journey that you need to navigate alone.

WARNING

My first caveat is to wait to share your news with highly opinionated people. It takes courage to plan a career break, and the beginning stages can be a delicate time. You don't want their fears and limiting beliefs to derail your momentum, so wait until you feel solid in your decision and are able to handle any potential negativity they may bring. My second caveat is to consider the impact of your news before telling those who are connected to your job. Be mindful of the potential consequences if word were to get out before you've told your manager or given notice.

TIP

If you don't have anyone in your network or inner circle that you feel safe sharing your news with, broaden your reach to connect with people on a similar quest. You may find them through social media, online groups, meetups, retreats, and so on.

Giving Your Notice and Leaving Your Job on Great Terms

Resigning from your job can be one of the most stressful parts of planning a career break. Your brain might offer you vivid visions of worst-case scenarios: being let go on the spot, permanently ruining your career, being monetarily penalized at bonus time, or being branded a failure who just couldn't hack it. But this doesn't have to be your reality. A thoughtful strategy and good timing can make giving your notice a positive experience. Every client who followed the strategy I'm about to share with you has said, "It went better than I expected." Your happy ending is possible, too!

If your main goal is to leave on great terms, you'll need to be two things: confident and considerate. Confidence comes across in your message (what you say) and consideration is shown in the timing of your message (when you say it). This section explains how to exude both qualities and shares a few examples of opportunities that can arise in the midst of giving your notice.

WARNING

Everything I'm about to share works best if you're in good standing at your job. If you're not, this approach won't harm your standing but it likely won't be enough to improve it either. However, it will hopefully help you part on neutral terms.

Knowing what to say

Contrary to popular belief, the best approach isn't searching for the perfect words and crafting a buzzword-filled speech. It's likely you'll forget half of it when the nerves kick in while you're delivering the news. Plus, it can come across as overly rehearsed and less authentic. You're taking a break, not jumping over to a competitor, and you have a great opportunity to gain an advocate in your manager. If you create an opportunity for your manager to understand how much this break means to you, you'll gain their support and leave on great terms.

To give your notice, follow a similar approach as outlined in "Breaking your news to others" where you start by sharing your "nugget of truth" or big why, but keep it focused on you (not them) and share what you hope to achieve with your break. Sharing why this break is so important to you and focusing on what you hope to gain from it will inspire your manager's support. If you drift into sharing the ways your current path, role, job, and so on hasn't been a good fit or disappointed you and focus on what you don't want, your message can get lost. Obviously, if they ask for feedback or make a counteroffer, you can share your honest experience, but I don't recommend starting off with this information when you first break your news.

Following are several examples that modify the purpose statements from the previous section. Note the focus on self and the uplifting tone:

>> I'm proud of how I've showed up for my career, but I'm ready to take a step back and reengage with things that bring me joy. I want to be braver and go for some of my big dreams.

>> I'm feeling really burned out and know that taking care of myself is the best way to come back stronger. I want to use this time to evaluate my path and reflect on my new definition of success.

>> I decided it was time to travel around the world. I know I'm going to learn a lot, and I can't wait to see what unfolds!

>> The people I love the most really need more time with me right now, and honestly, I need more time with them, too. I'm grateful for this time to connect with them and be fully present, which will help me feel ready and excited to return to work.

>> I realized that I'm burned out and need to focus on taking better care of myself. I don't want to wait any longer. I'm excited to see a restored, renewed, and inspired version of me emerge!

>> I'm ready to take some time to focus on the things that are good in my life and reconnect with myself in a way I haven't before. I want to thoughtfully explore what I want to come next.

This approach makes it easier to share authentically and confidently, to remember what you want to say in the heat of the moment, and to potentially gain an advocate in the process. Focusing on your simple truth and your hope for the future, like the previous examples show, is a great way to start the conversation when it's time to resign.

Once you've shared your nugget of truth (purpose) in the conversation, you can move on to sharing what you plan to focus on during your break (themes). If they seem engaged and interested, you can let the conversation flow organically, providing additional details about your break.

To prepare yourself to give your notice, reflect on your why and write down one or two bullets to summarize your answer. It's less about the exact words you use and more about the intention and energy behind your words. Connect with the essence of those bullet points and rewrite them to focus exclusively on you and what you hope to create through taking this break. You'll have a fruitful conversation, even if your nerves kick in. If you're still nervous after working out your bullet points, you can practice giving your notice with someone you trust to gain confidence and feel more at ease.

Taking a break is an exciting adventure! When you get ready to share your news, it's acceptable to convey that excitement and invite your boss to join you in celebration —"I've got some big news. I'm excited to share that I'm taking a career break. It was a big decision and one that obviously impacts you and the team, but (insert your nugget of truth here)."

Knowing when to say it

The default when leaving a job is to give a two-week notice, and many think this applies for resigning to take a break, but it doesn't. Giving two weeks' notice is a wasted opportunity. Giving more notice increases your odds of leaving on great terms. The best time to give notice is when you feel confident and set in your career break plan and timeline (your start date).

Demonstrating consideration for your team and company is the best way to ensure that you leave on great terms. Imagine being your team or your manager and receiving a two-week notice. That would likely feel chaotic and not leave enough time to revise the role or find an adequate replacement. Allowing your company time to prepare for your departure and a more seamless transition demonstrates partnership and consideration.

There is also a personal benefit to giving your notice sooner rather than later. It frees up your energy. You no longer have to spend time pretending you're invested in your five-year plan or the company's upcoming initiatives. You can shift your focus and energy back into your work and preparing for your upcoming break.

TIP

I recommend giving no less than a one-month notice. My clients average six to eight weeks.

WARNING

You know your situation best, and there might be a unique reason why you prefer to give less notice (like working in a career with sensitive information that would require you to leave immediately after giving your notice). You'll need to use your discretion to determine the best time to resign, but I encourage you to consider giving more notice than you initially planned.

ANECDOTE

When I left for my career break, I gave my company an eight-month notice. I knew I'd reach my savings goal in seven months, and that meant I'd finally be ready to take my break. I gave ample notice for three reasons: I was on a rotation program and wanted to avoid a short-term move into a new position; I wanted them to have adequate time to replace me; and I wanted to stop pouring energy into caring about the company initiatives. During those last seven months, I was better able to focus on my job and received my best review. I felt an incredible sense of freedom to not have to put energy into pretending I was staying and hiding my excitement about my upcoming break.

It can feel scary to imagine giving more notice. You might fear being let go early or penalized in some way. But if gaining support and ending things on a high note is important to you, give advanced notice to communicate your desire to support the company in the upcoming transition and not leave your team in a tight spot. This makes it easier for everyone to get behind you and support your new adventure.

POSITIVE AND SURPRISING OUTCOMES

Every client I've coached through the process of giving their notice had things turn out better than they'd anticipated, with generally positive results. Almost always, their managers took a moment to appreciate their contributions and reflect on their value to the team. Some of them have even been offered unexpected opportunities during their resignations. Here are some examples:

- A fully remote position in a company that previously did not offer remote positions
- A new role and promotion within the company
- A significant raise
- A newly created part-time role to extend the transition
- A six-month leave of absence to ensure an easy return to the company after the break was over
- A short-term contract position offered during the break

Receiving an unexpected offer while giving your notice can be enticing. But you've arrived at your decision to take a break after thoughtful planning. See the offer as a compliment and evidence that you'll have options when you're ready to return to work, but don't be swayed from your mission. Stay true to your career break purpose and themes. They are leading you to a better future.

Announcing Your Break

After you've shared your plan to take a break with close friends and family and have given notice at your job, it's time to make an announcement! Announcing your break will make it easier to let the rest of your network in on the secret. If you utilize social media, this is a simple place to share your news.

I recommend this step because it expands your ring of support. Offers to host, play tour guide, make connections, or give helpful travel advice may start rolling in. Plus, it invites others to be a part of your journey, which will be very helpful during your re-entry period. Your network will be more engaged with you and feel invested in your journey, making it easier to reconnect as you begin seeking new opportunities.

Figure 7-1 is a great example of a career break announcement.

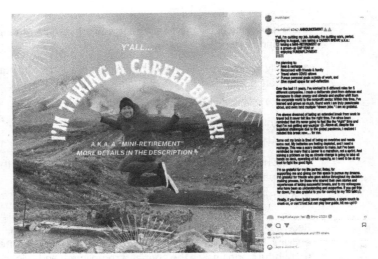

FIGURE 7-1: Career break announcement shared via Instagram.

Chapter **8**

Managing the Logistics

A s you begin preparing for your break, you need to think through key details and logistics necessary for your transition. In this chapter, I provide guidance and walk you through logistics that will help you feel ready to take the break. Using this chapter to thoughtfully prepare can yield big benefits like

» Feeling more confident about your break

» Reducing your stress during the preparation phase

» Ensuring a smoother transition into your break

» Minimizing last-minute chaos as you start your break

» Creating a better overall experience during your break

With thoughtful preparation, you'll experience less stress and career break drama, which means you'll have more time and energy to make the most of your break and enjoy this amazing experience.

WARNING

Don't let the details bog you down. While this chapter better prepares you to navigate a break smoothly, it's impossible to prepare for every possible hiccup or problem that may arise. Much like parenthood, when it comes to career breaks, a lot can be learned only through experience — so use this chapter to prepare as best you can, and let the rest unfold when you're on your break.

ANECDOTE

During my career break, I arrived in Bangkok days before my yoga training in Bali and lacking one critical item — a yoga mat! I'd been traveling light and didn't want to carry a cumbersome mat around the world with me. But now I was desperate to find a mat. I had some concern about finding a suitable option in just two days, but I was able to find one after a few failed attempts. If I'd tried to perfectly prepare for my break, I likely would have stressed over the logistics of securing and traveling with a yoga mat. But everything worked out with a little problem-solving. You don't need to prepare for everything ahead of time. You're resourceful and will figure it out, just like I did.

TIP

I'm going to cover some common logistics that might spark new ideas for you. Be sure to capture these ideas, so you can build on them and create a customized to-do list of your own.

Navigating the Practicalities of Preparing for a Break

Handling the administrative tasks in your personal life while preparing for a break helps you avoid expensive mistakes and a bumpy start to your break. It also makes it much easier to enjoy your break experience. In this section, I share important logistics to help get you career-break ready.

Adjusting your recurring expenses

Saving money becomes even more important when you begin preparing for a break. One way to make sure you'll spend your money wisely, both before and during your break, is to reevaluate your recurring expenses. Conducting a financial audit reveals opportunities to align with your new lifestyle and financial situation, helping you keep more money in your bank account. Proactively adjusting your recurring expenses by dropping unnecessary or irrelevant costs allows you to save more.

You'll have more free time on a break, which means some convenience-related expenses may no longer be worth the investment. It's also possible that your priorities will change as you prepare for your break, creating a desire to spend less. Whether you decide to adjust them during the preparation phase or after your break has started, examining your recurring expenses helps you see what to change to prevent money leaks.

Here are some common recurring expenses to examine as you prepare to start your break:

>> Annual and monthly fees and memberships: credit cards, public transit, parking access, gyms and fitness studios, and club stores (e.g., Costco)

>> Caretaking expenses: pet sitters and child care

>> Donations and monetary gifts

>> Insurance: health, life, car, homeowner

>> Maintenance services: lawn care, automobile

>> Subscriptions for online apps and services: television streaming services, grocery delivery apps, online newspapers, cloud storage, music streaming

>> Subscriptions for physical products: groceries and supplies (pet food, skincare), medications, subscription boxes, meal kits

>> Utilities: phone, gas, electricity, internet service

ACTIVITY

Review your bank and credit card statements for the previous 12 months. Then create a list of your recurring expenses. When you have your list, examine each item on the list. Envision being on a break (doing whatever you plan to do), and ask, "Will I need or want this?" If the answer is no, set a date to cancel it. I recommend immediately adding a reminder to your calendar so you won't forget. If the answer is yes, be sure to include it in your break budget and explore ways you can reduce it. This activity takes time, but it sets you up for big savings when you're no longer collecting a steady paycheck.

Evaluating your health insurance options

If you're launching a sabbatical or live in a country with government-provided healthcare, you likely won't need to worry about securing health insurance while on a break. For some, starting a break means losing health insurance benefits due to a lack of employment or because they plan to travel internationally. If taking a break will involve losing your health insurance, you need to think through the options so you're prepared for the transition. Coverage rules differ by country, so research your specific situation to know for sure. In the United States, giving up employer-sponsored health insurance can be one of the biggest obstacles to taking a career break. But it doesn't have to be. Several solutions can provide healthcare coverage while you're on a break (most of these are U.S.-specific):

>> **COBRA coverage:** This option extends your current employer-provided health insurance. It can be a preferred option if you'll need to continue your coverage (to use specific doctors and/or medications that aren't covered by the other options). But it's often the most expensive option. You pay the full premium without any employer subsidies or assistance.

>> **Health co-op:** This is a member-owned health insurance organization. Members (i.e., patients) pay premiums to the co-op to help cover the cost of care for all members. Co-ops aren't run for profit, so costs are often lower than traditional health insurance. But they also follow different regulations and may not provide safeguards for your care if the co-op runs out of money.

>> **Health Insurance Marketplace:** This service, run by the U.S. government, provides access to health insurance and enrollment (www.healthcare.gov). Options vary by state, and you may qualify for income-based tax credits (subsidies) to reduce your monthly premiums, making health insurance more affordable. With your impending loss of salary, you may qualify for a significant subsidy when choosing this option.

>> **Medicaid:** Depending on your estimated income for the year, you may qualify for Medicaid coverage, a government-provided healthcare coverage. You'll need to check your state's income guidelines to know for sure.

>> **Out-of-pocket/None:** If you plan to use travel insurance for your health-related expenses or opt to forgo health insurance altogether, you'll want to research any state mandates and penalties for being uninsured and factor this into your total cost (in addition to any healthcare expenses that may

arise). This can be an incredibly expensive option should you have any unplanned healthcare needs.

>> **Private insurance broker:** This option provides support for finding a suitable health insurance option. A broker provides guidance on your insurance options and assists in the enrollment process. Because they're often compensated by insurance companies, there's usually no fee for you to use their services.

>> **Spousal or family coverage:** If you're married, in a domestic partnership, or are a qualifying dependent, it may be possible for you to secure coverage by being added to your family member's health insurance plan.

>> **Travel-related insurance:** Many travel insurance options also include coverage for health emergencies. If you plan to travel during your break, this may be a suitable option for healthcare coverage. As always, research your options to find the best fit (see "Evaluating your travel insurance options" later in this chapter for specific suggestions).

TIP

The loss of a job with employer-provided health insurance is usually considered a "qualifying event," which means you can enroll in a new insurance plan outside of the standard open enrollment window (end of year). But do your research; you'll have a limited amount of time to make this change after leaving your job.

You'll want to consider affordability, accessibility, and the unique aspects of your situation when making your decision. Here's a list of things to consider as you weigh your options:

>> **Anticipated healthcare needs while on a break:** Consider the healthcare services you anticipate needing while on your break to make sure your coverage option provides an affordable way to cover them and that these expenses are accounted for in your career break budget.

>> **Healthcare expenses** (premiums, copays, deductibles): To estimate the total cost of your options, consider the out-of-pocket expenses you'll be responsible for.

>> **Pre-existing conditions:** If you have any pre-existing conditions, make sure you're considering options that will cover them.

- >> **Prescriptions/medications.** Consider the out-of-pocket costs and availability for any necessary medications (especially if you require specific brands).

- >> **Provider network/preferred doctor(s):** If you have preferred doctors or specialists that you'd like to continue seeing while on a break, check whether they're in-network and ensure that you'll have an affordable way to see them if they're not.

TIP

For health–related benefits like dental and vision coverage, you can consider skipping coverage if you're able to go the length of your break without them. Using your employer–provided coverage to conduct exams, get new glasses, and so on right before starting your break may allow you to comfortably wait until you return to the workforce.

Making a plan for your stuff

Deciding what to do with your things can be a big hurdle to face when your break involves significant travel and/or relocation. This section helps you break down the process and gives you options to consider as you begin preparing.

Options for your home

If you currently rent your home and want to return to it when your travels are over, you can continue renting as usual or ask your landlord to sublet while you're away. If you currently own your home, you can consider the following options:

- >> **Get a housesitter:** Find a housesitter to take care of your home, plants, and/or animals while you're away. You can hire someone you know or find a well-reviewed professional via an online platform like Trusted Housesitters.

- >> **Rent it:** You can choose to rent your home on a short-term or long-term basis. There are pros and cons to each. As you make your decision, be sure to check your Homeowners Association (HOA) rules, if applicable, for guidance on your options (e.g., some require a permit to lease your unit and can have a lengthy waitlist).

  - • **Short-term:** If you pursue short-term rentals, you need to consider logistics like uploading and listing it on rental websites, sourcing quality photos for the listing, hiring a manager and/or housekeeper to prepare for new guests and any furniture adjustments (purchases, replacements and/or storage).

- **Long-term:** If you decide to offer leases, you need to consider logistics like hiring a property manager, home preparations and/or renovations, and deciding if you will rent it furnished or unfurnished.

>> **Sell it:** If selling your house is part of your financial plan to afford a break, you'll want to give yourself time to prepare for logistics like hiring a real estate agent, conducting inspections, and managing any necessary repairs, upgrades, or renovations.

Twila had plans of renting her home when her break began. But when she checked with her HOA, she learned they'd recently banned short-term rentals and only permitted rentals with a one-year lease term — plus there was a waitlist for permits. Luckily, she was first in line on the waitlist and was able to list it for rent before starting her break. Start the process early if you plan to list your home for rent!

If your HOA currently has a waitlist for rental permits, check to see if they allow hardship exceptions that will allow you to rent it while you're unemployed.

Options for your vehicle

If you plan to travel and leave your car behind, you need to determine whether you want to keep it and the best place to do so. Here are several possibilities of what you can do with your vehicle after you start your break:

>> **Store it:** Store it at a friend's or family member's property or pay to store it at a facility. Review your car insurance; you can likely lower your premiums or cancel your coverage while your car is in storage.

>> **Rent it:** You can rent your car through a car-sharing marketplace like Turo or Avail. The process is similar to listing your home for rent through Airbnb. Depending on the service you choose, you may need to secure additional car insurance for this option.

>> **Sell, donate, or lend it:** If you decide to get rid of your car, you can list it for sale, donate it to a local non-profit, or lend it to a friend or family member while you're away. Remember to adjust your car insurance!

Options for your personal belongings

If your break includes downsizing, moving, relocating, and/or traveling, you need a plan for your personal belongings. Here are some options to consider:

>> **Donate them or give them away:** Donate unwanted items to a local nonprofit and support an important cause, list them on zero waste/upcycle websites, or gift them to friends and family. If you're donating large items like furniture, your donation center may come pick it up for you.

>> **Sell them:** You can sell your items via consignment (clothes, furniture, and home decor) or list it for sale on platforms like Craigslist, Poshmark, and Facebook Marketplace.

>> **Store them:** Depending on the number of things you plan to keep, you may need to secure a place (with friends and family or in a storage unit) for your remaining items.

TIP

If the thought of downsizing seems difficult or causes you stress, check out Chapter 9 for help with adopting a supportive mindset around letting go of your belongings.

ANECDOTE

I sold nearly all of my belongings before starting my career break. I was living in Minneapolis and knew I wanted to move somewhere new (and much warmer) after my break was over. I used a mix of consignment shops, Craigslist, social media, and Goodwill to find a new home for my belongings. And what I chose to keep, I stored at my mom's house in an empty bedroom closet.

Managing caretaking duties

If you have or share responsibility for the well-being of others (for example, children, parents, and pets), you need to plan for their care during the break. Start by clarifying your expectations and vision for the break. What kind of break do you hope to have? From here, consider opportunities where you can include those you care for into your break experience and circumstances when you need to delegate your responsibilities or find support.

Here are a few questions to consider before brainstorming solutions and making arrangements:

>> Will travel be involved? If so, for how long?

» If you plan to remain at home, are there parts of your break that require solitude or relief from your caregiving duties?

» Is there anyone in your circle who would be willing to provide adequate care in your absence (family member, neighbor, friend, etc.)?

» Is there room in your career break budget to hire support?

Even with the limitations your caretaking duties may create, proactive planning can help you create a wonderful break experience that still meets your needs. More than half of my clients had pets, 29 percent had kids, and 59 percent had a partner or spouse when they took their breaks. It may feel challenging at times, but brainstorming solutions and sources of support is key. For example, you can

» Adapt your travel plans and destinations to better accommodate your responsibilities.

» Enlist friends and family for support, even if only temporarily.

» Hire a caregiver or support person to assist or relieve you (be sure to include this cost in your career break budget).

» Set both individual goals and shared goals for your break (see anecdote below for an example).

ANECDOTE

Anna and her husband were excited to plan a three-month family sabbatical. As they built out their break plan, it became clear that they each had unique individual goals in addition to their shared goal of enjoying time together as a family. By proactively discussing their individual and shared goals with each other, they were able to create more clarity around their needs and boundaries before the break. Knowing what they hoped to get out of this experience individually, as a couple, and as a family helped them design a break to meet everyone's needs. And with this plan, they were able to proactively create time together as a couple by arranging for a family visit for their kids.

Wrapping Things up at Work

In the months before starting your break, your focus will be on wrapping things up at work and tying up any professional loose ends. Thoughtfully preparing for your exit ensures you won't leave money on the table with your employer-provided benefits and allows you to go out on a high note. This will be especially important if you've taken a leave of absence and plan to return to the same employer once your break is over.

Maximizing your employer-provided benefits

If you currently have employer-provided benefits, you'll want to make the most of them before leaving your job. To ensure balls don't get dropped right before your break begins, take a moment to review your benefits and schedule any necessary appointments. Taking advantage of your benefits can save a significant amount of money and ensure that you're not walking into your break with unknown health issues.

Here are common employer-provided benefits that you may be able to take advantage of before you go:

>> **Financial benefits such as 401(k) matches, company bonuses, unused PTO (paid time off):** While preparing for your break, you may want to maximize your company's 401(k) match, adjust your break timeline to accommodate a big company bonus, and/or consider using any PTO that won't be paid out when you leave.

>> **Health-related benefits such as annual exams, physicals, immunizations, dental and vision exams, discounted services (eyeglasses, orthodontics):** Visit your doctor for an annual exam or check-up and to explore any lingering issues. This helps you avoid being surprised by a serious health issue during your break (and after you've given up your employer's health insurance). If your travel plans require vaccinations, consider scheduling them while you're still covered.

ANECDOTE

When I began preparing for my break, I still had more than a year before the start of my break. So, I decided to take the plunge and invested in invisible braces while I still had dental benefits. With proper planning, I was able to maximize my benefit and put money into an HSA (health savings account), which saved me hundreds of dollars in taxes. I also decided to pay for them in full, which provided an additional 10 percent discount. This approach saved me $2,000 in total, which I funneled back into my career break fund.

TIP

Be sure to review your employee handbook or benefits website to ensure that you're taking advantage of the benefits your company provides.

Leaving your job on a high note

As you're preparing to start your break, you can do several things to ensure you leave on good terms. Being thoughtful about your exit helps you avoid burning bridges and creates more possibilities (referrals, networking, glowing references) when you're ready to return to work. If you're taking a leave of absence (sabbatical) and plan to return after your break, this lays the foundation for a more peaceful break and graceful return.

>> **Thoughtfully communicate:** Think about your goodbye. When will you announce your exit? (Visit Chapter 7 for suggestions.) How will you share the news with your team? If you're taking a sabbatical, also think through your out-of-office message and who it will reference for support.

>> **Draft a continuity plan:** Think through your projects and responsibilities to create a continuity plan for the transition. Work with your manager to create a project list and project takeover plan. Support the team in transitioning your duties and proactively set expectations for your transition back to work.

>> **Set clear boundaries:** If you're taking a sabbatical, it's super important to set clear boundaries for your break. You'll want to proactively determine your level of availability. If you want to disconnect fully, be sure to set those expectations before you leave. Specifically, think through the following things:

- What systems will you keep on/check in with during your break? How often will you be checking in?

- Under what circumstances are you available to your employer? If it's emergencies only, think through what constitutes an emergency (and what doesn't).

- How do you prefer to be contacted for urgent matters (phone call, text, personal email)?

- Who will be able to contact you during your sabbatical? Having a central point of contact can help filter requests to ensure they are essential.

- Are there any periods of time when you're fully unavailable, even for emergencies (weekends, trips, activities without cell reception)?

Making Necessary Travel Preparations

Travel can be an amazing part of the career break experience. It provides an opportunity for growth, exploration, and fun! It's likely not a surprise that the majority of career breaks and sabbaticals include some form of travel. Among my clients, 68 percent traveled abroad at some point during their breaks. Travel requires additional preparation, so if it's a part of your career break or sabbatical plan, this section covers important logistics for you to consider during your preparation. You can find more specifics and examples to better prepare for long-term travel in Chapter 9.

Tackling your travel to-do list

You have a lot of tasks to work through when you plan to leave your home for an extended period of time and/or visit a new country:

» **Apply for an international driver's permit:** You may need this if you plan to drive or motorbike abroad

» **Copy and digitize your documents and paperwork:** Make copies and take photos of important documents. Save them digitally for easy access while traveling.

» **Make plans for your mail:** Whether you forward it to a new address, hold it at the post office, use a virtual mailbox to collect and go through it for you, or have a friend or family member collect it, you need a plan for your mail, especially those important items that may arrive while you're traveling.

>> **Notify your bank and credit card companies:** If you plan to access your accounts while you're traveling, be sure to contact the banks so that they know not to decline your withdrawals and charges.

>> **Open a bank account and secure a credit card with international travel benefits:** To minimize bank charges and maximize accessibility, consider opening accounts that cater to travelers (more in Chapter 9).

>> **Renew or apply for a passport and necessary visas:** Documentation for international travel can take several months to process, so be proactive about securing an up-to-date passport and any necessary visas.

REMEMBER

Passports must have at least six months validity remaining to be used for international travel.

>> **Renew your driver's license:** If your license will expire while you're traveling, consider renewing it before you go.

>> **Research and purchase any necessary gear or equipment:** Be sure to think through the extra items you may need while traveling (luggage, electronics, etc.).

>> **Schedule a tune-up:** If you're planning a significant amount of driving during your break, schedule a tune-up and make sure your car is ready to go and road safe.

>> **Schedule any necessary or recommended vaccinations:** If some of your destinations require vaccinations, be sure to make those appointments in advance. (Sometimes vaccines are back-ordered and take a while to restock.)

>> **Schedule final appointments with service providers:** Make sure to get your final appointments with providers such as massage therapists, hairstylists, and estheticians scheduled so you won't miss them.

>> **Sign up for travel insurance:** Research your options and consider purchasing travel insurance to help you with healthcare expenses and travel emergencies. (See the next section for specifics.)

TIP

Use this transition as an opportunity to organize and declutter your life by cleaning out closets, deleting old files, and donating unused items to create more ease and set you up for a fresh start.

Evaluating your travel insurance options

It's important to consider your insurance options as you prepare for your career break travels. Travel insurance offers financial protection and support for unexpected delays and mishaps that can occur during your adventures. Having this additional protection can make it easier to enjoy your break and navigate challenges that may arise. Travel insurance can help with the following:

» **Emergency assistance:** A 24/7 helpline that offers guidance during emergencies and provides support services (legal, medical, translations, etc.)

» **Lost or delayed baggage:** Receive compensation for lost, stolen, or delayed baggage to help replace necessities

» **Lost or stolen items:** Some policies reimburse you for or replace lost or stolen items (be sure to review the terms and limits of coverage for your valuable items)

» **Medical emergencies:** Coverage for medical needs like doctor visits, hospital visits, medications, and even emergency evacuation

» **Travel delays:** Receive compensation for costs associated with delayed flights (hotels, food, etc.)

» **Trip interruption or cancellation:** Receive reimbursement for nonrefundable expenses (flights, hotels, tours, etc.) should your trip be canceled for family or medical emergencies or even natural disasters

ANECDOTE

While biking through a vineyard in Mendoza, Argentina, I took a tumble and injured my knee. Hoping it would heal on its own, I continued traveling. Weeks later, I arrived in Paris with no improvement, so I made an appointment to see a doctor. Unfortunately, he wasn't able to help, and my knee continued to get worse. I eventually returned to the United States near the end of my break and made an appointment with an orthopedic doctor, who was able to treat my knee. Fortunately, I had travel insurance on my break (through World Nomads) and was fully reimbursed for all associated healthcare costs.

Travel insurance offers many options. Some provide medical coverage; others do not. It's important to consider your needs when exploring travel insurance options. Your age, citizenship, and travel plans will influence the availability and affordability of your options. Here are several popular choices and comparison websites for career breakers and digital nomads:

>> Allianz (www.allianztravelinsurance.com/)

>> Safety Wing (https://safetywing.com/nomad-insurance)

>> World Nomads (www.worldnomads.com/)

>> InsureMyTrip (www.insuremytrip.com/)

>> SquareMouth (www.squaremouth.com/)

While you may travel without additional insurance, it's important to consider your options and the potential impact on your finances before making your final decision.

TIP

If you plan to spend several weeks or months in one location, it can be helpful to research healthcare costs ahead of time. Your destination's healthcare cost may be lower than the cost of insurance, making it more affordable to pay out-of-pocket.

ANECDOTE

I came down with a brutal sickness after arriving in Mexico City. After a few days of over-the-counter remedies, I finally scheduled an appointment with a nearby doctor. He was incredibly kind and spent an hour with me, discussing my symptoms. At the end of our appointment, he prescribed seven medications, which I filled at the nearby pharmacy. The total cost for my appointment and medications came to $130 USD, without insurance.

TIP

Travel-focused credit cards often provide travel-related benefits that overlap with insurance coverage. Be sure to review your current benefits before purchasing a travel insurance policy and consider opening a credit card with travel benefits, if you don't have one already.

AUTOMATIC TRAVEL INSURANCE

You can purchase individual policies to cover your travel emergencies, but you may already have access to some of these benefits through your credit card. Research your credit card's benefits to see what might already be covered.

As an example, the Chase Sapphire Preferred and Chase Sapphire Reserve credit cards both reimburse you for inconveniences like

- Trip cancellation, interruption, and/or delay
- Lost baggage and/or baggage delay
- Primary car rental insurance coverage

And that's in addition to their travel-friendly benefits like lounge access (for the Reserve card), no foreign transaction fees on purchases abroad, and rewards points you can redeem for future travel expenses.

Chapter **9**

Planning for Extended Travel

W hile travel isn't necessary for a meaningful and transformative career break, many people include it because it's often exciting and provides stimulation for their minds and a shift of their perspectives. Sixty-eight percent of my clients chose to travel abroad during their break, but those who opted not to still had incredible, life-changing experiences. If travel isn't on your career break agenda, feel free to skip this chapter. But if it *is*, buckle up because it's time for a crash course on extended travel!

Travel can be an exciting and transformative part of a break. On a break, you can travel for longer periods of time than you can while working, which opens doors to new opportunities and provides time to explore more of the world around you. It also gives you a new perspective on life and can be an accelerator for personal growth. In this chapter, I share how to prepare, mentally and tactically, to take full advantage of extended travel, which helpful resources make planning easier, and how to overcome common extended travel obstacles.

TIP

You can use this chapter to prepare for both domestic and international travel. While it's not for everyone, international travel is a very popular aspect of career breaks and sabbaticals, but taking time to explore your own country in new ways can also be inspiring and rejuvenating.

Understanding the Benefits of Extended Travel

Extended travel is a really special way to experience new places. You can visit more locations, stay much longer, and travel more slowly, which translates into a more immersive and enriching experience. If you approach it with an open mind, it can be a huge catalyst for growth and provide amazing benefits like the following:

>> **Career enhancement:** Gain global insights, new language skills, cultural awareness, and a unique perspective.

>> **Enjoyment:** Have fun as you explore new cultures, taste new foods, and enjoy the mental stimulation of learning new things.

>> **Freedom:** Set your own pace, live simply, and experience new places with more ease and flexibility.

>> **In-depth cultural exposure:** Expand your worldview and gain empathy and a deeper insight into places you visit.

>> **New friendships and connections:** Meet interesting people, make new friends, and build your network.

>> **Personal growth:** Leave your comfort zone and predictable environment to uncover new strengths, boost your confidence, and shake up the status quo.

>> **Personal satisfaction:** Gain a sense of accomplishment as you realize your travel dreams.

Planning Your Extended Travel Itinerary

When it comes to planning your travel during a career break or sabbatical, the infinite possibilities might leave you swirling. With so many moving parts, it can be hard to make decisions. Plus, extended travel has unique challenges, so you can't approach planning it like you would a normal vacation.

This section helps you outline a flexible plan that allows room for growth and evolution. You don't want to over-plan extended travel because trying to stick to a packed itinerary can quickly become overwhelming. Also, your desires and circumstances are apt to change along the way.

REMEMBER

You never have to stay committed to a plan that no longer works for you. Even the best laid plans need to be updated at times. Whether you want to slow down, speed up, go home, or cancel your plans and travel somewhere else, it's important to pay attention to your evolving needs and stay open to adapting your plans. You can always change your mind; creating a plan doesn't mean you've sworn an oath to your itinerary.

Choosing your destination(s)

Your break is an amazing opportunity to chase your travel dreams and tick new places off your bucket list. If you've arrived at this chapter with a list of destinations already in mind, great! If you have some ideas but are still solidifying your plans, this section has some tips that will help you.

I have three simple rules for choosing your destinations:

>> **Make sure your destinations align with your own interests and values.** What's best for you can differ from what's best for someone else or what looks good on a social media post.

>> **Be clear on your intentions for each location.** Make sure you know why each destination is on your list and what you hope to get out of your time there (even if the answer is simply a beautiful view).

>> **Leave some wiggle room in your plans.** You don't have to pre-decide every destination; leave room to pursue new ideas that will appear during your break.

WARNING

Don't attempt to chase other people's travel dreams and visions. Choosing places that aren't aligned with your intentions and interests — no matter how trendy, popular, or amazing — is a recipe for disappointment (as is following other people's travel speed). Instead of aspiring to someone else's vision of a great travel experience, follow your inspiration. Travel to places that spark your interest and imagination and that allow you to pursue your career break dreams and themes. And be sure to do it at your own pace.

There are many sources for travel inspiration — something as simple as an article or photo may trigger your travel desires. Books, podcasts, vlogs and blogs, firsthand stories, TV shows, and movies are great sources of inspiration. You can also choose locations based on special activities and experiences you want to pursue.

ANECDOTE

Two of my favorite places from my career break were inspired by media: Peter Mayle tempted me to visit Avignon, France, with his food-centric odyssey in *A Year in Provence,* while a college viewing of *Evita* planted a seed of desire to visit Buenos Aires, the city that evoked passion for the main character.

Here are several inspired ideas that have shaped my clients' extended travels:

>> **Antarctica:** Exploring the expansive white wilderness while crossing the seventh and final continent off the travel list

>> **Argentina:** Watching the World Cup series with avid fans (and being lucky enough to be there when they won)

>> **France:** Studying abroad for a year and later using that opportunity to find a job and relocate there

>> **Guatemala:** Pursuing a growing interest in learning Spanish while living with a host family

>> **Italy:** Traveling to Sicily to visit extended family and reconnecting with their Italian heritage and then being inspired to pursue citizenship by descent

>> **New Zealand:** Crossing a country off their bucket list with amazing adventures like hiking Tongariro National Park (Mordor in the film *The Lord of the Rings*)

>> **Spain:** Studying Spanish with a homebase in Barcelona, while taking many weekend trips around the EU

>> **U.K.:** Completing a specialized program and course to become a certified equine healer

TIP

Some of your best ideas may come to you spontaneously or through interactions with strangers. So it's great to have a list, but don't try to predetermine every destination in advance. Leave room to incorporate new ideas.

Timing it right

First things first: I need you to know that there's no such thing as perfect timing for your career break travels. When you're hitting the road for an extended period of time, it will be impossible to predict every possible circumstance or calculate every configuration. Besides, even when you've put your ideal plan together, life and weather will do whatever they please and can change your plans at a moment's notice. So instead of agonizing over your choices in an attempt to make the perfect itinerary, focus on making a good decision with the information you have available to you at the time.

When it comes to determining your travel timing, several factors can heavily influence your experience. You'll want to consider them as you draft your plans:

>> **Holidays and events:** Holidays and events will significantly impact your travel cost and experience. They provide a unique opportunity to witness something special and celebrate with locals, but with this added benefit comes higher costs, more people, and lower availability. Be sure to check the holiday and event schedules for your destinations and adjust your plans based on your preferences. Examples include Las Fallas in Valencia, Spain; Diwali in India; and Carnival in Rio de Janeiro.

>> **Seasonality:** Traveling in high season (the most popular time to travel) versus low season can make for a *very* different travel experience. Seasonality affects the crowd size, cost, and availability of lodging, transport, and activities. High season offers ideal weather and lots of activities — think Europe in the summer or the Colorado Rockies in the winter. But with these benefits comes a higher price tag and lower availability. Low season will be less crowded and more affordable, but travelers may experience undesirable weather and have reduced access to activities and

accommodations. Shoulder season, the period of time between high and low season, may offer the best of both worlds. Guidebooks and travel blogs can help you assess the trade-offs and time your travels accordingly.

>> **Weather:** Weather can have a massive impact on your travel plans. It may affect your mood and overall experience (too hot, too wet, too cold) in addition to the accessibility of your destinations. At times, severe weather (hurricanes, monsoons, blizzards) can make travel impossible. You don't have to (and probably can't) avoid all bad weather, but you'll want to consider the possibilities so you're adequately prepared (even down to your packing list).

TIP

If getting started feels hard or overwhelming, choose a high-priority activity or trip and book the necessary flight or hotel arrangements. This big investment will give you a firm push and starting point to build from. The other pieces will start to come together from here.

ANECDOTE

Lynn struggled to choose a start date for her break. There were reasons to move the date up and reasons to delay things a bit longer. With one big international trip in mind, she decided to book her flight, which made everything more real and firmed up her dates. This one big step made her trip feel concrete. She could then start arranging other details and future plans around her extended visit to Sicily.

Putting your travel plan together

After you have a list of destinations, it's time to start putting your travel plan together. I recommend creating a calendar that captures your daily location (see Chapter 6 for an example). This approach helps you catch issues before booking your travel arrangements (like not leaving enough time to transit from one country to another before joining a tour or meeting up with friends). Plotting your daily location also helps you keep track of where you'll spend each night to ensure that you have you've got reservations for a place to stay.

My biggest piece of advice during this stage is to resist the urge to overplan. Overplanning for longer-term travel can build up your expectations and create a lot of stress and rework down the road. By leaving space in your plans, you'll remain flexible and can more easily adapt to change. This is important because things won't always go according to plan, especially during longer-term travel. This isn't necessarily a bad thing — sometimes things turn out even better than you hoped — but it's something to keep in mind as you develop your itinerary.

REMEMBER

Overloading your itinerary before you've started traveling means leaning heavily into recommendations and suggestions instead of your own intuition. Leave space to discover something special and meaningful that can change how you see life. Sometimes the best travel experiences happen in the moments in between your planned activities, so leave room for magic and serendipity to happen! Sometimes these unplanned moments become the highlight of your entire trip.

WARNING

There is an important caveat to this rule: If you require special accommodations (dietary, physical, etc.), you need to do more planning upfront. My gluten allergy required more upfront research to ensure I had a few safe places to eat. If your ability to travel safely is in jeopardy, please do the necessary research and take precautions to find adequate solutions and options.

Making your money last longer

When it comes to money, managing extended travel expenses will be significantly different than those of a regular vacation. On a shorter trip, you'd likely plan out key details ahead of time and prepay big expenses like accommodations and transit. But when you leap into the world of extended travel, you have more unknowns to account for financially. Because you're traveling for a longer period of time, you won't necessarily preplan all your events or prepay your expenses. Plus, your plans can change along the way. So, it's important to have a few helpful strategies in place for making your money last longer as you explore the world more openly. The following strategies can help you travel better when pursuing longer-term travel.

Determining your travel speed and homebase plan

Your travel speed and homebase plan greatly affect your finances and thus the overall length of your travels. As you draft your plans, consider these factors, especially if you're searching for ways to extend your money and travels.

When it comes to choosing your travel speed, it can be fast, slow or a mix of both:

>> **Fast travel:** This vacation-style travel pace is what you're likely used to. With it, you move from place to place daily or weekly and fill your time with activities. This pace allows you to see and do more, but it racks up travel costs more quickly than slow travel and can eventually lead to burnout when done over the longterm.

>> **Slow travel:** This travel speed allows more balance and lets you live more like a local while you immerse yourself in your destinations. When slow-traveling, you stay put for at least a month in each destination. This pace allows you to spend less on accommodations and meals out. Choosing destinations with a lower cost of living and traveling slowly can significantly extend your travel funds.

>> **A mix of both:** With this approach, you look to your finances, the cost-of-living and travel expenses, and the length of your wish list for each destination to determine the adequate amount of time for each location. You'll move through some destinations more slowly, staying a month or longer, and you'll breeze through others in just a few days.

Where you plan to set your homebase will greatly impact your finances. If you plan to maintain your current homebase or establish a new homebase separate from your travel destinations, you'll face a significant additional cost. If, however, you opt to get rid of your belongings or store them during your travels, this frees you up financially as your travel destination(s) will become your homebase and removes duplicative expenses.

Tracking your expenses

Keeping track, even loosely, of what you're spending, can help you avoid overspending. Having a general sense of your running expenses compared to your budget will help you make smart trade-offs that won't jeopardize your break or your travel experience. This information is vital when you're traveling for an extended period of time and frequently changing your cost of living, routine, and daily expenses.

TIP

For help with budgeting and setting up a budget tracker, see Chapter 5.

Remembering your travel goals

Keeping your career break and travel goals in mind helps you decide which activities and experiences to invest in. With a plethora of choices, you'll want to check in with your goals (I recommend at least monthly) and prioritize your ideas. Exciting options will compete for your precious time and money. Being clear about what's most important to you will help you make good decisions more easily.

TIP

If you ever feel uncertain about which activities to invest in and which to skip altogether, explore what feels most necessary to your overall well-being and the pursuit of your career break themes. (See Chapter 4 to develop your themes.) Some opportunities may feel exciting but require sacrificing other more important goals and ideas on your list. Stay in touch with what's most important so you can channel your funds accordingly.

Clarifying your travel priorities

When it comes to travel, you should consider and prioritize three important aspects: convenience, money, and time. When you're working, you may decide to spend more money for extra convenience and/or to accommodate a limited vacation schedule. But on a break, you'll have ample time and added flexibility but limited funds to support you. In this new situation, you may be willing to give up some convenience (comfort and ease) and spend more time researching affordable options to save money and travel longer. You'll likely need to sacrifice some of one to have more of another, so it's important to understand what you value most as you begin making your travel plans.

REMEMBER

Managing longer-term travel expenses requires a shift in perspective. While your default may have been paying for convenience, you now have more time to be creative and resourceful in finding ways to travel for less. Here are a few examples of how you can shift your travel priorities to make your money last longer, using a one-month trip to France in the summer as the starting point:

>> Consider slower and cheaper modes of transportation (for example, regional trains in lieu of flights or bullet trains)

- » Reduce the length of your trip (3 weeks) or replace it with a more affordable option (Greece)

- » Spend more time in each location to benefit from an extended stay discount (Airbnb's monthly discount)

- » Stay outside of the popular areas and use public transit to visit them during the day

- » Travel during a cheaper and less touristy season (fall)

- » Vary your accommodations to incorporate cheaper options (hostel, longer-term rental, hotel, etc.)

REMEMBER

Having more time offers many benefits: You can take advantage of last-minute deals, travel during off-peak seasons, find cheaper travel with alternative dates, and move through countries more slowly to save money.

ANECDOTE

I'd originally planned to visit the Cinque Terre (a tourist hotspot) during my month in Italy. But I soon realized the accommodations didn't fit my budget, so I did some quick research and discovered the nearby town of La Spezia, an easy 10-minute train ride away with cheaper lodging. I booked a great place and found a gluten-free bakery within walking distance of my hotel (an exciting win!). When I set out to explore the Cinque Terre, I found it completely overrun with tourists and felt immense gratitude for my peaceful home. Sometimes going a bit off the beaten path can create an even better experience, in addition to saving money.

Setting up your travel accounts

Before you begin traveling for a longer period of time, you'll want to set up special accounts to make your life easier and your transactions more effective. Your specifics will vary by your country of residency, the places you plan to visit, and the amount of time you plan to spend in each, but this list provides an overview of the basic travel-related accounts you'll want to look into set up

- » **Bank accounts:** Search for options you can access online and that let you withdraw money in local currency with no transaction or ATM fees. Charles Schwab High Yield Investor Checking Account and Betterment Checking Account are a couple of examples.

- » **Communication:** While some prefer using local SIM cards, you can also choose a service that provides affordable international coverage (for example, T-Mobile or Google Fi for travelers with U.S.-based mobile plans). It's also important to have a communication app (for example, WhatsApp, Google Voice) to coordinate your arrival for things like prearranged taxis or Airbnbs and to affordably contact your home country in case of emergency.

>> **Credit cards:** It's important to make sure the credit card(s) you travel with don't charge foreign transaction fees, which can add up quickly. Consider card options that also reward you for using them (for example, Chase Sapphire Preferred or Reserve cards, Citi Premier, and American Express Gold).

>> **Mobile wallets:** These apps can simplify the payment process by enabling contactless payments via your smartphone (for example, Google Pay, Apple Pay).

>> **Money wires and transfers:** You can send and receive international transfers using different currencies with lower fees and competitive rates (for example, Wize, Revolut)

>> **Points and miles accounts and credit cards:** These will make your travel dollars go much further. You can source points to later redeem for flights, hotels, and activities. Opening an account now means accruing more points (for example, Chase Ultimate Rewards, Amex Membership Rewards, Citi ThankYou Points) before you begin traveling.

TIP

If you're a U.S. citizen with plans to fly, look into TSA Pre-check or Global Entry to expedite your travel experience. Having Global Entry will grant you TSA pre-check for domestic flights with no additional cost. There are also travel-focused credit cards, like the Chase Sapphire Reserve and the Amex Platinum that will reimburse you for the expense of enrolling in either of these travel programs.

Using points and miles to travel for less

This topic is so complex it deserves its own *For Dummies* book, but for now, I'm going to simplify this juicy and exciting topic to give you the lay of the land and help you direct your focus.

Using points and miles helps you in two unique ways:

>> It can make your travels free or more affordable.

>> It can improve your travel experience by giving you access to experiences you wouldn't otherwise be able to afford.

You can use points or miles to pay for flights, hotels, and even some activities. How you redeem them and the value you receive from your redemptions varies based on the company you're using, but there are two ways to approach amassing points and miles: sourcing them directly from the travel providers (an airline or hotel) or via a third-party bank (Chase Bank or American Express). Your best option depends on how you plan to use the points or miles, but you can also collect them through both avenues at the same time.

ACTIVITY

Choosing which credit cards and/or accounts to open can be overwhelming, so start with one aspect of your trip that you'd like to make more affordable or upgrade and search for points or miles that will help you accomplish this goal.

ANECDOTE

I got into points and miles soon after deciding to take a travel-focused career break. Because I knew very little, I began following several experts via daily emails and educating myself on the options. I realized that flights were going to comprise a big chunk of my travel budget, so I focused on learning specific ways to reduce my airfare costs. Because I was living in a Delta Airlines hub at the time, I found it easy to collect Delta Skymiles. So, I boosted my accumulation factor by securing one of their higher-end credit cards and prioritizing them when searching for regular flights (pre-break). When my break began, I was able to use just 80,000 miles to travel roundtrip from the United States to Singapore on the very nice Korean Air. I also began collecting Chase points to help reduce my hotel costs while traveling around the world.

TIP

Because a lot of factors will influence your approach (including your country of residency), I recommend finding experts to follow for ideas and advice and to stay up to date. Many send daily emails with the latest information and special offers. A few of my favorites that have helped me are

>> Miles to Memories (https://milestomemories.com/)

>> The Points Guy (https://thepointsguy.com/)

>> View from the Wing (https://viewfromthewing.com/)

ACTIVITY

To get started, sign up for two or three expert newsletters and search their websites for articles covering the basics. Educate yourself and then begin scanning the daily or weekly emails for interesting ideas and special offers.

Today is the best day to start. The sooner you begin, the more points and miles you will collect.

Using expert travel apps and tools

This section highlights several tools to help you save money and travel more easily. As technology advances so do the options available to you, so be sure to do your own research as you may discover new and customized options for your specific adventure.

Research tools

The following apps, tools, and websites help you conduct effective, personalized research to inform your travel plans:

>> **Facebook groups:** Great sources of information specific to your unique circumstances and travel destinations (for advice on healthcare in a specific country, the best neighborhoods to stay in, rooms for rent, traveling with a disability or dietary restriction, etc.). To find a group, search relevant keywords for things like:

- **City** (Digital Nomads Buenos Aires)
- **Country** (Vietnam Travelers)
- **Identity** (Travel Hacking Moms, Black Expats in Brazil)
- **Limitations** (Gluten Free Travel Around the World)

>> **Gas Buddy:** This app will help you locate the cheapest and closest fuel options when taking a road trip.

>> **GoogleMaps:** You can use this app or website to plan and organize your travel routes by proximity.

>> **Rome2Rio:** One of my absolute favorites, this app and website shows you all the possible ways to get from one place in the world to another (including ferries!) and provides associated costs and links to purchase tickets.

>> **Social media searches:** You can find up-to-date recommendations and suggestions by searching keywords on platforms like YouTube, Instagram, and TikTok.

>> **Travel blogs:** Learn from others who traveled to the places you hope to go. (*Nomadic Matt* [www.nomadicmatt.com/] is one of the best and most comprehensive.)

CHAPTER 9 Planning for Extended Travel 189

Booking tools

When it comes to booking your accommodations and transit, it's helpful to compare costs before purchasing. The following websites will help you do just that:

» **Flights:** Beyond the airlines' own websites, you can use a travel aggregator to compare across various providers:

- **Google Flights:** This is a powerful tool that has many filters to help you narrow your options. It also allows you to view a calendar with the lowest daily prices so you can easily find the cheapest dates.

- **Skyscanner:** The best feature of this tool is its "explore everywhere," which allows you to search the world to find the cheapest places to travel to on your given dates (great for flexible travel plans).

» **Accommodations:** Beyond individual hotel websites, you can search online vacation rental sites and OTAs (online travel agencies) to compare multiple options at once:

- **Airbnb:** One of several shorter-term rental sites, this can be a good option for longer stays because it often offers weekly and monthly discounts.

- **Booking.com:** A helpful aggregator with competitive pricing that allows you to search multiple accommodation types (beyond just hotels).

- **Hostelworld:** A great resource for exploring hostel options (sorting by reviews and ratings can be especially helpful for avoiding negative experiences).

Miscellaneous tools

Following are four helpful tools that can make your travels easier to organize:

» **Polarsteps:** This app automatically tracks your route and travel stats and calls up photos you've taken at different locations, making it easier to reflect on your adventures. You can also add blog style notes and share your progress with friends.

>> **Shazam:** This app is great for capturing and labeling unfamiliar songs as you travel the world. You can use it to create a playlist to remember your break when it's over.

>> **Splitwise:** This expense-sharing app is great for keeping track of shared experience so you can accurately and easily split bills among friends and fellow travelers, even across multiple currencies.

>> **Tripit:** This app and website stores all of your travel details in one place for easy reference (which is especially helpful when you're booking out of order and struggling to keep track of everything).

TIP

A note about entertainment: When you're traveling without Wi-Fi or internet, it's helpful to have a few entertainment-based apps available to pass the time. Consider podcast apps, audiobook apps, and library apps that let you access audiobooks for free (for example, the Libby app). Be sure to download them and set things up before you go offline.

Preparing for Your Extended Travels

Extended travel requires significantly more mental and logistical preparation than shorter vacations because there are many additional steps and things to account for. This section helps you build your confidence as you put together a plan, prepares you for a smoother start to your longer-term travels, and helps you create a better overall experience.

TIP

Be sure to check out Chapter 8 for practical travel tips, a practical travel "to-do" list, an overview of your travel insurance options, tips for making a plan for your belongings, and tips for managing your home while you're away.

WARNING

Don't fixate on having everything figured out and arranged before you start traveling. It actually isn't possible with longer-term travel because there are too many moving parts; with an extended timeline, unforeseen changes are likely to occur. Instead, put together a solid plan that builds your confidence and helps you feel prepared. Don't get stuck in the details. They always have a way of working themselves out after you get started.

Embracing a travel mindset for a better experience

The importance of adopting a travel-friendly mindset cannot be overstated. Extended travel can accelerate your growth and become a highlight of your break experience. It can stretch your comfort zone and expose you to many new things. But to enjoy the journey and navigate the challenges ahead, you need to approach it with an open mind and travel-friendly mindset. This section covers the aspects of a travel mindset that you should adopt to feel grounded and prepared for your upcoming adventure.

Realizing there's no right way to travel

There's no right way to approach travel. Having a great trip depends on your ability to create the experience you really want and not confuse it with the one you think you should have. Following others' advice and recommendations can leave you trying to recreate their experiences instead of designing your own, which leads to disappointing results.

To discover your own way of navigating extended travel, you'll need to clarify what you want from the experience and then give yourself permission to go for it. For inspiration, here are four unique examples of navigating travel during a break, based on real client experiences. You can use them to spark your own ideas and expand your consideration set.

ANECDOTE

» **Having a homebase and taking shorter trips:** Stephen's wife opted to continue working while he took his break. His ideal break included lots of travel, but with pandemic restrictions and his desire to spend time with his partner, he decided to break his travels up into shorter trips (lasting several weeks) and intersperse them between longer stays at his homebase in the United States.

» **Big international trips during the travel phase:** For one client, travel was an important reason for taking a break. She traveled abroad at the beginning of her break, for a total of four months, and then returned to her homebase and partner in the United States. She spent the remainder of her break at home, focused on her other themes with a few short overnight/weekend getaways mixed in.

>> **An indefinite travel adventure:** Extended international travel was the main feature of Kim's break. She spent her first month preparing for her big trip and enjoying her last few weeks in her home city. She then headed out on an indefinite adventure, beginning with a stop in the Azores. As I did, Kim let some of her travel plans unfold instead of booking everything in advance.

>> **Traveling and relocating abroad:** Twila's break kicked into high gear six weeks after she started her break. After time at home preparing for her international travels, Twila boarded a plane and began her whirlwind journey. Along the way, she decided to take a leap and pursue residency outside of her home country, using her travels to scout out possibilities.

Knowing what you really want

It's important to think about what success means to you before you start traveling. Designing with the end in mind will make it easier to have a satisfying experience. Similar to creating a successful career break plan, you'll want to answer some important questions as you begin planning your travels.

As you consider what you'd like to get out of your travel experience(s), you can reflect on your

>> Bucket list and travel dreams

>> Career break themes (see Chapter 4 for more on this)

>> Interests, likes, passions, and curiosities

In addition, here are two prompts with examples to help you with the exploration process:

>> **What are your intentions?** For example, experiencing joy and ease, facing and overcoming new challenges, personal growth, building connection and community

>> **What do you value?** For example, being in nature, immersing in city life, having food experiences, engaging in physical activities, learning a new language, living like a local, experiencing warm weather or colder climates, learning and being exposed to new things, and so on

Exploring these questions and prompts helps you establish things like how quickly (or slowly) you'd like to move around, what you'd prefer to be doing, and where you want to invest your time and money. Getting clear on these things helps you avoid being heavily swayed by other people's suggestions and glamorous recaps and led to travel plans you won't enjoy. For help creating your ideal travel experience, be sure to check out the "Planning Your Extended Travel Itinerary" section earlier in this chapter.

WARNING

Don't be distracted by glamorous social media content or the desire to create an experience that others will envy. It's tempting to chase after what others have but that pursuit could leave you feeling empty. The best experience you can have is one that's meaningful to you. So, take time to get clear on what YOU want and create a plan to get it. Don't try to re-create someone else's travel experience.

ANECDOTE

I've learned a lot about my longer-term travel preferences over time. I like to move slowly and leave space in my schedule to discover hidden gems. I enjoy the freedom of wandering through cities and towns at my own pace, so multiday group tours aren't a fit for me except where the language and/or culture is hard to navigate as a foreigner or solo female traveler. I also appreciate warm weather and plan my travels accordingly. Books are a great source of travel inspiration for me. Some of my best trips have been inspired by a great story. And finally, food is one of my biggest travel motivators. I'm happy to invest in food tours and adventure to new countries in search of a great meal.

Giving yourself permission to do it your way

As you solidify your priorities and determine what you most want to get out of your travel experience, remember to give yourself permission to do it your way.

REMEMBER

You can approach travel in many ways: longer versus shorter trips, nomadic life versus having a homebase, living like a local versus traveling like a tourist. Tuning into your values and preferences helps you adopt a travel style that suits your personality and desires. Not paying attention to this critical information could have you believing you're not cut out for extended travel, when really the problem is HOW you're traveling, not travel itself.

When it comes to giving yourself permission to do it your way, here are two important things to remember:

>> **Trial and error is OK.** Not every place or activity will be a winner, but every travel "fail" teaches you more about your preferences, and you can use this information to adjust and improve your future plans.

>> **Discomfort isn't necessarily a problem.** When everything is new, you will definitely have moments of discomfort. Give yourself some grace and time to adapt before deciding you have a big problem to solve.

ANECDOTE

I had a lot of fear about traveling to Vietnam alone (based on various stories and experiences I'd read about online). But in the end, my love of food won out, and I decided to go. Honoring my feelings meant traveling in a way that felt good to me, even if it wasn't the cheapest option. I bought a one-way flight to Hanoi (instead of a roundtrip) and promised myself I would leave the moment I felt unsafe. I booked my accommodations just one or two days in advance and slowly made my way down the coast. Three weeks later, I arrived in Ho Chi Minh, having had the most incredible experience. Vietnam became one of my favorite career break travels.

Letting go of your expectations and embracing what is

It's easy to romanticize travel with visions of glamorous journeys and perfectly planned itineraries dancing through your mind. In reality, your experience will likely be incredible but also not what you expected. If you're able to let go of your expectations and stay present, you will open yourself up to

>> Being delighted by life and experiencing many positive and memorable surprises along the way

>> Being more open to unplanned adventures that lead to hidden gems, new friends, and favorite memories

>> Enjoying the ups and downs of travel without making everything feel bad or wrong and beating yourself up when thing don't go according to plan

Whether it's travel delays, unexpected weather events, holidays, protests, or a multitude of other issues, longer-term travel will, at times, be unpredictable. Some surprises will be delightful, whereas others may disappoint you. If you want the most enjoyable experience possible, you can't force your experience to meet your expectations. Instead you need to embrace and appreciate what is, even when it's vastly different from what you'd envisioned. This will increase the joy and appreciation for your travels. If this is something you struggle with, try any of the following to help you:

>> **Approach things with a sense of humor:** Try zooming out to marvel at the topsy-turvy nature of the universe. Sometimes your toughest moments will become your best and funniest stories.

>> **Find the lesson** You're always learning, especially when you encounter failure and disappointment. Search for the lesson each mishap teaches you and use it to inform your future travels.

>> **Make peace with uncertainty:** You're not responsible (nor capable) of knowing exactly how things will go. So lean back and enjoy the journey, trusting that you have what it takes to figure things out.

REMEMBER

The longer you travel, the easier this all becomes. Your confidence and travel skills grow over time, and setbacks and challenges you face strengthen your resiliency. It may feel uncomfortable at first, but you're honing a life skill that will serve you, even beyond the break.

ACTIVITY

A tool I use to help clients reframe disappointment is practicing the belief that things are happening FOR you, not TO you. What if you believe that your canceled flight is actually creating a chain of events that lead to a better overall experience? Focus your brain to collect evidence that this could be true (that is, your travels are turning out even better because of this unexpected change), and you will start to shift your feelings and perspective.

Downsizing your life

Preparing for longer-term travel offers a unique opportunity to downsize your life, physically and mentally. It won't necessarily be easy or without some angst, but the gifts of extended travel are amplified when you seize this chance to strip things down to the essentials and reexamine your life. By choosing to downsize your life, you can

>> **Access financial freedom:** Having less means needing less space to house your belongings and spending less to maintain or replace them. This means you spend less and require less money to maintain your life.

>> **Be present and enjoy the moment more easily:** Worrying and thinking about your "stuff" can distract you from what's really important and keep you from being present in your own life.

>> **Feel lighter, literally and metaphorically:** Having and traveling with less can feel like a deep sigh of relief. With less to struggle with physically and mentally (watch for the tourists struggling up the stairs with their oversized suitcases), you'll find yourself feeling grateful that you have so much less to lug around and take care of.

>> **Reconsider what you need to be happy:** When you travel, you'll make do with a lot less and witness happy people living with less than you're accustomed to. This will have you rethinking what's essential for your own happiness.

TIP

For support with the tactical aspects of handling your belongings and managing your homebase while traveling, be sure to check out Chapter 8.

I hope you'll seize this opportunity to let go of things that you've outgrown (including outdated beliefs) so you can consciously decide what to include in your life going forward. As someone who's sold most of her earthly possessions twice in the last decade, I know that it's not easy, but I've learned it's definitely worth it. This is a chance to leave your old life and way of thinking behind and make room for something better.

REMEMBER

You can mindfully add things back into your life later on. This lighter existence can be temporary if you want it to be. You don't have to live the rest of your life with fewer things. View this as a big experiment and get ready for all that it will teach and show you!

The first time I sold my things was right before my 20-month career break started. I had a beautiful apartment full of high-end decor and furniture — things I wasn't sure I could replace. I felt sad thinking of the financial loss, and it took time to feel ready to part with them (one or two of my favorite pieces found their way to my mom's home for safe keeping). But as I worked through selling, consigning, donating, and throwing away, the excitement for my upcoming adventure helped me stay positive. By the end of my break, I was excited to begin my next chapter and didn't mind having to start over again. In fact, just a few weeks into my break I struggled to remember the things I'd gotten rid of.

Packing for a long trip

Packing for longer-term travel is an adventure unto itself. The first stages can be delightful, purchasing new clothes and gear to prepare for your upcoming trip. But slowly the feeling of being overwhelmed starts to creep in, as you face the reality of cramming your entire life into just one or two bags for several weeks or months of nonstop travel. There will be frustrating moments, but this section can help. I share a simplified approach and philosophy to packing for longer trips.

TIP

Many detailed packing lists are available online. With a simple search, you can find lists customized to your unique situation.

No matter your specific needs and requirements, my philosophy on packing is less is more (#teamcarryon). Your brain may want to convince you to be overprepared and overpacked, but this can hinder your ease, mobility, and joy (just ask the tourist struggling to haul their oversized luggage onto trains, up stairs, and along cobblestone streets).

Following are benefits to traveling with a carry-on (backpack or suitcase) rather than larger luggage:

>> Having less to keep track of and worry about
>> Having less to unpack and repack at each stop
>> Saving money on transit costs
>> Traveling lighter and with greater mobility

On my break, I traveled the world with a small backpack for my essentials and a larger 40L Osprey backpack (that was carry-on size) for everything else. With this combo, I was able to easily navigate my surroundings and avoided paying extra to check a bag on my flights.

If you're attempting to lighten your load, I recommend focusing on these four qualities when packing for extended travel to maximize utility and minimize space:

>> **Functional:** Pack things that are comfortable and durable. Make sure everything has an important purpose. Extended travel can involve a lot of walking, so this is especially true for any shoes you bring along.

>> **Multipurpose:** You can save space by including items that serve more than one purpose. For example, a simple sarong can also become a scarf, a bathing suit cover, and a skirt.

>> **Layers well:** When it comes to your clothes, packing things that can be layered well (worn under or over other things) will save space and help you adjust to different temperatures and conditions as you travel.

>> **Versatile:** Include clothes, shoes, and accessories that can be dressed up or down, according to the occasion. This helps you pack less and save space.

As you plan what you need to take with you, consider the following categories:

>> Accessories

>> Clothes and shoes

>> Electronics

>> Essentials

>> Gear

>> Medication

>> Occasion-specific

>> Toiletries

Packing for longer-term travel requires a more mindful approach, especially if it's your first time. Don't wait until the last minute. Start packing at least a few weeks ahead of time!

FACTORS THAT INFLUENCE YOUR PACKING LIST

What you need to bring with you will vary based on a variety of factors:

- **Intended activities:** What you plan to do during your break (hiking, swimming, birdwatching) dictates what kind of gear you need

- **The terrain:** The type of places you plan to visit influence your packing list. Beach travel may necessitate sunscreen, bathing suits, and a hat, whereas a trip to the mountains requires hiking boots, a rain jacket, and a head lamp.

- **The weather:** The weather can be unpredictable, especially when you're planning far in advance. You can research general averages but it's best to pack layers and be prepared for anything.

- **Travel pace:** Your travel pace dictates how often you're unpacking and repacking. If you're planning to switch locations every few days, you may need lighter luggage and more ease than someone traveling slowly.

- **Your physical needs:** You need to consider any medications and supplements for your health, neck pillows and earplugs for your comfort, as well as any devices or equipment for your support.

ACTIVITY

Lay out every item that you'd like to take with you on an empty bed or floor to see it all together. If it's too much to fit into your backpack or suitcase, try removing a couple of items every day. You can remove items that don't have a strong purpose or fit the four space-saving qualities mentioned earlier. You can also remove items that stick out like a sore thumb (pants that don't go with any of the shirts you've chosen) and unnecessary duplicates. Slowly chip away at your pile until what remains fits into your bag(s).

Handling Issues Like a Travel Pro

To help you make the most of your travels and ensure you don't let drama or obstacles derail an otherwise amazing experience, this section covers four big extended travel pitfalls to watch out for and how you can avoid them.

WHAT IF YOU DON'T LOVE TRAVEL OR WANT TO CALL IT QUITS?

There's a very good chance you'll enjoy your extended travel experience, even despite any challenges that may arise. But it's also possible that you'll learn you don't love travel or a nomadic lifestyle as much as you thought you would. This is OK, too. Travel will teach you many things, including the fact that being a world traveler, as glamorous as it may appear, may not be for you. Feel empowered to try out extended travel and prepare to avoid the common pitfalls, but please don't feel like you have to love extended travel to have an enjoyable and transformative break. Life moves in seasons, and it's possible that the current season of your life doesn't require travel.

Avoiding travel fatigue and burnout

Two related and incredibly common obstacles longer-term travelers will face are travel fatigue and travel burnout. Crazy as it may sound, it can be hard to keep things interesting when you're non-stop traveling around the world. If you're not careful, extended travel can become a grind and lose its sparkle. You may start to feel exhausted and become numb to the awe-inspiring sights and sounds over time.

There's a simple solution to help you avoid both of these travel obstacles: Set a sustainable pace for your travels and embrace variation in your experience. This will keep your interest and engagement high and help you avoid exhaustion and indifference. In this section, I share three ways to approach setting a sustainable pace and incorporating more variation into your days.

REMEMBER

Avoiding travel fatigue and burnout requires pacing yourself like you're living a regular life and not on a vacation. You'll have to slow down and create more balance to have the energy to enjoy the experience and learn about yourself and the world around you.

TIP

Taking care of your health is also an important aspect of avoiding travel burnout and having a great experience. Be sure to check out the next section for easy steps to stay healthy while you're traveling.

Slowing down and incorporating "regular life"

When traveling for an extended period of time, it's important to adopt a slower and more sustainable pace that reflects a "regular life." If you don't, you will surely burn yourself out. So instead of rushing through your destinations in an action-packed adventure, try giving yourself enough time in new locations to get your bearings and enjoy some familiarity. This also helps calm your nervous system.

Just like you would at home, you will need downtime to recover and continue processing your experience, in addition to time for handling administrative things. Instead of trying to YOLO (you only live once) your way through your break, give yourself permission to incorporate these important aspects of your normal life.

TIP

Incorporate downtime into your schedule. Dedicate time for handling and enjoying "regular life" activities like catching up on rest, staying in bed, watching TV, continuing your normal exercise routine, catching up on emails, and connecting with loved ones. These pockets of time will provide you with a sense of normalcy, adequate rest, and a more balanced life that allows you to enjoy your travels.

Setting one daily intention

An easy approach to enjoying your travels without overplanning and creating travel fatigue is to set one main intention for the day. To do this, you simply prioritize an intention and allow your day to form and unfold around this activity or event. For example, you might be excited to find the best coffee in the city. Your main intention one day could be to visit a highly reviewed cafe in continuation of your research. (I'm obsessed with food, so this is often a focal point for me.)

ACTIVITY

Set an anchor (focal point) for your day. No activity or experience is too small. Plan for one thing you really want to do or accomplish. Figure out your ideal timing for this activity or experience and then create a route to arrive at your starting point. Remember to take your time. There's no rush. Stay open to fun and interesting things you can incorporate into your experience.

When I spent a month in Buenos Aires, I had many days that were guided by a simple intention. One day, I voyaged to a new neighborhood to explore one of the world's most beautiful bookstores that was once a theater (El Ateneo Grand Splendid). Instead of creating a jam-packed day and rushing over via taxi, I wandered on foot, discovering new restaurants and shops along the way. With nowhere to rush off to after I'd finished checking out the bookstore, I continued exploring and found a new favorite gelato shop on my way home.

If you tend to be an over-planner, I highly recommend giving this a try — even if you normally love planning and structure. Creating the space to allow things to unfold can bring some serious magic into your life. You may meet new friends or discover once-in-a-lifetime experiences.

Flaneuring to enjoy your travels more

Flaneuring is a French term and delightful concept that involves wandering and taking leisurely strolls. Unlike most of life, when you're flaneuring, you're aimlessly wandering for fun with no specific destination or outcome in mind. Instead, your focus is on soaking up the beauty you would normally miss because you're distracted by things like your thoughts or your phone. At its essence, flaneuring is about being present to the sights, sounds, tastes, and smells all around you. Instead of mindlessly wandering to your next stop, it challenges you to be mindful of all that you're experiencing along the way.

Flaneuring can help you cultivate more calm, joy, presence, and gratitude during your travels, which makes for a refreshing change of pace. Instead of focusing on a mission, you're free to observe the world around you and focus on what you're feeling and experiencing because of it.

To give flaneuring a try, set aside a morning or afternoon to just wander. Pick a starting point (your hotel, a cool cafe, or a bakery in a fun neighborhood) and start strolling. Put your phone away and notice life around you. Pay attention to what you're feeling and let your desires guide you. Are you getting hungry? Let your stomach guide you to food. Are you feeling tired? Let your feet guide you to a nearby seat to sit and observe. Are you thirsty? Find a spot for a refreshing beverage and try something new. Allow yourself to aimlessly wander for a couple of hours and marvel at what you notice.

An important caveat is making sure you're flaneuring in safe areas. Choose an area that is generally safe to aimlessly wander. If you're somewhere that doesn't feel safe, save the opportunity to flaneur for another day.

Here are two ways I approach flaneuring, with my safety in mind:

» **Do it during the day:** Because daytime is generally safer, I do most of my flaneuring during the day. I do aimlessly wander in the evenings, but only when I feel confident in my safety (families out for an evening stroll is often a good sign).

» **Ask an expert for guidance:** I ask the hotel staff or my Airbnb host for feedback on any areas I want to visit. If they feel it's unsafe, I usually avoid it.

ANECDOTE

With lots of good food and so many people out for an evening stroll, Milan was a perfect place to flaneur. Along my aimless strolls, I caught snippets of conversations in Italian, smelled delicious foods, and took in the beauty of the city alongside the water. I allowed myself to be present and appreciate and observe the beautiful and simple things around me.

Avoiding health issues while traveling

Staying healthy doesn't have to be hard. In fact, longer-term travel can facilitate a healthier lifestyle if you're intentional about integrating healthy practices into your day. It may require more work upfront to set a habit, but it's worth it because it will help you avoid medical intervention and expenses, create a more enjoyable travel experience, and give you more energy to enjoy your day. And because you're traveling for a longer period of time, it's critical to focus on supporting your health more than you would on a regular vacation.

Here are several areas to focus on to support your health:

» **Food:** Be sure to stay hydrated and to incorporate healthy items into your day (vegetables, protein, and so on). It can be helpful to prepare some of your meals at home to create more nutritional balance.

» **Movement:** Move your body daily, even if it's a simple walk. Exploring on foot and via public transit are great ways to get to know a city better and get more movement in your day.

Plus, it can also save you money. If you already have a daily exercise routine established, try to keep up with it when traveling.

>> **Rest:** When you're traveling for a longer period of time, it's important to incorporate rest and give your body time to recover, especially after long travel days and/or time zone changes.

TIP

Be sure to consider your travel insurance options. Should anything happen to you while you're away from home, it's important to have a plan for your healthcare expenses. You can find more details and recommendations in Chapter 8.

Avoiding boredom and indifference

One of the unexpected obstacles of longer-term travel is navigating boredom and indifference. No matter how incredible your surroundings are, your excitement may fade as you become used to your new lifestyle. And as much as you want to continue enjoying your adventures, you may struggle to be impressed by the interesting and beautiful things you see. But you can remedy this with variety and gratitude.

Variation creates appreciation. Creating a contrast will make it easier to notice and appreciate your circumstances. Variety will spice things up and prevent life from feeling stale, thus making it easier to feel grateful and more engaged with your surroundings. As an example, you may eventually start to feel isolated if you stay only in hotels. A night or two in a hostel-type environment can give you instant connection and make it easier to find dinner partners. And when you're back to the quiet of a hotel room again, you'll appreciate the solitude even more than before.

REMEMBER

Variation can make simple and mundane things feel novel again. And from this feeling, you'll be able to connect more deeply with a sense of gratitude for your circumstances.

Try to intentionally mix things up, even if it means stepping outside of your current comfort zone. For inspiration, here are several ways you could introduce variation:

>> **Activities:** Whether your focus is history, food, or nature, consider mixing things up and incorporating new interests.

>> **Level of adventure:** If you're an adventurous person, try incorporating a few leisurely experiences; if you're not particularly adventurous, try pushing yourself to try something new that's a bit beyond your current edge.

>> **Mode of transit:** Extended travel is great for traveling more like a local. Instead of searching for the fastest and easiest route, slow down and take a more scenic route

>> **Travel style:** If you're planning for a hotel-based experience, try mixing in a few hostels or homestays to meet new people and switch up your experience. (You can book a private room in a hostel if privacy is important.)

>> **Type of destination:** Create a contrast within some of your destinations (urban areas, remote locations, beaches, mountains, deserts, and so on) to continue appreciating the change in landscape and energy of your surroundings.

ACTIVITY

Take time to appreciate aspects of your current situation that may be different than what you were previously experiencing. List 10 things that are good about your present moment or experience and try to appreciate them individually.

WARNING

Don't take variety to the extreme. You don't have to constantly create massive change; this will lead to exhaustion and feeling overwhelmed. Instead, incorporate it in doses and view the contrast as the toppings on a really tasty ice cream sundae.

Avoiding loneliness and friction with others

Whether you decide to travel alone, with others, or a mix of both, it's important to understand the difficulties you may face and develop a plan to manage them. For more practical tips on managing loneliness, you can visit Chapter 10.

Traveling solo

One of the biggest fears of solo travel is dealing with loneliness. While it might seem counterintuitive, solo travel can create more (not less) meaningful connection. When you travel alone, people will find it easier to engage with you, and you'll find yourself more willing to step outside of your comfort zone to make new friends, all of which helps you to feel more immersed in your travels.

Being alone is not the same as being lonely. Loneliness is a condition we wrestle with even in the company of others. It's possible to feel lonely while in a group or sitting next to a loved one. Being alone doesn't mean you have to feel lonely. Some time alone to process things and the freedom to follow your own desires without consulting or compromising with anyone else can be meaningful and satisfying.

ACTIVITY

If you're feeling lonely, be curious as to whether you're really feeling lonely or just noticing that you're alone. If you're just noticing that you're alone, get curious about whether it's uncomfortable because it's different or because you don't wish to be alone right now. If it's uncomfortable, view it as an opportunity to experience new parts of yourself; if you don't want to be alone, you can try any of the following ideas to create connection:

>> **Call home.** If you're missing home, connecting with a loved one back home can be restorative. As a bonus, it may also remind you of the mundane moments you've temporarily left behind and give you a much-needed travel boost.

>> **Sit at the bar for your next meal.** This will make it much easier to engage in conversation with others, while giving you something to divert the focus and keep things casual.

>> **Spend the night in a hostel.** Even if you book a private room, surrounding yourself with fellow travelers in a hostel can make it much easier to find adventure buddies and dinner partners when you don't want to be alone.

>> **Take a tour.** Whether it's a topic of interest or just a free walking tour, being around other travelers who speak your language and share your interests can be restorative.

>> **Take a walk and smile at others.** When you're feeling alone, simply taking a walk outside and exchanging smiles with others can create a feeling of connection.

TIP

If you're staying somewhere for a while, it can be worthwhile to focus on building a community. You can check out expat Facebook groups or join a local gym or yoga studio. Connect with like-minded people and spend your time doing things you enjoy with others who share your interests.

Traveling with others

Whether you're traveling with a partner, your children, friends, or strangers, you need to be thoughtful about how you approach and manage your travel experience.

On the positive side, having a travel partner(s) comes with benefits like having someone to help you navigate unfamiliar places and handle stressful situations and to create memories with and share the highs and lows of your experiences. But traveling with others also presents unique challenges, specifically managing multiple needs, desires, roles, and responsibilities. When you're traveling with others, you'll want to proactively manage your communication. Before you begin traveling, it's helpful to discuss topics like

>> **Personal strengths:** Understanding and communicating your personal strengths can help inform your travel roles and responsibilities. It also establishes opportunities for you to support the group.

>> **Roles and responsibilities:** Divvying up the responsibilities ahead of time helps avoid confusion and enables you each to prepare for your upcoming tasks.

>> **Standard operating procedures:** Before things get heated, it's important to establish a protocol for handling frustrations, disappointments, and concerns. Consider how you'll establish a safe space for these to be expressed.

>> **Travel goals and desires:** Understanding what your travel partner(s) want to get out of this experience will help you support each other's goals and inform when it might be best to split up or navigate an experience solo.

At some point, you'll likely make friends with fellow travelers and decide to partner up, giving you someone to share meals and experiences with. Travel buddies can make your travels more enjoyable, but don't feel bad if you realize you've outgrown the connection. The partnership may have an expiration date, and that's OK. You can separate and return to doing your own thing again. Whatever you do, avoid compromising your own needs and desires and remember that having transitory travel buddies is a natural part of the travel experience.

Take time to get clear on your own needs and desires before beginning your break travels. Knowing what you want to experience will help you consider the drawbacks or trade-offs of any compromise, which helps strike the delicate balance between cooperation and honoring your own needs.

If you're traveling with a partner, consider incorporating some solo time into your plans. During your break, you'll be together almost 24/7, which can be a sharp contrast to your previous experience. You may need and want some time alone to decompress from long days, accomplish personal goals, and fulfill different (and possibly competing) needs and desires.

During my break, my boyfriend accompanied me on several of my travel adventures. He was an incredible source of calm and confidence. I leaned on his uncanny sense of direction and fluency in Spanish to help us navigate new places. I was great at flaneuring and allowing the day to unfold, so I helped us find balance and avoid travel burnout. But even with our complementary skills, it wasn't always easy. For example, we had completely opposite approaches to food. I had a gluten allergy and didn't mind paying more for a great meal. He preferred tasty and affordable food and generally loved gluten. This made meals a challenge, so our compromise was sometimes dining separately. This allowed us both to indulge and enjoy our experience in a way that aligned with our values.

4

Navigating Your Break

Discover best practices for creating a life-changing career break and enjoying the experience. You learn what to expect and how to handle any setbacks that may arise.

Discover ways to stay within your budget and avoid a money meltdown while on a break.

Avoid boredom and ensure you don't waste your time while on a break. Find out how to enjoy the free time and maximize your overall career break experience.

ou uays

» **Learning how to handle surprises and setbacks**

» **Navigating loneliness and making connections**

» **Creating lasting change and transformation**

Chapter **10**

Getting the Most out of Your Break

Taking a break is a big investment, so it's important to know how to navigate it well to maximize the benefits. In this chapter, you find out how to get the most out of your experience and create a life-enhancing break. Knowing what to expect and how to move through your break with less fear and more confidence will eliminate any worry that you're messing it up or doing it wrong. You'll be prepared to navigate common obstacles like self-doubt, loneliness, and boredom, which enables you to create a deep and meaningful transformation that lasts well beyond your break. You learn how to let go of the familiar and embrace a sense of adventure and curiosity to navigate an uncertain world full of possibility. Get ready to navigate your break like a pro for improved results and a better overall experience!

Surviving and Thriving in the First 60 Days

Starting a break can feel like jumping out of an airplane — both terrifying and thrilling. While on a break, you experience more freedom and opportunity than ever before but there's significantly less structure and routine than you're used to. It can be disorienting at first, but you'll get the hang of things quickly if you have a plan to navigate the early days. This is because your first 60 days will set the tone of your overall experience in the following ways:

>> Influencing your confidence and willingness to take more risks, try new things, and experiment

>> Anchoring your perspective for how positively (or negatively) you view your break

>> Testing your ability to handle uncertainty and discomfort

This chapter helps you develop a winning approach. While your own experience will be unique, this section provides a general idea of what you can expect over the first two months of your break. I'll share the commonalities I've seen over dozens of career breaks and sabbaticals to help you

>> Adjust more quickly when you face challenges that are harder than expected

>> Feel validated and less alone with any issues you face as you begin your break

>> Give yourself grace and navigate challenges more easily

>> Reduce the discomfort and confusion you'll experience during the entry period

Adjusting your expectations

No matter how you think your break will go, it's bound to surprise you, especially in the first few weeks. Because it's a brand-new experience, you're going to learn a lot through trial and error. One of the best things to do as you begin your break is let go of any preconceived notions of how it should go or what it should look like. Unmet expectations are the root of frustration and disappointment, so instead of setting yourself up for disappointment, practice accepting and enjoying things as they unfold.

As an example, you may have visions of blissful naps and incredible bursts of productivity but in reality struggle with pushing yourself to do too much or feeling guilty about taking it easy. Maybe you envision crystal-clear boundaries to protect your time but in practice struggle to honor them with others. Instead of feeling guilty, pushing too hard, or being critical of yourself, accept that it's a learning journey and give yourself permission to do it imperfectly and still enjoy the process.

ANECDOTE

Richard had an easy start to his break but hit a slump within days. He felt bored after working out, relaxing, and shoveling snow all in one day. The transition into infinite free time was overwhelming. His default was to fill his time with doing things, but he'd run out of ideas and was struggling with boredom. However, at the end of his first week, things started to shift. The burnout and exhaustion caught up to him and he decided to slow down. He granted himself days with double naps and more quality time with family and friends, and he began to embrace a more "do-nothing" approach to his next few weeks. This allowed him to start recharging on a much deeper level.

REMEMBER

Give yourself grace and try not to have expectations for how you will feel and what you will do (or not do) during this transition. Your first 60 days are a big adjustment. It's OK if they're messy. Accept what is and know that things will feel easier in time. You will find your rhythm. Don't be startled by the difference between how you thought your break would go and how it actually unfolds. It will still be a great experience!

Resting and restoring without resistance

One of the most challenging aspects of taking a break is adequately resting and restoring. After years of chasing goals and moving at a frantic pace, it can feel extremely uncomfortable to slow down, be present, and let go of the relentless need to be productive. But this will be critical, especially in the first few months, to your ability to experience a full recharge during your break.

A break offers a deep level of restoration and healing. To access it you'll need to prioritize rest and restoration in the first two months of your break (or longer, depending on your themes and how you're feeling mentally and physically). The first few months of your break are a great time to prioritize self-care, nourishment, relaxation, and rest.

For a full recharge, disconnect from things that deplete you and (re)connect to things that replenish you. Focus on the following to find effective ways to rest and restore:

>> **Physical:** Allow your body time to power down, rest, and decompress as you begin your break. You'll also want to focus on nourishing your body and supporting your physical well-being.

>> **Mental:** Let your mind decompress and disconnect from as many stress inducers as possible. You can aid your recovery by engaging your mind in pleasant activities and leaning in to creativity and inspiration.

>> **Emotional:** Disconnect from, or minimize, relationships that burden you and give yourself permission to express yourself authentically. Seek support, if necessary, and pursue relationships that feel nurturing to you.

>> **Environmental:** Unplug or reduce your connection with external stimulus to give yourself an environmental detox. You can also use this time to create more restorative and peaceful surroundings.

While you might be looking forward to the additional time to pursue rest and restoration, it's OK if you're also at a loss for where to start, beyond getting better sleep and taking naps. Figure 10-1 provides a checklist of activities that you can experiment with to help you rest and restore. But don't to try tackle everything at once! Start with ideas that feel accessible and vital to your well-being and slowly build up from there.

Don't underestimate the power of rest. Adequate rest allows you to decompress and renew, plus it provides fuel for the rest of your break. Pushing yourself too hard too soon could land you back at square one and delay moving on to other focus areas of your break.

Emotional

- ☐ Disconnect from those who drain your energy or make you feel uncomfortable
- ☐ Exercise control and autonomy by leaving unplanned time in your schedule to experience time free from the needs and demands of others, including family
- ☐ Seek support to process and release emotional stress (support groups, therapy, coaching)
- ☐ Spend time with people who make you feel comfortable and free to be yourself

Environmental

- ☐ Create a more relaxing environment (sounds, scents, colors, lighting)
- ☐ Declutter your home to create more space, peace, and clarity
- ☐ Remove external stimulus (social media, screen time, phone ringer, and other notifications) for a set period of time
- ☐ Spend time in nature
- ☐ Visit places that feel restorative (your favorite coffee shop, happy places, locations with ideal weather, loved ones' homes)

Mental

- ☐ Engage in "mastery activities" that are mentally absorbing and also pleasurable (chess, writing, learning a language)
- ☐ Immerse in sources of inspiration to engage your mind (museums, podcasts, books, movies)
- ☐ Make time to appreciate beautiful scenery (sunrises, mountains, lakes, oceans)
- ☐ Meditate and/or practice breathwork
- ☐ Pursue creative and expressive outlets (drawing, journaling, coloring)
- ☐ Spend time alone to process, dream, reflect, and be present
- ☐ Write down your to-dos to help your brain stop thinking about them

Physical

- ☐ Create a healthy sleep rhythm and aim for at least seven hours of good sleep nightly
- ☐ Eat more nutritious foods
- ☐ Get a massage
- ☐ Incorporate gentle movement (walking, yoga, stretching)
- ☐ Incorporate pleasurable activities (hiking, swimming, golfing)
- ☐ Stay hydrated
- ☐ Take baths or long soaks
- ☐ Take naps

FIGURE 10-1: Activities to help you rest and restore physically, mentally, emotionally and environmentally.

Boredom and discomfort are not signs of restoration. After a few weeks of taking it easy, you may feel like it's time to start chasing big goals again like finding a new job, tackling a big home project, starting a new business, or making another big change. But before you launch into any big endeavors, it's important to take your time, be patient, and continue incorporating restorative practices into your days for the first couple of months. This work has the power to reshape your relationship to time and productivity. With it, you'll be more capable of creating and maintaining an enjoyable and sustainable pace after you return to work.

TIP

On average, it takes about three months to recover from the daily grind of full-time employment and detach from the extreme levels of urgency and productivity it likely required. If you're using your break for healing or suffer from burnout, it can take even longer to fully restore and heal yourself.

TIP

If you'd like to explore different types of rest in more detail, I suggest this interview with Dr. Saundra Dalton-Smith: https://goop.com/wellness/mindfulness/7-types-of-rest/.

TIP

If you're planning to travel or embark on a big adventure early in your break, try to give yourself three to six weeks at home or in a stable environment before you begin. This will provide time to start decompressing, pack, move, handle administrative tasks, and finalize travel plans before your trip.

ANECDOTE

For logistical reasons, I started my three-month road trip almost immediately after beginning my break. To compensate for having less downtime upfront, I extended my stay at my first few stops, spending one week in each location. I also gave myself more rest days after visits with friends and removed some destinations to slow down the pace of my trip. I then spent two months at home with family over the holidays to have more time to rest and recover and process the grief of losing my brother. Afterward, I felt more prepared to leap into a nonstop eight-month trip around the world.

REMEMBER

Give yourself grace during this time. The early part of your break is meant to help you recover and ease into this new experience. If you're used to pushing through and accomplishing things even when you're exhausted, this may feel uncomfortable at first. You won't be a lazy sloth for the entirety of your break, but right now you need more rest. Honor this need. Give yourself lots of downtime and enjoy this temporary life of leisure. You've earned it!

WHY YOU NEED REST

Rest isn't a privilege you need to earn. It's your right. Human beings are meant to rest. With it, you feel happier and operate at your best, much like professional athletes who depend on rest and recovery to optimize their performances. While it might not look like much from the outside, rest is NOT doing nothing. A lot happens underneath the surface when you're resting. It can be especially productive during the first few months of your break because it helps you adjust and decompress after years of sprinting through life and functioning through feelings of being overwhelmed and burnout. Enjoy your rest with satisfaction and the knowledge that you are taking exquisite care of yourself.

Moving through your first two months

While each person's break experience is unique, there are several universal truths about all breaks. Being aware of them can help you feel more prepared and know what to focus on during the first two months of your break.

You'll experience a range of emotions

You may feel electrified by your newfound freedom, and moments later lament the loss of familiar routines and structure (and feel terrified by the uncertainty it creates). From "I've totally got this" to "I don't know what I'm doing," emotional swings are normal. Try not to waste time worrying about them or thinking something is wrong if you have them.

REMEMBER

It's OK to feel a bit off. Experiencing highs and lows is normal. Your mind is processing the change, so don't criticize yourself for any feelings you have, no matter how uncomfortable.

Your activity level will ebb and flow

The content of your days will vary. Some will be active (running errands, doing tasks, accomplishing goals), and others will be more restful. You may need more restful days than you'd originally planned for, or you may have enough but feel guilty when you try to enjoy them. You may have an amazing and seamless first week and then struggle with being overwhelmed and lacking motivation in week two. All of this is normal. Nothing has gone wrong. It's just part of the process of learning how to be on a break and create a more natural and intuitive flow for your days.

Your focus will continue to evolve

As you move through the first few weeks of your break, your focus will naturally evolve and deepen. It's important to be thoughtful about how you approach your first two months as they set a tone for your overall experience. These first two months are a great time to focus on things like the following:

>> **Celebrating your break:** Acknowledge the work it took to get here and embrace the freedom in your life and schedule.

>> **Decompressing:** Think of it as taking a few deep, slow breaths after years of shallow, frantic breathing.

>> **Enjoying life with ease:** Give yourself time to adjust, while keeping things simple and easy.

>> **Finalizing the details:** Put a finer point on key details, your travel itinerary, and your break plans in general.

ANECDOTE

On the first Monday after starting her break, Danielle woke up and walked to the kitchen, where she promptly laid down. As she spread across the kitchen floor, she stared up at the ceiling and felt a profound sense of freedom. She perceived laying on the floor on a Monday morning, with no one to answer to and nowhere she had to be, as an expression of her newfound freedom.

ANECDOTE

Kim's rest-oriented theme was Nourish, so while mapping out the timeline of her break, she decided to spend the first month of her break in her home city, focusing on this theme. That month gave her time to decompress and to enjoy a more leisurely pace as she finalized her upcoming travel plans and booked her first international flight to the Azores. Giving herself a month at home allowed Kim to ease into her break and manage any stress and anxiety around her upcoming solo travels. It also gave her more time to say her goodbyes and enjoy her city as a tourist before heading out on a big adventure.

A GENERAL PROGRESSION OF THE FIRST EIGHT WEEKS

The following is a general overview of how many of my clients' breaks have progressed. This is by no means a standard you need to follow. Your experience will likely vary (which is totally fine), but this break-down gives you an idea of what to expect and provides tips for what you may want to focus on as you move through your first two months:

- **Week 1:** Your first week will likely feel exciting and a bit messy as you navigate life with ample free time and without an anchoring work schedule.

  Focus on getting your bearings and enjoying your freedom. Don't worry about starting an ambitious daily routine or overloading yourself with errands. Instead, do things that help you celebrate the start of your break and tune into a feeling of gratitude.

- **Week 2:** You're still in the early stages of decompressing; be sure to move through this week without self-judgment.

  Focus on incorporating structure and routine into your day. Don't overwhelm yourself with tasks. Keep it simple. Starting a support-ive morning routine will help you achieve a sense of accomplishment and avoid feeling aimless. (See Chapter 12 for help in designing a morning routine.)

- **Weeks 3 and 4:** As you start to get the hang of things, you can be more intentional about how you spend your time and energy

  Focus on incorporating activities that align with your themes. You'll also want to start a consistent check-in routine to reflect on your break and process the things you're learning and experiencing as you go (see Chapter 12 for help with this). This is also a good time to check in with your finances to see how things are going.

- **Weeks 5 through 8:** You're likely feeling a bit steadier and clearer, and it's really sinking in that your break is more than just an extended vacation.

  Focus on continuing your intentional activities (that is, fulfilling your purpose and themes) and enjoying this new experience. Don't be afraid to switch things up and make tweaks to create a

(continued)

(continued)

routine that suits you. Remember to keep incorporating restful activities (like those listed in the previous section) into your day to support a full recharge. If your break plan includes travel, this is a great time to make the final arrangements and get started.

Navigating the Ups and Downs

A career break is an exciting journey full of twists and turns. To have the most enjoyable experience and create the best outcome possible, you'll want to be prepared to handle the surprises, setbacks, and mind drama that may arise during your break. In this section, I share tools that I've used to support clients through some of their biggest challenges and trouble spots during their breaks like:

>> Being diagnosed with serious health issues that require extra care and downtime during their break

>> Feeling lonely, uneasy, and/or a bit lost during their break

>> Having a family member fall ill during the break

>> Knowing how to meaningfully fill the empty space and free time in their days

>> Losing a loved one while on their break

>> Receiving an unexpected job opportunity and deciding whether to end the break early or turn the offer down

>> Wanting to prematurely end to the break because they're worried they're falling behind in their career

With all of the excitement, energy, and effort you've put into your break, it's easy to forget that unexpected obstacles may arise. The same ups and downs that happen in regular life can (and do) happen during your break — a break is still real life. But if and when it does, you don't have to abandon your break. Instead, remember that the ups and downs are normal, and you can get through it by taking one small step at a time.

REMEMBER

When life gets hard or tosses you a big challenge, you don't have to throw in the towel. You can focus on how your break has prepared you to handle these challenges with more ease. Search for evidence that being on a break was exactly what you needed to help you navigate this experience.

My brother unexpectedly passed away just days before my break began. The start of my break was nothing like I envisioned: planning a funeral, putting career break money toward funeral expenses, and navigating a tsunami of grief. I was doing my best to survive the most difficult experience of my life while starting my break. But instead of spiraling down a hole of anger and resentment, I focused on taking care of myself as best I could and focused on how grateful I was to be on a break as I dealt with all of this. To move forward, I had to let go of the old vision for my break and accept what was. I was never going to feel prepared to handle this life event, so I conceded that if it was going to happen, this was actually the best time for it. I had $40,000 in the bank, no job to report back to, and a thoughtful plan for my time off. And at the end of the day, I still managed to have an incredible and life-changing experience during my break.

Kisha took a break with the intention of finishing the novel she'd been longing to write. She'd made incredible progress several months into her break, when a recruiter reached out with a contract opportunity that paid significantly more than her previous salary. She reflected on her break's purpose as she weighed the decision. Ultimately, she opted to return to work (temporarily) with the goal of building up her savings and returning for a longer break to finish her novel when the contract had ended. Having a clear purpose made it easier for her to consider the trade-offs and make an informed decision.

Following the golden rules of adopting a break mindset

A career break creates the opportunity to embrace a new way of life — one with more balance, more joy, and more ease. Adopting a positive attitude and supportive mindset will help you ensure a successful outcome. Here are six rules you can follow to create a supportive career break mindset:

>> **Allow all of your emotions.**

You'll feel many things as you move through your break. Acknowledge them (name them) - even the "icky" ones — and allow them to pass through (more details are provided later in this section). Don't hold on to them. Criticizing yourself for having them or pretending that they don't exist only gives you more to unpack and deal with later on.

» Don't make yourself wrong.

Whether you take three naps in one day, decide to cancel long-awaited travel plans or have an anxiety-fueled meltdown on a hard day, don't make yourself wrong for how you move through your break. There will be lots of ups and downs, so know that it's normal and unavoidable. Give yourself grace, learn from the stumbles, and use them to improve your approach and create the experience you want to have.

» Embrace spontaneity.

You've invested in your freedom, so make the most of it! Allow yourself to say yes to things or change your plans with only a moment's notice. Enjoy the present moment and the flexibility you have to follow your nudges and seize opportunities as they arise — a treat that isn't possible when you're working full time.

» Let go of your expectations.

Your break is an exciting new adventure, and it will yield amazing benefits that you can't yet imagine. To really appreciate and embrace these, you need to let go of how you think it should look and enjoy the new discoveries and experiences.

» Stay curious and cultivate a sense of gratitude.

Starting from a place of curiosity and a willingness to learn new things will make your experience more enjoyable. This allows you to observe and learn without judgment and keeps you engaged with the world around you even when it feels confusing. Your break is a huge learning opportunity, and connecting with gratitude and delight along the way will help you see life in a new light and appreciate the gifts of even the most ordinary days.

» Trade up for better problems.

Our brains are problem-solving machines. They will create problems when there are none to be found, which means you'll never be problem-free (not even on a career break). The good news is that your goal isn't to eliminate all of your problems; it's to create better problems to solve. When you're facing problems during your break, stop to ask yourself if they're better problems than you had before your break. If the answer is yes, count that as a success and know that you're heading in the right direction.

ACTIVITY

To start incorporating the previous rules into your break, choose one rule that feels relieving and freeing to imagine. Next, set an intention to practice it over the next week. Write it down and remember it each morning; then apply your chosen rule throughout the day.

Staying connected to your vision

Things may get a little bumpy from time to time while you're on your break. One of the simplest and most powerful things you can do when you feel overwhelmed, lost, or confused is take a moment to connect to your original vision for the break. It's possible that new circumstances may require you to adjust your plan, but it's important that you first connect to your purpose statement and themes before making any big decisions (see Chapter 4 to develop these critical elements). This will help you remember the bigger picture and reconnect to your personal definition of success. From this grounded place, you'll be clearer about what (if anything) needs to change for you to keep moving forward.

REMEMBER

Your purpose statement and themes serve as the North Star for your break. It's very unlikely that these will change during the break because they are an essential truth about what you want and need in this season of your life. So be sure to keep them in mind as you make big decisions and revisit them anytime you feel unclear about how to proceed.

ACTIVITY

To reconnect to your vision, write down your purpose statement and themes. Reflect on your progress for each one: How have you already fulfilled it, even if only partially? Then, for each theme, ask yourself "is this still true?" And for every "yes" ask the follow-up question, "What are some new ways that I can approach fulfilling this?" Write down your ideas and get creative with your answers. Brainstorm new ways to approach your themes if your circumstances require a change of plans.

TIP

If you're struggling to stay connected to your vision and motivated on your break, seek out others on a similar journey to feel supported. The Sabbatical Project's Facebook group is a supportive resource. If you need help rebuilding your confidence and belief or charting a new direction, I also recommend reaching out to a career break or sabbatical coach for professional guidance.

Accepting your feelings and managing your fears

An important part of navigating the ups and downs of your break is being able to ride the emotional waves. You may find yourself in a challenging moment during your break, with guilt about feeling frustrated and disappointed. But a break is still real life, and as such, you're going to be exposed to the full range of human emotions. Allowing yourself to acknowledge your fears and accept any difficult feelings that arise will help the hard moments pass sooner and the joyful moments linger a little longer.

You can put your energy to better use, like solving problems and enjoying your experience, when you give yourself permission to feel your feelings instead of wasting energy trying to avoid them. Difficult feelings don't mean that you're ungrateful or failing at your break. They're a sign that you're a normal human being. So give yourself permission to have a big cry or frustrated scream, if you need one. Expressing your emotions allows you to process your feelings and move through them much more quickly, so they won't stick with you and sour your break.

ACTIVITY

If you notice yourself feeling really upset or struggling with a lot of negative emotions, try this exercise. Write down every feeling you're experiencing. Are you sad, frustrated, scared, excited, hopeful? After you've named each emotion, it's time to feel them. Put your hand over your heart and speak the following mantra: "Right now I feel ___, and that's a right way to feel." It may sound silly, but the simple act of acknowledging and allowing your feelings will help you process and release them more quickly (so you can get back to enjoying your break).

Fear will rear its ugly head many times during your break. You may feel fearful about running out of money, finding another job, not wanting to go back to work, being judged, feeling lazy, ruining your career, and so much more. This is normal. So, while I can't help you eliminate your fears altogether, I do have some tools up my sleeve to help you manage them:

» **Acknowledge your fears.** Similar to the exercise where you acknowledge your emotions, write down your fears one by one. Listing them helps you recognize the irrational fears you don't actually believe (and want to let go of) and acts as an emotional release, getting them out of your head and onto the page.

» **Put fear in the backseat.** If you like visualizations, imagine your fear in the front seat, desperately grabbing at the steering wheel and trying to decide where you'll go next. Fear never leads you to the best destinations, so sternly ask it to climb into the backseat and strap its seatbelt on. Listen to what it has to say (what it's afraid of) but remember that its concerns are only meant to help you make an informed decision, not to choose your destination.

» **Celebrate your wins.** It's so easy to dismiss your progress and downplay your accomplishments and experiences during your break. What once felt nearly impossible no longer feels noteworthy. You can counteract this tendency by making a conscious effort to celebrate your wins. Reflecting on your wins will help you see how strong, capable, and resourceful you are, and it will bolster your belief that you can figure things out.

» **Practice gratitude.** Tapping into feelings of abundance and gratitude can help counteract your fears. Focusing on what you're grateful for reminds you that you already have more than enough and that, even in hard times, a lot of good can be found around you. This can alleviate some of your worries and stress and create a sense of calm.

» **Remember your re-entry period.** Your re-entry period (as discussed in Chapter 4) is the part of your break when you have dedicated time to figure out what comes next. If you're not in the re-entry period but are feeling stressed about what to do after your break, gently invite your fear to come back later. You can defer your big questions and anxiety about the future and get back to the current job at hand — enjoying your break.

TIP

For more tips and guidance on managing fear, see Chapter 3.

AVOIDING CAREER BREAK ENVY

Even when you've planned an amazing break, you may find yourself struggling with compare-and-despair syndrome. No matter how fantastic your travel plans are or how healing your journey is, if you were raised in a competitive or individualistic culture, your brain is used to assessing your progress by comparing your experience to those of your peers.

In the absence of having metrics to evaluate your break and facing uncertainty about what you will return to, it's easy to fall into the trap of not appreciating your break experiences and instead focusing on what someone else has or has done on theirs. But this leads to feelings of inadequacy and self-doubt, which are not helpful.

If you've used Chapter 4's guidelines to develop your plan, you can rest easy knowing you've designed a road map to your best break. The results will be incredible, but your journey won't look like anyone else's because it's uniquely yours. So, embrace the uniqueness and stay true to your needs. This will make it much easier to enjoy your experience and avoid the sinking feeling that you're doing it wrong.

Dealing with Loneliness during Your Break

Taking a break means breaking away from the status quo and following a unique path, which can sometimes feel isolating. Giving up the daily meetings and similarity in routine with those around you can leave space for loneliness to creep in. In this section, I share three ways to address feelings of loneliness and prevent them from ruining your break.

Resolve it and build connection

If you're feeling lonely, focus your energy on building connection. The following are several easy ways you can approach this:

>> **Be of service:** Offer a helping hand to a person in need; do something kind for someone or something else.

- » **Send thank-you messages:** Email or handwritten notes enable you to reach out to someone and tell them how much you appreciate them.

- » **Make a courageous hello.** Be brave. When you see someone next to you, say hello.

- » **Make time for your friends and family.** Go out of your way to connect and strengthen relationships.

- » **Say "yes" to new people.** Be open and willing to try something new when someone reaches out to you and expresses an interest in getting to know you.

- » **Attend an event that interests you.** Pursue things that catch your attention and find like-minded people.

- » **Share your story.** Be open and vulnerable, and tell people about who you are and what you're up to.

- » **Reach out to someone who makes you feel good.** Call, email, message, or video chat people who make you laugh or radiate positive energy.

Reframe it in a more positive light

While loneliness can feel uncomfortable (painful, even) you can reframe it to cast it in a more positive light. Start by noticing the difference between being alone and being lonely. Are you feeling lonely? Or are you just alone? Alone can sometimes be a great thing (see the next approach for more on this). Don't fool yourself into thinking there's anything wrong with being alone.

If you're feeling lonely, it's good to acknowledge the feeling but don't infer that there's anything wrong with you or your break. You can feel incredibly lonely in a room full of people or sitting next to someone you love. Feelings of loneliness are part of the human condition because we're social beings in search of connection. Instead of viewing it as a bad thing, neutralize loneliness by remembering it's a part of the human experience and review the preceding section for ideas to create more connection.

Embrace it and enjoy your alone time

There are certain aspects of your break that are best experienced in solitude. It's during this time that you can focus deeply on your needs and not worry about incorporating or fulfilling the needs and desires of those around you. In moments where you're feeling lonely, try leaning into this alone time in one of the following ways:

>> **Celebrate it and take advantage:** Do something you prefer, or can only do, solo.

>> **Get to know yourself better.** Take yourself out on dates to discover new things you enjoy and do things you've always wanted to do or try.

>> **Treat yourself well.** Spoil yourself with kindness and care.

If you're looking for ways to manage loneliness while traveling, be sure to visit Chapter 9 for targeted advice.

TIP

Ushering in Change and Transformation

One of the best gifts a career break offers is the opportunity for personal transformation, and in this section, I share three practices that can help you achieve it. If you weren't loving life pre-break (working too hard, feeling misaligned, lacking connection, not having interests outside of work), this is your chance to hit the reset button and create a more meaningful and enjoyable path.

Taking a break sets the stage for transformation, but experiencing a significant change also requires leaning into uncomfortable moments and exploring new ways to resolve them. Quite often the hardest part of your break will offer the biggest lesson you need to learn to create the life you want. So when you feel stuck in your break, try viewing it as a reflection of where you might be getting stuck in life and seize the opportunity to overcome it. You may struggle with setting boundaries, overworking, ignoring your intuition, or believing you're lazy if you take time to rest. During your break, you'll have a lot more time and energy to focus on addressing these challenges in a new way and leaving them behind for good.

The moment you feel ready to quit or abort your break, you could be on the verge of a breakthrough. Changing old habits and patterns is hard work, but taking a break will give you an opportunity to face this challenge, and choosing a new way to approach it can lead to your breakthrough moment.

REMEMBER

ANECDOTE

One client's break had been an incredible and insightful experience. . . until the moment she stuck her toes back into the job-search waters. After months of freedom, joy, and balance, she suddenly felt pressure to find a great job ASAP. The preparation triggered a stress response, and for a moment she reverted to her old approach for handling work stress — pushing ahead full-steam and trying to do everything "right." But this approach didn't feel good anymore and would ultimately lead her back to burnout. So, she slowed down and incorporated self-care and creative pursuits. She played competitive tennis and launched a blog about her career-break experience. With a more balanced approach to her job search, she landed a job she was excited about starting, enjoyed the last few months of her break, and brought a more grounded version of herself into her next chapter.

Practicing presence and patience

Coming off the hamster wheel and into a break can be a jarring transition. After the initial rush of freedom, you might struggle to enjoy the present moment without feeling guilty or bored in the process. Or you might struggle with the uncertainty and long to rush to the end of your break and figure out what you'll do next. A positive change IS coming, but it won't happen on a schedule. Getting the most out of your break will require patience and presence. Be mindful of doing the following specific things:

>> **Being patient with yourself.** This time is ripe with change and personal growth, so give yourself lots of grace and time to adjust.

- Don't judge yourself for feeling scared or frustrated. It's completely normal to wrestle with moments of anxiety and self-doubt during a break.

- Your break will feel messy at times because it's a completely new and uncharted experience and because life is messy sometimes and your break is still real life.

- Don't feel compelled to compensate for downtime. You don't have to earn the right to rest. Practice giving yourself permission to slow down and savor the small moments of your break.

>> **Being patient with your break.** Your break will have highs and lows, and as you move through it, your focus will change. Allow it to unfold and let your days be unique

experiences. Enjoy them for what they bring and try to avoid vigilantly waiting for a breakthrough or big change to occur. (As they say, a watched pot never boils.)

» **Reframing boredom (don't make it a villain).** Boredom can create feelings of anxiety and discomfort, but it can also be a gift. To reframe your perspective on it, try approaching moments of boredom with curiosity. What's in the stillness? Uncomfortable thoughts and feelings? Creative ideas? A deeper level of relaxation? Learning to explore boredom (instead of running away from it) can offer new insights that lead to change.

ANECDOTE

Chad entered his break, excited to slow down and recover from burnout after an intense career in healthcare. His first few weeks were filled with new discoveries and exploration. He tried new things (like beekeeping), spent more quality time with his family, and allowed himself to relax. But a few weeks into his break, everything changed. He suddenly felt agitated by the slower pace and lack of clarity in his next career move, even though his break had only recently begun. His brain wanted to default to the familiar ("old") way of doing things — pushing hard and overworking for results. But those results came at a high cost. This time, the real work was to explore his discomfort and the thoughts that compelled him to continually rush through life. After a weekend of reflection, he realized that he'd been demonstrating his value by doing as much as possible. But this approach didn't create joy, nor was it sustainable, so he decided to consciously practice a more mindful way of utilizing his time and viewing his worth, developing a more aligned approach to life and work.

ANECDOTE

Juliana had an amazing name for her rest-related theme: *dolce far niente* (the Italian phrase for the sweetness of doing nothing). With such a beautiful name, I was excited to see how she embraced this theme. Spoiler: It was similar to my other clients — with confusion and discomfort. Of her four themes, this was the most challenging one for her to fully embrace. With a mix of delight and guilt or peace and angst, she attempted to relax and enjoy the freedom to be idle. But it took a lot of practice and a willingness to be uncomfortable. Several months into her break, she finally started to enjoy her idle time and discovered the magic of allowing her days to unfold before her.

If you're struggling to enjoy your free time or are distracting yourself with overplanning and overdoing, I have four activities to help you stay present and be more patient with yourself and this slower pace:

>> Ask "what do I need/want right now" and honor that need or desire.

>> Focus on quality questions like the following and see what comes up.

What am I avoiding right now?

What thought or feeling is under the surface here?

What about this moment feels so uncomfortable?

Why am I working against the rest and ease I want?

>> Scan your five senses, and you'll be back in the present by the time you finish.

What do you smell right now?

What do you taste right now?

What do you hear right now?

What do you see right now?

What do you feel right now?

>> Take a moment to reflect on your relationship with productivity. How has it impacted your well-being, happiness, and sense of self-worth in the past? Is this a relationship you want to continue or to redefine?

Being intentional with your time

If you want to achieve personal growth and create a life-improving experience, you need to be intentional about how you spend your time on the break. You can learn more about exactly how to do this in Chapter 12. This section focuses on two simple practices that can help you navigate moments where you feel stuck or frustrated so you can continue your journey of change and self-discovery.

Have healthy boundaries

Healthy boundaries are critical for protecting your time and honoring your intentions to learn, grow, and relax while on a break. This is especially true if you have others depending on you during your break. Protecting your time can be a challenge because it can often appear that you have more time to take on additional responsibilities. But in reality, a break includes a lot of time for rest and internal processing, which are important to your overall success. So, while it might not look like much from the outside, a lot of meaningful things are happening on the inside, and these changes are significant, even though they aren't immediately apparent.

As you start your break, proactively create boundaries to ensure you're able to spend your time wisely. Watch out for the common traps listed here to ensure you get to do the things you need and want to do during your break:

>> **Allowing others to fill your time for you:** Others may see your break as unlimited downtime and try to shift more responsibilities onto you. Remember that your break is meaningful and important. It deserves the same attention and protection you'd give a full-time job.

If you're taking care of others (kids, parents) you may experience moments of caretaker guilt and feel the need to focus your time on caring for others. Avoid this trap. You need time to focus on your own well-being, too. Trust that pouring back into your own cup will enable you to be a better caretaker or parent and to model healthy boundaries for others. Use this break to your full advantage!

>> **Feeling guilty about doing "nothing":** To compensate for feeling guilty (or lazy) you may try to fill your time in an effort to feel busy and productive, but this is actually counterproductive. Allow yourself time to lean into your purpose and themes and enjoy this amazing experience.

>> **Overprioritizing administrative tasks:** With time to address the to-dos in your life, it can be tempting to spend your break catching up. It's helpful to handle the important tasks you've overlooked, but don't let the to-do list overshadow your needs and desires for the break.

>> **Taking on too many responsibilities:** If you find yourself thinking, "I have the time, so I might as well," make sure you're predominately spending time on things that align with your break purpose and themes and not overcommitting yourself to things that don't.

If you have caretaking duties while on a break, it's best to predetermine what those will be before your break begins. Communicate with those involved when you will and won't be available to set expectations and ask for their support. To avoid conflict and confusion, be explicit with what you will and won't be in charge of. You can put it in writing for an additional level of clarity. Be mindful of scope creep and address it when necessary.

Decide how you want your day to go

Did you know that you have the power to determine how your day will go? By setting an intention for your day (career-break theme, feeling, state, or goal), you can connect with what you most desire to experience or feel — joy, delight, curiosity, and so on. When you consciously decide and proactively focus on what you want to create more of, you won't have to wait for the perfect external circumstance to live into your intentions. Instead, you begin cultivating them on your own, no matter the circumstance.

As an example, if you wanted to feel more joy, you could focus on things like the following:

>> **Daily check-ins:** Quickly check in with yourself at the end of each day to reflect on the moments you felt joyful.

>> **Permission to do it "just because":** Give yourself permission to explore, do, and try new things just because they spark your interest. Don't try to capitalize on them, such as by worrying about making them financially rewarding down the road to justify your investment.

>> **Set an intention each morning:** Each morning you can set an intention to feel more connected to joy. From here, consciously work to infuse it into everything you do and experience that day.

>> **Start a fund for your intention:** If there's one particular theme or feeling you're struggling to indulge, allocate a weekly amount of money to spend and invest on that one thing. You can spend your Joy Fund on things that bring you happiness or allow you to explore joy.

Lynn had an amazing trip to Sicily, but when she returned home, she found herself passing time in a way that didn't feel meaningful. Without the tangible and immersive experience of travel, she struggled with how to best fill her time and considered ending her break early to pursue new goals. But as we reviewed her themes and assessed her days, it became clear there was still a great opportunity for her to benefit from the break. So she became more intentional with her time. She revisited her themes, experimented with a new morning routine, and started setting an intention for each day. She also created a Connection Fund to give herself permission to invest in building and deepening her relationships. With the new approach, even simple days full of rest had more purpose.

TIP

When your break involves time at home or in a familiar environment, it can be easy to default to old patterns and/or prioritize administrative tasks. You'll need to thoughtfully structure your time and be proactive about setting intention(s) for this time.

REMEMBER

Even simple activities and periods of rest can be meaningful and fulfilling when you do them with intention. For example, taking a nap because you're tired and know that taking care of yourself is one of the goals for your break feels way better than mindlessly laying down for a nap and waking up with a sinking feeling that you've just wasted your afternoon.

Processing and adapting to change

There will be a lot to process throughout your break. This is normal and to be expected. During this time, you'll pave the way for lasting change by shedding parts of yourself that no longer fit with how you want to live (overworking, people pleasing, denying yourself rest and joy). You may also make shifts in areas such as the following:

>> **Your perspective on productivity:** Realizing that you're more than just what you do and letting go of the urgent need to constantly be producing is powerful. You may discover that it feels good to deeply care for yourself and that it's easier to do big things when you feel balanced and restored.

>> **Your relationship with money:** Discovering how much less you need to be happy and satisfied in life frees you to make new and exciting choices. Giving the money you earn a purpose beyond just providing safety and being a metric of

success can pave the way for improved well-being. If you need help with this, visit Chapter 5.

>> **Your relationship with yourself:** Loving yourself more deeply can help you reconnect to the fun, silly, and unique parts of yourself that you've lost touch with. You may see how amazing you are when you've healed your burnout and are living a life that feels aligned.

>> **Your self-identity:** Rediscovering who you are and what you love doing outside of your job is important. Letting go of labels that keep you stuck in jobs or careers that leave you unhappy and dissatisfied can be transformative. You'll learn how to nurture your life outside of work.

REMEMBER

Your biggest breakthroughs often come through your most challenging experiences. Here, your brain will want to take the "old" approach to solving problems, but that yields more of the same old results. If you want to create different results, be sure to do things differently.

ACTIVITY

When you're in a tough spot and feeling a lot of discomfort, disappointment, or fear, ask yourself, "What if I'm on the verge of a breakthrough?" Journal for 5 to 10 minutes to explore how this might be true. It will help you shift into a more positive and supportive state of mind.

Putting your life in a new perspective and adapting to significant change can be immensely rewarding but also challenging. To support yourself through this process you can

>> **Stay open:** Explore new things, try new approaches, and expose yourself to new ideas. By staying open, you'll learn life-changing lessons and allow yourself to pivot or adjust your career-break plan, as necessary.

>> **Embrace curiosity:** Experiment without judging your results. You can then use this information to make any adjustments.

>> **Reflect on your experience:** Allow for time alone and without distraction to reflect on what's working and what's not and help you solidify the changes that will lead to a better life.

You always have the power to change your mind and update your plan as you move through the break. You might decide to start a part-time job or side hustle, extend your break, or accept a new opportunity. My best advice to help navigate these forks in the road is to avoid making a decision driven by fear and to revisit your purpose statement and themes to understand how well you've fulfilled the original purpose of your break.

Be kind to yourself and give yourself grace. You're learning as you go, and that's hard work. If you're feeling stuck and worried that things will always feel hard, know that change can happen quite quickly — if you stay committed to yourself and the purpose of your break.

Chapter **11**

Avoiding a Financial Meltdown

Maintaining a healthy relationship with your money while you're on a break can be challenging. If you aren't used to budgeting, you may struggle to track your expenses and find yourself overspending. Or if you're really good at staying close to the money, you may feel panicked spending money while watching your account balance steadily decline.

Whether you lean toward overspending or underspending, this chapter helps you avoid letting money drama sabotage your break. In this chapter, you find out what to watch for when it comes to managing your money during a break. Your break experience is an investment in your well-being and a better future, and this chapter helps you avoid squandering it or letting money anxiety ruin your experience.

Sticking to Your Career Break Budget

Having a great plan for your break is half the battle, but when your break begins, you'll need to make sure your money lasts long enough to bring your vision to life. You can achieve this by sticking to your career break budget and being mindful of your spending habits. In this section, I outline a process to help you stay on track and avoid overspending.

Checking in consistently with your finances

If you aren't used to budgeting or tracking what you spend, it may feel stressful to think about consistently tracking and managing your expenses. But discipline is an important part of successfully managing your money while you're on a break.

Consistent check-ins keep your finances on track and alert you when adjustments need to be made. If you don't check in with your finances, you risk being caught off guard by overspending and having to end your break early or navigate debt. You can avoid this financial disaster by consistently checking in and using one of the following methods to track your numbers.

Tracking your expenses

With this method, you track everything you're spending money on during your break. This approach requires more effort, but it provides a more detailed and accurate snapshot of your savings, spending decisions, and overall financial situation. This additional information helps you make informed decisions while navigating your break.

ACTIVITY

Track your expenses via app, spreadsheet, or even good ol' pen and paper. During your check-ins, total up what you've spent since the previous check-in and compare this number to your original career break budget. Are you staying on track? If you're over budget, brainstorm adjustments that could reduce your future expenses. Figure 11-1 provides an example of this approach.

Tracking your account balance

This method is simple and straightforward. You track and compare changes to your account balance(s) during your break. Tracking the gradual decline provides snapshots of your overall spending, but it doesn't provide specifics to better understand exactly *how* you're spending your money. If you stay on budget, this method can be fine, but if you need to make adjustments to your spending, you'll need to dig deeper into the details for answers. Also be aware that there may be a significant lag in your account balance, especially if you're using credit cards to pay for things.

1. Estimate your total expenses since your last check-in.

Food	$300
Accommodations	$800
Travel	$200
Entertainment	$100
Ongoing expenses	$200
Miscellaneous/other	$200
Total	$1,800

2. Divide by the time since your last check-in.
$1,800 ÷ 3 weeks = $600 per week

3. Compare to your break budget.

Break budget	$500 per week
Current expenses	$600 per week

4. Reduce spending to get back on track (for example, find cheaper accommodations for next destination or revisit current itinerary for ways to reduce costs).

FIGURE 11-1: Tracking your break expenses and comparing them to your budget.

ACTIVITY

Determine your current account balance (if using multiple accounts to fund your break, sum for one overall number) and subtract it from the previous balance taken during your last check-in. This is roughly what you've spent on your break since your last check-in. Compare this number to your original career break budget to see if you're on track. If you're over budget, explore adjustments to reduce your future expenses. Figure 11-2 provides an example of this approach.

TIP

If you want to develop a budget to inform your spending habits and help you stay on top of your finances, visit Chapter 5 for steps to create a well-informed career break budget.

Determining the frequency

After you've determined your method for monitoring your career break spending, as outlined earlier in this section, you'll need to set your check-in frequency. It's important to choose a time period that seems both accessible and informative so you'll stay consistent and well-informed.

Career break account balance as of May 1	$50,000
Career break account balance as of June 15	$47,500

1. Subtract current balance from previous check-in balance:
$50,000 − $47,500 = approximately $2,500 spent

2. Divide by time elapsed since your last check-in.
$2,500 ÷ 6.5 weeks = $385 per week

3. Compare to your break budget.

Break budget	$500 per week
Current expenses	$385 per week

4. Continue your great spending habits to extend your break, have additional money available for a more expensive portion of your break, and/or add to your itinerary.

FIGURE 11-2: Tracking your account balance(s) and comparing it to your budget.

Here, I offer three suggestions. Choose whichever one feels best to you or create your own. It's possible that each phase of your break may require its own unique cadence.

>> **Daily:** When you're traveling to places with a relatively high cost, or experiencing high variability in your day-to-day expenses (such as by traveling quickly through destinations with different currency), checking in daily or every other day can help you keep a close eye on things and avoid accidentally going over budget.

>> **Weekly:** This frequency is a good standard for your break, especially when traveling. Your expenses each day may vary, but with a weekly cadence, you'll catch a sharp uptick before it becomes a big problem.

>> **Monthly:** If your days are more predictable or your expenses are relatively steady — such as when you're living at home or slow traveling — a monthly check-in is a suitable option.

ACTIVITY

When you've set a cadence, set a recurring appointment on your calendar to remind you of your check-ins.

Make sure your budget is realistic and doable. It doesn't matter how good it looks on paper, if it's not achievable and underestimates your necessary expenses, it won't work. If you run into problems, you can always revise your budget to be more sustainable and realistic, even if you have to shorten your break by a month or two. It's better to have a fulfilling and successful five-month break than a lackluster and disappointing six-month break.

Prioritizing the average

Over the course of your break, it's normal for your expenses to vary, especially if you're traveling. Some days, weeks, and/or months may be significantly more expensive, and you may have some unexpected expenses along the way. Plus, it's difficult to estimate the costs for places and things you've never experienced before. You'll likely overestimate the cost for some parts of your break, while underestimating others. This is why I recommend paying the most attention to your average. How does the average compare to your career break budget? By focusing on the overall average of your expenses, you can create more ease and flexibility. A temporary uptick in your spending doesn't have to be a big deal.

For example, if a portion of your break surpasses what you originally budgeted, you may be able to absorb that increase because you've underspent on an earlier portion. If that's not the case, you can creatively seek ways to reduce your future expenses and bring the average back in line by

>> Adjusting your itinerary to replace costly activities with more affordable options

>> Cutting out short trips and/or future destinations to save on travel costs

>> Reducing the length of upcoming travels and trips and/or reducing expenses for future travels (such as lodging)

>> Replacing expensive destinations with more affordable options

>> Shifting eating habits and finding more affordable options (cheaper restaurants, more "at home" meals, and so on)

I fell in love upon arriving in Avignon, France. I'd booked an expensive (to me) five-night stay at a beautiful apartment in town, and between the architecture, gorgeous weather, and incredible food, I wasn't ready to leave when it ended. But my budget had taken a big hit due to my upgraded accommodations and 60€/day food habit, so I knew I'd need to compensate by reducing my spending. Because I reviewed my budget daily, I easily set a new target that would bring things back in balance. I moved into a nice hostel for three more nights in the charming medieval town without overshooting my overall budget.

TIP

Keep track of the average amount you're spending and don't fret too much about an overbudget day (or week). You can make adjustments to compensate for it later on, if necessary. See the "Determining the frequency" section earlier in this chapter for information about deciding how frequently to compare your spending to your planned budget.

REMEMBER

You're allowed to make trade-offs and update your budget as your break progresses. It isn't necessarily a bad thing to spend more than you projected you would, as long as you feel good about your decision. The key is making intentional trade-offs so you don't regret them or shortchange yourself on your break. Consistently checking in with your finances will help you do this.

Determining your red zone number

One of the most helpful things you can do as you're preparing for a break is to establish your "red zone" number. This number is the lower limit of your financial comfort zone — the minimum amount of money you feel comfortable having in your account while you're on a break. Think of it as the panic button for your break. Approaching the red zone number alerts you that it's time to wrap up your break or seek a cash infusion to keep it going.

You may never hit this number while on your break, but if you do, it simply means it's time to reflect and plan the next step of your journey so you don't end up in financial turmoil. As you set your red zone number, it can be helpful to consider the following:

>> A longer-than-expected re-entry period (delays in securing a new job, lead time for starting a business, etc.)

>> Expenses to restart your life post-break (rent, deposits, moving and relocation fees, career services, etc.)

>> Financial obligations (outstanding loans, others depending on you for financial support, upcoming expenses, etc.)

>> Money set aside for emergencies and unforeseen expenses that may arise in the near future

ANECDOTE

My initial red zone number was $10,000 USD. I estimated that to be enough for a slightly longer re-entry period (in case I struggled to find a job) and to afford one to two months of rent plus a security deposit before securing an income. It also left extra for unforeseen expenses.

If you enter the red zone, reflect on your break and evaluate the options for your next move. The following are questions you can use to guide you through the process:

>> **How have I spent my career break fund?**
  - How do I feel about my answer?
  - What goals have I accomplished?
  - Do any goals remain?

>> **Do I feel ready to end my break? If not**
  - What do I hope to accomplish with more time?
  - Do I need to adjust my career break plan?
  - Are there options to generate more money to continue my break?
  - Can I/do I want to adjust my red zone number?

After you've taken time to reflect, you're ready to determine your next step. It will likely be one of the following:

>> Adjust your red zone number and downshift your break lifestyle to afford more time for your remaining pursuits.

>> Begin exiting your break and moving into the re-entry period (Chapter 13 covers exactly how to do this).

>> Pursue your options for creating additional money or income to extend your break.

ANECDOTE

When I hit my $10,000 red zone number, I was in Denver, Colorado, taking classes and considering new career paths. As I reflected on my break, I realized I wanted to continue exploring my options. Because a friend had been kind enough to offer me a free place to stay for the rest of my break, I felt comfortable lowering my number to $5,000 and continuing my break for three more months. I didn't worry about applying for jobs until I hit my new $5,000 limit.

Giving Yourself Permission to Spend Money

Even when you have more than enough money in your bank account and are sticking to your budget, money anxiety can appear. Seeing your bank account decrease month over month, while feeling uncertain about what you'll do after your break ends can bring up feelings of guilt and fear and a perception of being irresponsible. Plus, if you've been sacrificing or ignoring your needs to advance your career, take care of others, and/or upgrade your lifestyle to keep up with your peers, it can be uncomfortable to allow yourself the privilege of investing in your happiness and well-being.

It's important to know this is a normal part of the career break process. Nothing has gone wrong if you're feeling stressed about money and struggling to give yourself permission to spend it. Many of my clients have struggled with this, too. In this section, you find out how to move beyond your financial anxiety and grant yourself permission to invest in your break and realize its full benefit.

For many, a career break introduces a new and unfamiliar financial dynamic — spending while not earning. In this new reality, you may find a fresh perspective and profound shift in how you relate to money. You may realize that even without a steady income stream, you have more than enough. You may also discover you need less to survive and thrive than you originally thought.

TIP

If you struggle to give yourself permission to spend money, try viewing your discomfort as an opportunity to learn something new about yourself and your relationship to money. Stay curious as you explore the meaning and significance of money in your life and see what comes up!

REMEMBER

Money is more than just a proxy for success and safety. It can also provide you with the means to pursue personal growth and improve your well-being. Investing in a well-designed break can help you access more happiness and fulfillment than mindlessly saving to amass a bigger bank account. Don't be afraid to spend some of your hard-earned money on this break. Investing in your future is putting it to great use!

ACTIVITY

Find a quiet and comfortable place and take a few deep breaths to prepare for a visualization exercise. Start by closing your eyes and remembering when you were saving for this break. Connect with how good it felt to watch your bank account increase. Thank the part of you that had the discipline to make this dream happen. When you're ready, imagine yourself moving through your break while conserving your money and working to spend the least amount possible. No treating yourself to new experiences, no travel adventures, and no investments in your well-being. Now, visualize yourself at the end of your break after saying "no" to almost every possibility. How does it feel to imagine ending your break with very few experiences but a surplus of money? Do you feel satisfied with the experience? Is this your optimal outcome? If you feel dissatisfied with this hypothetical outcome, I encourage you to let your money serve its purpose: amplifying your joy and well-being. Spend your money and enjoy this gift!

Focusing on the facts

When you feel resistance to spending money or are stressing about the cost of your break, it's helpful to look at your actual numbers. This objective approach helps you discern fact from fiction and ensure you're making a rational decision about your next step.

Determining the facts requires uncovering the truth about your expenses and overall account balance. Compare your numbers to your original career break budget and red zone number for context. When you have this information, you're ready to explore a bit deeper:

>> How much have I spent so far?

>> Does this number match my budget? Is it over or under?

>> Does my spending align with my intentions for this break? Do I feel good about the things I'm investing in?

>> How much money do I have in my bank account(s) right now? Is this enough for me to continue my break?

>> Where is my fear coming from? Is it real, or is my brain trying to solve a fictional problem?

REVISITING YOUR RED ZONE NUMBER

Knowing your red zone number can help you avoid sabotaging your break due to money anxiety (see "Determining your red zone number" earlier in this chapter to set your number). If you're thinking of prematurely returning to work before fulfilling your purpose for this break, revisit your red zone number. Are you really in the danger zone or just feeling uncomfortable with the steady decrease in your savings account? If you haven't reached the red zone, remind yourself that you still have more than enough to continue your break.

After you've examined your numbers and worked your way through these questions, take time to reflect on the whole picture. If you still feel concerned after looking at the facts, you can adjust your plan to reduce your spending and/or prepare for an early exit.

REMEMBER

Investing in a thoughtfully designed career break is a good use of your money. The version of you that created the financial means to make this break happen can absolutely rebuild your financial resources when this break is over. You haven't lost anything you can't replace.

TIP

If you struggle with money anxiety on your break, consider starting a separate career break account. A separate account will help you create a visual distinction between your emergency fund (or post-career break money) and your career break savings. And this distinction can make it easier to give yourself permission to spend your dedicated dollars on a fulfilling career break experience.

Recommitting to your break

If you struggle to feel good about spending money on your break and enjoying this time off, reconnect to your big vision for this break. Remembering why you took this leap can help you recommit to your break and the goals you're pursuing. If you still find yourself struggling, try the following:

>> **Reconnect to your vision by revisiting your why.**
Remember how you felt before your break and how you

hoped things would be when your break was over. You're on your way to making your dreams come true. Notice and appreciate the alignment between your values and your financial decisions.

>> **Reframe your break as an investment.** Think of the benefits you stand to gain from this time off (visit Chapter 2 for a list of great benefits) and connect with the knowledge that you are worthy of this investment.

>> **Remember the re-entry period.** If you've planned for a re-entry period (see Chapter 4 for guidance on developing your re-entry plan), you've dedicated time and money to sort things out and plan your next step. You don't have to have all the answers before your re-entry period begins. That's what a re-entry period is for!

ACTIVITY

List the reasons you originally decided to take a break. If you developed your purpose and themes in Chapter 4, reflect on these answers. When you've made your list, reflect on your progress. Have you realized your goals and desires for this time off? Is it truly time to quit? Is the benefit still worth the financial sacrifice? This activity will help you gain perspective on your break and decision about what to do next.

Giving yourself a numbers detox

If you're used to checking your numbers often (bank account balances, investment accounts, 401(k) returns, and so on) and/or closely following economic news and trends, you may find it hard to stop stressing about money and enjoy your break. A dwindling bank account intermingled with gloomy financial predictions can weigh you down when you start your break.

If you find yourself struggling to let go of the fear and anxiety, I highly recommend a two-week numbers detox. This means NO checking your numbers, tuning in to economic predictions, or following the financial news for two weeks. It can be a tough adjustment, but this approach creates more space to ease into your break and reduces stress associated with your big change.

ANECDOTE

One of my clients was very good at managing her money and took a conservative approach to her finances. Deciding to take a career break was a big decision for her — one that had been many years in the making. But as her break began to unfold, it became clear that her constant financial vigilance, which had been helpful for growing her savings account, was making it nearly impossible for her to enjoy her break. So we implemented a two-week numbers detox. While it initially caused anxiety, she honored the process, and soon her outlook and feelings about her break became more positive. Sometimes you have to disconnect from familiar habits to create space to enjoy your break.

Chapter 12

Spending This Time Wisely

What will you do with the unstructured time during your break? If you're living independently, you might daydream about the freedom you'll have when you're on a break but also worry about facing boredom and becoming overwhelmed by choice. On the flip side, if others depend on you, you may worry about managing your responsibilities and balancing their needs with your own. Either way, this chapter can help you make sure you don't waste this precious opportunity.

In this chapter, you'll discover a simple process to navigate the balance between structure and freedom and manage your time well. It will have you rethinking your relationship to free time and understanding why leaning into fun and rest is just as important as achieving your career break goals. Spoiler alert: This is one of the most life-changing things about taking a break.

Let's begin with an agreement of what "spend this time wisely" really means: It's staying engaged and accountable to your career break themes (see Chapter 4 for details on these), while also allowing yourself to slow down and relax without guilt. It's about meeting all of your needs, including the deeply personal ones.

By the end of this chapter, you'll know what it means to spend your time wisely and feel prepared to make the most of your break. You'll be able to relax, kick back, and fully enjoy the experience.

Structuring Your Free Time

Starting a career break is exciting but it can also feel overwhelming. If you don't have any major responsibilities to worry about, it might feel amazing to envision months off with nothing to do and no one to report to. But the reality of that freedom can also feel a bit startling. Which makes sense – this might be the first time in your adult life that you've had an expanse of free time. So, of course you aren't a professional "free time spender". . . . *yet.*

If you *do* have some major responsibilities to manage during your break, you might struggle with the opposite — carving out the space and time to meet your needs while meeting the needs of others. For you, using your time wisely during a break requires healthy boundaries and proactive planning.

No matter your current circumstance, it can be paralyzing to face an infinite amount of choice for how to utilize time during your break. This is why incorporating a gentle structure into that freedom is important. It helps you ease into a lifestyle of abundant free time without losing your mind or panicking that you'll become a permanent couch potato. And it helps you create healthy boundaries that allow you to balance the demands and responsibilities of life while fulfilling your career break goals.

Developing a morning routine

When you're living your best career break life, each day can look wildly different from the last. Some days you might hike a mountain, attend a yoga retreat, or learn a new skill, while other days you might binge your favorite show or be on the phone reconnecting with friends. There will be an ebb and flow to your days while on a break. Some will fly by, and others pass more slowly. While this variability can be energizing, it can also be disorienting and make it challenging to start each day off on the right foot. You might also find that you struggle with missing the sense of accomplishment you felt while working (even if you didn't love your job).

One easy solution can solve both of these problems: Develop a fun and supportive morning routine. A morning routine helps you stay centered and begin each day with a "win." It provides a sense of accomplishment early in the day, which makes it easier to enjoy the day, especially if it's a day of rest.

REMEMBER

Having a consistent morning routine helps establish a healthy boundary. You get to set the tone for your day before reentering the chaos of life and allowing the day's events to pull you off course. If you're caretaking others during a break, this will be essential. At the end of your break, you can carry your routine into your next chapter and continue creating a powerful start to each day. This is one way you take the benefits of a break with you after it's over! If you're thinking, "Ugh, I hate morning routines!" please know you're not alone. I, too, once dreaded the morning routine. But after experiencing its magic firsthand and subsequently testing it on my clients, it's been proven to be a powerful tool for navigating a career break. Even if you're skeptical, I urge you to try it out for two weeks before deciding to forgo it. I'd hate for you to miss out on the big benefits of having one!

REMEMBER

A daily morning routine can feel especially supportive during this time of transition. It creates a sense of normalcy during a period of your life where many things are anything but normal. Uncertainty and unfamiliarity abound, especially if you plan to travel abroad, so having a small touchpoint where you make space to take care of yourself each day can be very nourishing.

It's very important to keep your routine fun and manageable. Don't bog yourself down with a list of things you think you "should" be doing. You don't need to drink green juice and meditate for an hour, if that doesn't appeal to you. Instead, focus on things you enjoy or that are at least tolerable and have big benefits. Start with something short and simple and build up from there.

WARNING

Don't create a routine based on what you think you "should" do. Complicated, aspirational routines don't last. Create one you like and keep it simple. It will reduce your chances of giving up.

It's also helpful to frame your routine as an experiment. Be willing to try, fail, and learn! You can adjust and improve as you go. Please know that you aren't obligated to keep things you don't like or that just don't work for you. You are always free to change it up.

TIP

For learning purposes, I recommend trying out any new ideas or habits for a solid week (it's important to give yourself a few data points of information before you cut something out). When you have at least one week under your belt, reflect on what worked well and what didn't. Then swap out or adjust whatever isn't working and stay curious and open as you replace it with new ideas.

TIP

When designing your morning routine, choose two or three words that describe how you want to feel as you start your day. Brainstorm activities that help you connect to these feelings and start with a few of the ideas you like most.

Here are some suggested words to help prompt your morning routine:

>> Motivated

>> Calm

>> Positive

>> Hopeful

>> Centered

>> Loving

>> Energized

>> Excited

>> Joyful

>> Grateful

>> Abundant

>> Focused

>> Sharp

>> Restored

>> Confident

>> Prepared

The following are activities to help you design a morning routine. Keeping your routine to 10 to 20 minutes a day is plenty, especially if you're new to having a morning routine:

>> **Make your bed.** This simple action packs a big punch. It gives you a tangible accomplishment first thing in the morning; it helps organize your space; and it ensures you don't unintentionally hop back into bed.

>> **Drink water.** Staying hydrated is important. If you aren't a water fan, make a commitment to drink one or two glasses before your regular morning beverage. You can also try drinking it warm with a splash of lemon juice to help it go down easier.

>> **Move your body.** Whether it's yoga, stretching, walking, or dancing to your favorite song, putting your body in motion gets the energy flowing. Just 5 to 10 minutes of movement can make a big difference.

>> **Practice mindfulness.** You can incorporate a few minutes of deep and slow breathing, a guided meditation, or journaling to calm and center your mind. If you prefer, you can also sit in silence. Whatever your choice, mindfulness practice gives your mind space to prepare for the day. If you're new to meditation, the Insight Timer app is a wonderful place to start.

>> **Set an intention.** Decide what you want to focus on or how you want to feel as your day begins. Consciously choosing how you want to face the day will set a great tone for your day.

>> **Listen to music.** Music is a powerful mood influencer, so choose a song that reflects the way you want to feel and let it play!

TIP

Allow yourself one to two weeks of being on your break before starting a morning routine. Initially, you might take a ton of naps or sit idly for hours on end — this is all OK! It can take a few days to decompress and feel ready to add some structure. Put a morning routine start date on your calendar for one to two weeks out. That way you won't forget. Then sit back and enjoy the beginning of your break!

Having a consistent check-in routine

While the morning routine is the secret to getting a great start to your day and feeling a sense of accomplishment (see the preceding section), having a consistent check-in routine is how you process and maximize the impact of your break. If you don't leave adequate time for reflection, you'll likely miss the changes taking place during your break. Instead of waiting until your break is over to start processing your experience, you should be checking in with yourself along the way.

If you're like my clients, you may find it easy to gloss over the celebration-worthy moments on your break and to minimize the changes taking place within you. To feel like your break is a success, you have to stop to acknowledge your wins, big and small, as they happen. By giving them a moment in the spotlight, you draw attention to the fact that even though you sometimes feel like you don't know what you're doing or where this path leads, amazing things are happening, and you are creating miracles with this time off.

REMEMBER

Many changes will occur during your break. Some will take longer to see, and others will be obvious early on. Expect your perspective on life and work to shift, know that new strengths will emerge, and get ready to release old beliefs that no longer feel true. How you see yourself, how you value your time, and what makes for a worthy sacrifice are likely to change. So much growth is waiting for you on this break, and you can speed it along and amplify its impact if you take a moment to acknowledge and celebrate it.

A consistent check-in routine creates space for you to reflect and process your experience. When challenging emotions and fears arise, it gives you a safe place to process them. It shows you the lessons you're learning as you move through your break. It keeps you more in tune with what's really going on and helps you raise a red flag if things don't feel right. Simply put, this habit will have a big, positive impact on your break.

TIP

Here are three quick steps to design your own check-in routine. You can choose your cadence — daily, weekly, biweekly. Whatever you choose, remember that consistency is key.

1. **Choose your check-in cadence.**

You can do check-ins weekly, biweekly, or monthly. There is no "right" amount of time. Choose an interval that feels good to you and seems manageable so you'll stick with it for the long run. If your break is shorter than three months, I recommend weekly check-ins. If it's longer, I recommend checking in once every two weeks. No matter what cadence you choose, I highly recommend checking in at the halfway point of your break.

2. **Decide what you will evaluate and reflect on during your check-ins.**

You can reflect on your purpose and themes, celebrate recent highlights from your break, evaluate your progress and how you're feeling about the break itself, and/or consider what isn't working and needs to change. You can also journal about your feelings and experiences. If you're longing for a quantitative measure of your progress, choose a few personal goals to track, like the number of books read or hours spent reading, days of meditation, friends you've caught up with, and so on. Feel free to abandon these metrics if they start to feel forced or in conflict with the enjoyment of your break!

3. **Preschedule your check-ins.**

As soon as you've chosen your cadence, set a recurring appointment on your calendar that starts when your break begins. This will help you stay accountable and ensure you don't forget your check-ins when you're on your break.

Here are several helpful check-in questions to consider:

>> What am I most proud of since my last check-in?

>> What have I learned about myself since my last check-in?

>> What is currently working really well?

>> What isn't currently working well?

>> What was the biggest lesson I learned since my last check-in?

>> What is my biggest dream for this next period of time?

>> Am I living into my purpose and themes? If not, what can I do to better address them?

>> What are three highlights from this past month?

>> Why am I grateful for this break? List three or more reasons.

>> How am I feeling about my break right now?

Revisiting your themes

Your career break themes are the anchor points for your break (see Chapter 4 for more details about career break themes). Fulfilling them leads to a successful experience, so it's important to revisit them often. As you move through the break, reflect on and stay connected to your themes. Are you investing your time, money, and energy into things that align with them? If you are, give yourself a high five and keep going! If you aren't, don't beat yourself up. You can easily get back on track. Spend some time reviewing your wish list and prioritizing things that will help you fulfill your themes.

REMEMBER

It is especially helpful to revisit your purpose and themes when big life changes — positive or negative — happen. You may receive an exciting job opportunity or startling news about a loved one's health. During times like these, strong feelings arise that can threaten to blow you off course. While you may long to chase the new opportunity or to give up on your break because things suddenly feel too hard, it's critical to take a moment to consider your themes before deciding what to do.

No decision is necessarily wrong, but it's important to be intentional about changing or early exiting your break. Impulsive decisions aren't helpful here. You don't have to agonize over or overthink your decision; just take some time to clear your mind and ask yourself a few of the following questions:

>> **Have I adequately fulfilled my themes?** If the answer is yes, it might be the right time to end your break. If the answer is no, but you feel it's best to end your break anyway, consider how you might incorporate your themes into your next chapter, adapting your wish list to this new circumstance.

>> **How does this new circumstance that I'm facing influence my themes?** Have they made your themes feel more important or less? Do they shift your priorities? Do they change your definition of success or just require you to rethink how you go about fulfilling your themes?

>> **If I knew that everything would work out and there were no wrong decisions, what would I most want to do right now?** Before making a big decision, it's important to be clear on your ideal outcome. Sometimes it's not possible to achieve this, but being clear about what you want helps you get much closer.

Revisiting your themes is also very grounding. You can connect back to them anytime you feel lost or confused about what you should do with this time.

Incorporate this practice into your regular check-in routine for ease and simplicity.

TIP

Protecting your time while managing big responsibilities

If you'll be contributing to a household or maintaining caretaking duties during your break, you need to be strategic about how you'll handle these responsibilities and commitments so they don't overtake your break.

WARNING

If you aren't proactive about creating space and setting boundaries, you'll likely end up replacing one full-time job with another. Don't let an endless stream of to-dos, chores, and others' needs eclipse your goals for this time off.

Following are some suggestions for how to protect your time during a break while still managing your responsibilities. They can help you create more harmony in how you balance your needs with the needs of others and any household duties you may have.

» **Establish pockets of "me time" — time specifically for you and your career break goals**

- *Define your "me time":* Decide what your "me time" will entail. What kinds of things will you do during these pockets of time? What things do you prefer not to do? Reflect on your wish list and themes for ideas and suggestions.

- *Create and schedule blocks of time:* Review your obligations and/or family calendar to determine when to schedule your pockets of "me time." Try to schedule it in blocks or large chunks of time so it feels more expansive. If you have children, school hours can be a great option.

» **Get help and ask for support**

- *Hire help:* If you're able to, hire help to give yourself more free time. You can add this expense to your break budget because the extra help is meant to make it possible for you to fulfill your career break goals. You can get support for meal prep, housekeeping, child care, or anything else that competes for your precious time.

- *Ask your village for support:* The amount of time required to caretake others can sometimes expand. Whether it's a partner, friend, or family member, remember your village is your team. Reach out when you need help. Even though you're currently not working, your break is serving a big purpose, and you deserve to be supported when you need a helping hand.

>> Include others in your plans

- *Think more broadly about your themes:* If you'll be caring for others during your break, expand your approach to fulfilling your career break themes. Think of ideas you can do alone *and* with others. One of my clients had two approaches for her "recharge" theme: She meditated and hiked in solitude to recharge on her own and took quiet family walks and led group mediations to recharge with her kids.

- *Incorporate others into your wish list activities:* If you'll be responsible for others during your break, think through ways you can include them in your plans. Start with something you want to do (a wish list item) and expand it to include something they could do concurrently. One of my clients reconnected with her passion for art. She sketched while her two small children colored alongside her. You could walk your pet or take a stroll with your kids to incorporate a theme of restoring your health.

>> Set clear boundaries and create personal space

- *Create a contract:* If you share responsibilities with another person(s), create a contract to agree formally on how you'll split duties during your break. When are you available? When are you not available? What will change during your break? What stays the same? Discuss this before the break for a smoother transition and less frustration and disappointment.

- *Create a sanctuary:* Having your own physical space to disconnect and nourish yourself can help you achieve your career break goals. It can be an entire room or just a corner space. Communicate a clear boundary about what does and does not happen in this space. Try rearranging your furniture, removing clutter, and adding candles or floor pillows to help set the mood.

- *Take some time away:* If you're able to take a solo mini-getaway, I highly recommend it. The physical distance away from the chaos of home can quickly re-ground and restore you. It doesn't have to be an exotic location — book one or two nights at a hotel across town.

REMEMBER

Boundaries can be healing. They provide you with the time and space to meet your own needs, which then allows you to be more generous with those you love. When you pour into your own cup first, you'll have more to give to others.

Enjoying Your Experience

A career break grants you the space to learn a lot about yourself. Removing the typical day-to-day responsibilities and "on autopilot" nature of being a working adult gives you time to discover who you are separate from the work you do and the jobs you've held. It also provides space for you to have adventures, explore new ideas, and cultivate new interests and passions. It lets you indulge the sparkly side of you that you might have tucked away while pursuing your corporate career.

You've already discovered the importance of having a simple structure to foster your growth and support your career break goals. But it's equally important to be adequately prepared to enjoy this amazing experience. And that's what this chapter is all about!

A career break is a gift — and one that you most certainly will want to enjoy. It would be a waste to bury it under a mountain of to-dos for fear that you need to justify your time off. But you'd be surprised how often I see this happen. Luckily, it won't happen to you because you have this book and are about to learn three keys to enjoying your break (which is critical to spending this time wisely).

As counterintuitive as it might seem, I've seen many career breakers struggle with this part. So while it's simple, it's not always easy. Because we're often taught to work hard, push through, and keep going until we hit retirement, we don't have the chance to practice deep rest or ample play. In fact, these practices often go against beliefs we're taught about being productive and efficient with our time. Well, buckle up. You're about to unlearn some stifling beliefs.

If you've ever stopped to ask yourself, "Do I deserve this break?" the answer is YES, you do deserve it. So let's talk about how to actually enjoy it.

Granting yourself permission

It can be a challenge to let go and fully enjoy this time. You may worry that taking a break makes you a lazy person or that you'll get too comfortable and struggle to go back to "real life" when it's over. Or maybe you feel guilty ignoring household chores or having downtime while your partner is still hard at work. But this kind of thinking will actually limit the impact of your break.

Giving yourself permission to experience a life filled with joy and ease can feel very foreign. It may feel uncomfortable to make space to rest, play, and just be. While it may not look productive from the outside looking in, I assure you that a lot is happening under the surface. The results will be more apparent toward the end of your break, and they will be more than worth it. Some of my clients' biggest breakthroughs come from this practice. (See Chad's case study at the end of this chapter for a real-life example.)

You don't need to feel guilty for wanting time apart from being a caregiver or partner. That's a big part of what this break is for: self-discovery. If you're not careful, you may default to a pattern of putting your household or child-care duties ahead of your own needs. Remember, your break has a purpose, and you need time to fulfill it. You can take on more responsibilities during this time off but be sure to reserve time for your needs and desires, too.

WARNING

Your brain will try to trick you into believing that it's better to keep one foot in the productivity-obsessed working world. You don't want to get soft and lose your edge, after all. But straddling both worlds and trying to ration your joy and ease means missing out on the best parts of your break and minimizing the benefits. You need to give yourself permission to experience the best life has to offer you. The secret to a life well lived is making the most of what you've got for as long as you have it. So instead of shying away from joy, fun, rest, and ease on your career break, you've got to dive in, head first! Swim around and notice how good life feels. To reap the full benefits of your break, you have to lean into them while you have the chance.

AN ARGUMENT FOR GIVING YOURSELF PERMISSION

Imagine you've won a free vacation at a five-star spa with a world-famous pool. The infinity pool looks out over the Caribbean Sea, with butlers taking care of everything. It's paradise, and you've dreamed about lounging by this very pool for years. And now you're here! But soon after arriving, the breathtaking view makes you realize how gloomy and ill-suited your home in the suburbs feels.

As much as you'd love to spend your days in this tranquil oasis, you decide to stay indoors for the entire trip. After all, swimming in this pool will likely spoil you and make it harder to return to "real life" when this vacation is over. What if you return home and can't stop thinking about how amazing that pool was? That would be pure torture.

So you manage to avoid the pool and return home a week later. To your surprise, you still can't stop thinking about the pool. And on top of the reminiscing, you're now feeling pangs of regret that you never gave yourself permission to enjoy it. You realize that you aren't any better off for denying yourself the experience — it's quite the opposite. You missed out on this once-in-a-lifetime experience and now you regret it.

If you had given yourself permission to enjoy the pool, you'd still feel disappointment after returning home from this amazing trip. But you'd have the joy and memories from this incredible experience, and you may also find the inspiration to create more magical moments just like this one now that you know it's possible.

Practicing being present

It's normal to experience waves of stress and doubt during your break. Your brain is a great problem solver, and if it can't find a problem in the present moment, it will look to the future, scanning the horizon for potential danger. *What if I don't find a job after my break? What if I run out of money?* It will also look back to the past and question your decisions. *Should I have waited to quit my job? Did I make the right choice?* The future problems don't exist yet, and the past is unchangeable, so worrying about these situations doesn't improve nor maximize your break experience.

You don't want these unhelpful worries to rain on your career break parade and stop you from enjoying this time. What can you do to navigate these waves? You can come back to the present moment where (almost always) everything is fine — or likely even better than fine.

REMEMBER

Being able to fully enjoy this experience will require you to bring yourself back into the present moment often. This practice works wonders to help you reduce stress and enjoy your break. It also helps you feel more gratitude and a greater sense of ease. When you're present, you are available to experience and appreciate the small moments that make life so sweet. Plus, it makes the big moments that much better. This is especially true when you're on your break and experiencing a high volume of great moments.

ACTIVITY

Here's a simple activity that will help you bring yourself back to the present moment any time. Try this when you're feeling stressed or notice your mind drifting away:

1. **Stop what you're doing and take three deep, slow breaths.**

2. **Go through your senses and see what you notice.**

   What do I taste right now?

   What do I hear right now?

   What do I smell right now?

   What do I see right now?

   What do I feel right now?

3. **Take another deep breath and release your stress with the exhale.**

TIP

If you're struggling with this activity, try this instead: Ask yourself, "What is good in this moment?" and come up with at least three answers. Staying present takes practice. Lucky for you, a break is a great time to hone this important life skill.

There can be great joy in spending time with loved ones during your break, especially when you're practicing presence. Stretch yourself to find gratitude in even the most mundane moments, and your enjoyment will likely increase.

TIP

If you have small children (or find yourself in their presence during your break) they offer a great opportunity to practice being in the present moment. They're wired to stay present and can help you do the same. You'll get to see the world through their eyes. It's possible your mind will want to wander by the 50th round of their game of choice but that's what makes it such good practice. Plus, seeing them bloom in your undivided attention will make for an extra sweet reward.

Slowing down

A career break is a chance to rethink your relationship with efficiency and time. In the working world, the default is spending the least amount of time accomplishing the most you possibly can. But this approach doesn't leave much (or any) room for ease and joy. It's true that time is a finite and precious resource, but spending it trying to maximize your output doesn't necessarily lead to a happy and fulfilling life.

Chances are, you've taken on the belief that you need to do more with less, but the "fat" that gets trimmed in the process is often the stuff that makes life feel good. Your break is an opportunity to slow down and reconnect with the things that matter most. You get to consider a new approach and perspective on how you spend your time. Taking a break from the workforce means having more time for the things you want to do — the things that bring you joy and connect you with the things you value most.

In life, people often take the highway, metaphorically and in reality. We're searching for the fastest and most direct route possible. But on a break, you have more control over your day. Your time is still finite but it's no longer a scarce resource. You have ample amounts of it available. This means you finally get to slow down and enjoy the scenery. Literally and figuratively.

Figuratively, you have permission to take your time. You can linger or get sidetracked without fear of negative consequences. Now, if you're used to running through life at top speed, this can be quite challenging at first. But try to remember that your to-do list is self-created. You can update it, amend it, and delete things from it as you see fit. You can slow down and stop to smell the roses, enjoying the small details and joys of life that you may have been too busy to notice before.

You literally have time to truly take the long way home and enjoy the drive. If you'd like to practice slowing down and making space for mini-adventures, I highly recommend taking a new, non-highway route home next time you're out running errands.

ACTIVITY

Next time you head out to run an errand, take an alternative route to get there. This activity works whether you're heading somewhere you've never been or just across town.

First, you place your destination into Google Maps. Next, select "Route Options" and then select "Avoid Highways" to see alternative routes to your destination.

This activity will lead you to discover scenic routes, new shops and restaurants, new neighborhoods, and beautiful places that you didn't know existed. It will help you shift out of autopilot and the default to "get there as fast as possible." Instead, you'll start seeking opportunities to slow down and enjoy the ride. You'll find yourself having more adventures and feeling more inspired. Just a few extra minutes can open you up to a whole new world.

ANECDOTE

When I lived in Minneapolis, I tried this often and discovered many interesting neighborhoods. I found restaurants and shops that I'd never been to before, plus a ton of inspiring scenery. I got to know the city on a much deeper level, explored new places, and practiced slowing down more often.

TIP

If you need help slowing down and savoring life, you can try this activity anytime (even if you're not on a break).

Avoiding the Common Pitfalls

The first part of this chapter talks about what to do on your break. In this section, I explain what *not* to do. You discover the common mistakes career breakers make when it comes to spending time wisely and find out how to avoid them.

Surprisingly, the most common mistakes career breakers make when it comes to managing their time are centered around trying to do too much. Unconsciously, they default to what's familiar and try to re-create their old work dynamic. But a career break is a chance to leave that demanding and often unhealthy dynamic behind and prioritize their own well-being.

Many worry they'll become complacent and end up doing very little on their break. They recognize the break is a gift and want to make the most of it. They also fear being seen as lazy by others. To appease these fears, they cram in as many activities and commitments as possible. But the most harmful mistakes I've witnessed involve overdoing it and treating your break like a full-time job. If you have a solid career break plan (see Part 2 for how to create one) and are committed to fulfilling your career break themes (developed in Chapter 4), you will avoid the trap of becoming a full-time couch potato who wasted their break.

WARNING

Trying to do all the things all at once will ruin your break. Instead, focus on striking a balance between doing and resting. And understanding the common pitfalls will help you do just that.

Overscheduling your time

Because you're likely used to juggling a lot of responsibilities and mapping out your life down to the minute to make sure it all gets done, it's easy to continue overscheduling yourself into your break. But this easy default creates more exhaustion, even if the new responsibilities are more exciting and fun.

Your break is a chance to exit "busy mode" entirely and see what emerges when you leave space for yourself. Think about how it feels to have a booked calendar. When the appointment notification dings, you may suddenly feel resistance to moving on to the next thing but think, "I don't want to do this, but it's on the calendar, so it's part of the plan, and I'm doing it." You may do this so often that you don't even hear that voice anymore. Instead you just push through and move on.

But that approach doesn't leave space for you to tend to your needs. It doesn't leave space for you to have inspired ideas and creative thoughts. And it doesn't allow you to do whatever feels good to you in that moment. Instead, you're beholden to the you from two weeks ago who put this item on your calendar. But your break is an opportunity to live differently. It's the perfect time to create more space for you and your needs.

Allowing whitespace (i.e., free time) in your days and weeks means having time to meet your needs and desires in real time. If you're tired, take a nap. If you're craving fresh air, go outside for a walk. If you miss your best friend, give them a call. It also provides space for your new ideas and deeper thoughts to emerge.

TIP

If you struggle with what to do during this free time, ask "What do I need right now?" or "What would feel good to me right now?" and start with whatever answer comes up.

There is magic in new and unexpected opportunities that will appear during your break, but you need to be available to say yes. This is especially true if your plan includes travel. Not overscheduling will leave you with time to explore and meet new people, take unexpected detours, and relax when you're feeling overwhelmed. It makes it easier for delightful surprises and adventures to appear.

ANECDOTE

During my break, I traveled alone on a one-way ticket to Vietnam. I arrived in Hanoi with a very loose plan to head south toward Ho Chi Minh on my 30-day visa. During my cruise in Halong Bay, I met two students from the Czech Republic who were traveling in the same direction. We became fast friends and planned to meet up across four different cities. Together, we had many fun adventures that I couldn't have imagined before starting my trip.

This can be a challenging exercise if you love planning, but please remember that this break is an opportunity to discover new parts of yourself and to grow. So, it's an incredible time to lean into more spontaneity and to leave space to fully show up for your present moment.

Striving to be productive

We have a complicated relationship with productivity. While it might feel true that in corporate culture "the more you do, the more valuable you are," our worth and value are not determined by this metric. We are worthy and valuable even when we're not "doing."

If you're feeling exhausted or burned out when you start your break, you'll need to include time for relaxation and rest (which can feel unsettling if you're used to going at 100 miles an hour). It can be hard in the beginning to shake the foreboding sense that you're behind or not doing enough. Your body and mind may still be on high alert, even though you aren't in any danger of missing deadlines or dropping balls that you've been juggling. It's safe to rest now.

Some career breakers end their break experience still feeling tired and burned out, because they didn't dedicate time to rest and restore. They replaced the work hustle with fun and adventure or chores and career preparation to make sure they stayed productive. Their fear of not being productive enough had them overworking on their break, creating a disappointing ending. Don't let this be you!

You don't have to prove you're being productive while on your break — to yourself or to others. You deserve to rest. Rest and relaxation may not look like much from the outside, but inside, healing and restoration are happening, and they are necessary for you to show up as the best version of yourself when your break is over.

If you're stressed about not doing enough, shift the focus from what you're doing (or not doing) into how you're feeling. Ask "How am I feeling right now?" and if you don't like the answer, take one action to shift your energy. You can go for a walk, talk to a friend, sit in a park, or listen to music to shift your mood.

It's important to give yourself downtime during your break. You will be learning a lot about yourself and the world around you during this time, whether you're traveling or staying put. You will experience and process a lot of thoughts and emotions, and you'll likely have a few breakthroughs, too. So it's critical to give yourself time to process it all — this is how you create lasting changes that will positively impact the rest of your life. Allowing downtime starts with reframing productivity and its role in your life, especially while you're on a break.

Turning it into a job

This last common mistake is easy to make because our brains crave familiarity. In the midst of leaping into this new adventure and facing a ton of unknowns, your brain will want to create a structure to navigate the uncertainty based on what worked in the past. It will want to turn your break into another job.

Your days of overworking, prioritizing others' needs over your own, and struggling to maintain healthy boundaries may creep back in. You may find that you're holding yourself hostage to prior commitments and pushing beyond your limits to get things done and check the boxes on your daily to do list. If you share responsibilities with a partner or take care of others, you may be tempted to trample over your boundaries and fill your "free time" with more chores and time spent taking care of others' needs. A career break won't magically bring your life into balance. You'll have to create new beliefs about what's possible and what you deserve and set new intentions for how you want to live. But a break is going to make this transition a lot easier. It will give you space to replace the old habits with new and better ones. It will snap you out of autopilot so you can see all the ways you were defaulting in patterns that weren't healthy and supportive. This break is like a clean slate, and you can start fresh, filling your life with better and more enjoyable routines and habits. In the beginning, you need to be careful not to bring these unhealthy habits with you into your break. Here's an easy activity to become more aware of the habits you'd like to leave behind:

1. **Grab a journal, and set a timer for eight minutes.**

   You can use a phone for the timer. You can also type your answers if that's preferable to writing them down.

2. **Take a few slow deep breaths.**

   This will help you feel more centered and connected.

3. **Start your timer.**

4. **Think about your job and typical work day.**

5. **Write down the things that felt challenging and out of alignment with the way you want to live.**

   Let your words flow. Don't edit for grammar or logic — just share whatever comes up. Examples: sitting at a desk all day, working until the point of mental fatigue, ignoring my body's needs like hunger and rest, putting everyone else's needs before my own, and having a ton of deadlines in my day.

6. **Reflect on what you'd like to leave behind as you start your break.**

7. **After the timer has ended, take a moment to reflect on your answers and note the habits that you'd like to let go of and/or replace.**

WARNING

Your break is not the time to raise the bar on yourself. Don't overdo it with a sparkling clean home or daily meals made from scratch if that wasn't part of your pre-break routine. Yes, you'll have more time available, but the goal is to direct it toward your career break goals and learning to take better care of yourself.

Meeting a case study: Chad's story

Chad hired me after years of nonstop and often intense work in the healthcare industry. He felt stuck in a rut and discontent with this career, so when his clinic announced they were closing their doors, he considered his wife's suggestion to turn down the new job being offered to him and take a career break instead.

A break hadn't been on his radar. He assumed he'd continue working until retirement but sitting with the idea made him realize it felt natural and right to take some time off. He felt lost in the weeds and unable to see his way forward with his career. Chad hoped for a sense of renewal and clarity during his five-month career break.

Chad wanted to make the most of his break but wasn't sure how to spend his time wisely. He sought a balance between a life of routine (like his pre-break life) and the unstructured freedom his career break offered. He started off strong, feeling grateful and excited by the large amounts of "me time" in his days. But it took effort to enjoy this freedom and make peace with having a very unstructured schedule. Chad worked on staying present and allowing white space in his days. During these unstructured periods of time, he checked in with himself to see what he needed and honored the answers that appeared. He also leaned on meditation, self-reflection, and journaling to support his growth. But worrying about what would come next created a fair amount of stress and left him feeling frustrated about his perceived lack of progress.

Where am I going with all of this? he wondered. He was used to pushing through, checking boxes, and accomplishing his goals as quickly as possible. He felt a growing sense of urgency to have all the answers just two months into his break. By asking some reflective questions, I was able to help Chad realize what his break was really about. In his words, "Why am I rushing through this and my life? To get to the end, which is what — death? And to do it with only minimal fun and joy?" His brain was putting a heavy focus on his fourth theme, designing his next chapter, and wanted to skip over fulfilling the other three (restore, reconnect, joy exploration).

Chad did the hard work to really see himself and his patterns so he could change them. He moved through this challenge instead of trying to go around it (i.e., change the circumstance to avoid it). This moment was pivotal to his transformation. He suddenly saw things differently. He realized he'd taken the stairs two-at-a-time for as long as he could remember and that he often rushed his daughter through dinner even when there were no pressing plans afterward.

With this new perspective and desire for change, Chad learned how to slow down. He flipped his default from rushing through life to taking time to fully enjoy it. In the midst of these big changes, his family adopted a dog and relocated 1,100 miles away to a new state. Chad's new approach to life was opening the door to new possibilities. Though he began his break feeling burned out and potentially done with his healthcare career, his break helped him return to his old profession with a new attitude and outlook. His perspective went from "I have to do this" to "I get to do this." He created a relatively seamless transition out of his break. While he worried about his re-entry at the beginning, it naturally unfolded and presented itself when he was ready. It took very little time to find his next job. Using the principles mentioned in this chapter, Chad spent his time wisely, and it paved the way for the most transformative and insightful period of his adult life.

5

Exiting with Ease and Grace

Find out how to transition into your next chapter smoothly and successfully.

Develop your career break story and discover the best way to explain your break to potential employers and navigate the job-hunting process.

Prepare to embrace a new vision for your life and sustain the positive changes — emerge refreshed, inspired, and motivated for what lies ahead.

Chapter **13**

Transitioning out of Your Break

Ending a break can feel like a bumpy ride. After so much autonomy, the thought of returning to work can be both exciting and stifling, while the limitless possibilities ahead can feel simultaneously exhilarating and overwhelming. But regardless of whether you're ready, the end will eventually come, and it will be time to prepare for what comes next. This is where the re-entry period comes in. You can use it as a ramp for returning from your break recharged, inspired, and happily employed. Specifically, you can use this time to

» Recover from extended travel or reground yourself after an extensive period of stretching beyond your comfort zone.

» Determine your next big goal and take action to start achieving it.

» Explore new career options, lifestyle changes, and/or income possibilities.

» Process your thoughts and feelings and reflect on lessons you've learned from this experience as you chart a course for your next chapter.

>> Reset your habits and routines to better prepare you for a healthy return to full-time employment.

In this chapter, you find out how to transition out of your break and into a future full of possibility. You'll take steps to ensure you start off on the right foot and are building momentum for a smoother return to work. You'll also discover real examples of different re-entry experiences to see what's possible. It's OK if you're feeling unsure of your next steps or goal. This chapter walks you through the process of preparing for a successful return to the working world.

If you're taking a sabbatical (instead of a career break) you can use this chapter to help you process your experience and apply the lessons you've learned, so you'll retain the benefits of your break as you return to your employer.

I started my re-entry period feeling very confused about what to do next. I hadn't received the lightning bolt of clarity I'd been hoping for during my break. I felt sad and frustrated at the thought of ending my break but my finances made it clear it was time to find a job. So I put in the work to set a new goal and make progress toward achieving it. Luckily, that work led me to receiving five job offers in five weeks and created the foundation for what I share with you in this chapter!

Kick-starting Your Re-Entry Period

You don't want to come skidding into the end of your break with only a few days or weeks left to find your next job. That level of pressure and urgency can create an air of desperation that turns off future employers and leaves you settling for less than you deserve. Plus, it makes for a chaotic end to an otherwise pleasant adventure. To find better balance and create better results, give yourself ample time to transition out of your break and back into work mode.

Your re-entry period will have two phases. How quickly you'll move from one to the other depends on your readiness to return to work and the amount of time and money you've set aside for your re-entry period. The more time and money you have, the slower this transition can be. This chapter helps you navigate phase one, and Chapter 14 helps you navigate searching for a new job in phase two:

>> **Phase one:** In this initial phase, you'll start winding down your break and mentally transitioning out of "break mode." You'll have time to process your break experience, reflect on your journey, and bring clarity to your new goal as you think through your next steps. This time also allows you to build a foundation that supports your pursuit of this new goal.

>> **Phase two:** During the second phase, you'll start taking action to achieve your new goal (landing a new job, launching a business, or becoming self-employed).

Avoiding a false start

Before you officially start your re-entry, I suggest you make doubly sure you're ready to reenter. You might be surprised to know that some of my clients have tried to exit their break early due to things like

>> A growing discomfort with unlimited ease and downtime

>> A (sometimes real, sometimes perceived) lack of money

>> A tempting job opportunity

>> An unforeseen crisis or change in circumstance

You may be arriving at the natural conclusion of your break feeling satisfied with your experience, and that's great! But if you're arriving at the end sooner than expected or without feeling satisfied with your break, it's important to make sure your brain isn't trying to sabotage you. For example, you may feel stressed by watching your bank account dwindle, but you're still on budget and have more than enough to continue your break. Or you might feel guilty about "doing nothing" and appearing unproductive but still have work to do on fulfilling your rest-related career break theme. There are definitely times when ending earlier is a good idea, but to avoid a false start, here are some steps that will help you discern what's really going on before you move forward.

Start by listing your current fears and concerns and then examine them for the truth:

>> If you're worried about money, check your numbers and compare them to your break budget. Do you have enough money to continue your break?

>> If you're worried about being unproductive and falling behind, reflect on your themes. Have you fulfilled them to the best of your ability?

>> If you feel uncomfortable with the high levels of ease and downtime, ask yourself why this is the case. Do you like your answer?

>> If you've received a tempting job offer, think through the trade-offs. Will the benefits outweigh the cost?

If, after reflecting on your fears, you decide to extend your break, visit Chapters 10 and 12 for suggestions on how best to utilize the remaining time. Otherwise, if you've decided it's the right time to begin your re-entry period, the remainder of this chapter can help you navigate it like a pro.

Setting expectations

As you begin preparing for life post-break, you'll likely experience a kaleidoscope of emotions as you sort through ideas of what to do next and make a plan to achieve your new goal. This is an action-packed phase that can feel quite messy or uncertain, so I recommend the following rules to set yourself up for a successful re-entry and create great results.

>> **Allow yourself to feel a range of emotions.** You'll likely have a multitude of feelings, and maybe even a tantrum or two, as you begin to exit your break. You may feel resentful that it's time to go back to work. You're not wrong to feel this. It's a normal part of the process. You get to have all of the feelings, even the uncomfortable ones, as you process this life-changing experience and prepare to launch into something new or return to something familiar as a new version of yourself.

>> **Don't rush this part of your break.** This is a legitimate phase of your break. You'll want time to process and reflect on your experience, determine your next steps, and ramp

back into work mode. Don't cut your re-entry period short. Give yourself enough time for these important steps.

>> **Make sure to celebrate your break.** Taking a break is a fantastic accomplishment and one that should be heavily celebrated. Don't forget to make time to really sit in the miracle of having had this time and choosing to pour into yourself and improve your life. You are making the most of your one precious life. Take time to intentionally reflect on and celebrate that.

>> **Prepare to face confusion and self-doubt.** As you begin to reflect on your experience and use this process to determine what you'll do next, it's easy to feel overwhelmed by the uncertainty of what lies ahead. Don't question yourself for the highs and lows as you work to build a life post-break. Remember that your break once felt overwhelming and uncertain, but look at you now!

>> **Stay curious and open.** As you begin this transition period, staying curious and open will help you consider new possibilities that a break can open your eyes to. Instead of allowing old definitions of who you were and what you liked to confine you, consider new ideas, be curious and willing to explore new things as you create your next chapter.

ANECDOTE

At the beginning of her break, Juliana envisioned a travel-based break that would most likely culminate in a career pivot. She was open to new possibilities and excited for a change. During the last few months of her break, she slowly began her re-entry period. She explored creative pursuits like blogging and writing and even supported a start-up company with her marketing talents. It took time, but as she moved through her re-entry period, she realized that her previous belief that success would mean starting a new noncorporate career was no longer true. After reflecting on her new goals, nonnegotiables, and career desires, she returned to the corporate world and accepted a position that married her past experience with her new post-break goals and desires.

Ensuring adequate time for your re-entry

You can't skimp on your re-entry period if you want to create a successful outcome post-break. It takes time to transition out of a break and back into the workforce. You'll need to process your experience to amplify your clarity and confidence as you begin pursing new opportunities. Otherwise, you may struggle to find a new job or backslide into unhelpful pre-break habits and patterns, such as overworking or having unhealthy boundaries. You've come too far to throw all that growth and clarity away. Realize the full benefit of your break by setting aside adequate time to re-enter.

Setting your parameters

Determining what an adequate amount of time means for you begins by defining your parameters. How much time and money are you willing and able to set aside for your re-entry period? These two numbers form the boundaries of your re-entry period, and when you've established them, you can move on to developing the details of your transition plan.

If you've already allotted time and money for your re-entry period (as discussed in Chapter 4), you're done with this first step. If you haven't yet allocated resources to your re-entry period, your first step is to decide how much money and time you'll dedicate to your transition. These numbers are a starting point; you can adjust them later, if necessary.

Applying the 1 for 6 Rule

If you're planning to return to something similar to what you were doing before your break, or you already have your next role lined up, you can estimate a suitable length of time to reenter, using the 1 for 6 Rule of thumb: For every six weeks that you're on a break, dedicate *at least* one week to your re-entry period, and make sure your minimum is at least one month. The 1 for 6 Rule allows time for you to

>> Mentally prepare to wrap up your break

>> Process your thoughts and feelings

>> Reset your habits and routines

>> Get clear on your next goal

>> Start taking action to achieve your new goal

TIP

If you're planning to explore your options and pursue new possibilities, be sure to read the next section for guidance on extending your timeline. The additional layer of new possibilities requires a longer re-entry period.

To apply the "1-for-6" rule, calculate the length of your break in weeks, excluding your re-entry period. When you have this number, divide by 6 to calculate your minimum re-entry period, remembering that your minimum should be at least one month regardless of the length of your break. For example, if you've had a 6-month break, you'd estimate that was 24 weeks long. Dividing by 6, you'll get 4 weeks as your minimum re-entry period (which meets the one-month minimum). This means you'll want to add *at least* 4 weeks to your break for transitioning, but you can absolutely give yourself more time, especially if you anticipate it taking longer to find your next role.

This rule serves as a guideline, but your finances or responsibilities may dictate a shorter timeline. If this is the case, you can jump to "Creating Your Transition Plan" later in this chapter to help you maximize the time you have available for setting up your next chapter.

Extending your timeline

If you're like me, or many of my clients who explored new possibilities for their post-break life, you'll need more time than the 1-for-6 Rule indicates. You'll want an extended re-entry period. If you hope to create a significant change in how you earn an income after your break, like starting a new career, jumping into self-employment, or taking up the digital nomad lifestyle, this additional time is critical for exploring your options before moving on to the tactical stuff. If you've set one of your career break themes around this desire, you've likely already started exploring new lifestyles and/or career paths. But if you're still figuring out what you want to transition into, I definitely recommend adding more time beyond the 1-for-6 Rule to shift from exploration into action.

You need to take several factors into account as you set a timeline for your extended re-entry. Here are several important things to consider:

>> How much additional time does your budget allow?

>> How much exploration and/or upskilling would you like to pursue? How much time might these take?

>> When it's time to begin searching for your next opportunity, do you anticipate a long cultivation period?

Based on my clients' experiences, an average length of time for an extended re-entry period that includes exploring new options is three to four months. Quite often, this exploration was one of the four themes for their break, so they began the exploration process months before transitioning into re-entry.

My re-entry period, after a 20-month break, was 4.5 months long. As I explored my options, I had many informative conversations, read career-focused books, and took community education classes on a wide range of topics, like fermenting vegetables at home. One of these classes, How to Build a Life Coaching Business, wasn't immediately relevant but would later become an important step in the journey that led to writing this book. If you're in an exploration phase, stay open to new ideas, opportunities, and conversations that expand your consideration set. Even if they don't create a pathway to your next job, they may plant important seeds that bloom in the future.

Creating Your Transition Plan

The re-entry period won't feel as wild and free as the rest of your break, but there's still a lot of freedom and autonomy during this phase. You'll phase into job-hunting or business-building steps but you don't have to go from 0 to 100 right away. Immediately shifting into eight-hour days of job searching, upskilling, and networking can make you feel overwhelmed. As you build your transition plan, remember your re-entry is a ramp, and you can take one step at a time up that slope instead of running full-speed toward your next goal. This section outlines a simple process to transition out of your break and into a successful next chapter at a steady pace.

Shifting out of "break mode"

As you begin your re-entry period, you'll need time to process your experience, integrate the insights you gleaned from your break, and mentally start to transition out of "break mode." This helps you feel grounded and ready to create more clarity on your next right step and find better alignment with your future goals. You'll also have time to recover from any reverse culture shock you may experience after returning from long-term travel. The following are a few examples of activities that will help you begin to transition out of your break.

- >> Connecting with loved ones
- >> Engaging in mindfulness practices
- >> Indulging in joyful interests or hobbies
- >> Reflecting on your experience and lessons learned
- >> Spending time in nature

TIP

Honor this time by keeping your activities simple and supportive. Before you begin to ramp up and busy yourself with achieving your future goals, take a week or two (at a minimum!) to ease into the transition. It will bring clarity and confidence as you design your next chapter.

Establishing a new routine

Your re-entry period is the perfect time to set new routines and habits that will support you in creating the life you want. Establishing these before you begin your new job or seize your next opportunity allows you to develop a new standard before work creeps back in and starts competing for your precious time. You can proactively determine how you want your days to begin and incorporate the new and different ways you want to experience your life (for example, daily meditation or movement, early morning silence or journaling, drinking a glass of water when you wake up, and so on).

REMEMBER

Proactively starting a new routine before you return to work will help you maintain more balance and thoughtfully design your day, instead of allowing outside commitments to design it for you. Even if you didn't have a daily routine through most of your break, the re-entry period is a great time to develop one so you can incorporate healthier habits that will become more automatic and thus easier to maintain after you start working again.

A great routine is both supportive and accessible:

- >> **Supportive:** A good routine helps you start your day feeling grounded with a clear mind and allows you to prioritize your well-being, both physical and mental.

- >> **Accessible:** A good routine is also accessible so you can do it consistently and without too much friction from competing priorities, like work and family.

Here are several great questions to reflect on as you begin designing a life-enhancing routine to carry forward the benefits of your break. You can also visit Chapter 12 for specific suggestions on designing a new morning routine.

>> Ideally, how much time would I like to commit to my daily routine? Is this number consistently achievable? If not, what is a more realistic commitment I could make?

>> What are three things (such as habits or beliefs) I want to leave behind as I move into this new chapter of life?

>> What are three things I've gained from this experience that I don't want to lose; how can I incorporate them?

>> What are three habits that pre-break me had that I don't want to carry with me into my next chapter?

Determining your next big goal

Once upon a time, taking a break was your big future goal, and now that you've achieved it (congrats again, by the way!) it's time to look forward and set a new one. Even if your next goal isn't career-focused, you'll need money to support your new goal (and life in general), so gaining clarify helps you focus your search on job opportunities that align with and support your new goal (instead of compete against it).

TIP

The common default is to return to something similar to what you did pre-break. You have the skills, experience, and network to make this a relatively smooth transition. But I want to encourage you to seize this opportunity to think bigger about your future and your life. Use your re-entry period to get clear on which goal aligns best with the new and improved version of you.

ANECDOTE

I came into my break unsure of what I wanted to do when it was over. As I began my re-entry period, I took time to explore interesting options, like becoming a holistic chef. But I eventually came to the realization that pursuing options like becoming a chef or life coach with $42k of student loan debt hanging over me felt nearly impossible. Paying it off would give me the financial freedom to pursue new dreams, and returning to the corporate world was the fastest way I knew to make this happen. So, I used my goal of becoming debt-free to inform my career search. I searched and applied for corporate jobs that felt more aligned with my personal values and goals than my last job but that also paid well enough to help me achieve paying off my debt. This clarity helped me be able to consider only opportunities I felt good about and sell myself effectively in interviews. Twenty-one months later, I paid off my debt, became a certified life coach, and started building my business.

Before we dive into how you can develop more clarity on your next big goal, remember these two important caveats:

>> **Don't search for the perfect answer.** It can be easy to agonize over this important decision, but much like your break, your next step is not permanent nor irreversible. If you don't like it, you can always change your mind and do something different. Don't raise the stakes so high you become paralyzed by indecision.

>> **Only focus on your next right step.** You can't possibly know how the next 25 steps after this one will unfold, so don't try to play a chess match with the universe and determine the best move 25 steps from now. Instead focus on what is currently true for you and honor that next step.

ACTIVITY

Are you ready to determine your next big goal? The following questions will help you expose your future goal. I recommend journaling your answers as a stream of consciousness, where you just write without filtering for grammar or logic.

>> Are there places where I find myself wanting to push beyond my current comfort zone and/or do something differently?

>> How has my career break changed me? What's something I can do differently to honor this change?

>> If I could break any rule for myself, which one(s) would I break and why?

>> What are my superpowers? What's currently holding me back from using them?

>> What are three new interests or passions I've discovered during my break?

>> What is currently my biggest dream for my life?

For many of my clients, tasting the freedom a break provides makes it hard to return to the old way of life. They don't want to go back to the grind. Instead, they use their re-entry period to pursue new career options that honor their new goal *and* the new version of them that's emerging. For example,

» Becoming a contractor

» Exploring self-employment

» Freelancing as a digital nomad

» Joining a start-up

» Launching a business

» Starting a new career

» Stepping up into a new role

» Targeting an adjacent career

» Transitioning into part-time work

» Trying something completely new

There's absolutely nothing wrong with returning to your old career, job, or company. But if a part of you is longing for something new or different, this is a great time to explore.

Planning your action steps

When you've determined your next big goal and which career option(s) you'll pursue to help you achieve it, it's time to plan your action steps. The easiest place to start is with a brainstorming session for small steps that could help you reach your goal. For example, you can consider the following questions:

» **What additional skills or knowledge might help you reach your goal?** Consider programs, certifications, fellowships, and so on that can help you upskill, improve your qualifications, and become a more competitive candidate.

» **What challenges might you face that you'll need to overcome?** Think through the potential obstacles and make a plan for how you can overcome or navigate them.

» **What preparations will you need to make?** Think about the tools, resources, and steps you'll need to prepare yourself for the job search or start a new endeavor.

» **What services or experiences can move you closer to your goal?** Consider sources of support and experiences that may enhance your capabilities and help you reach your goal faster (career coach, volunteering)

>> **Who might you want or need to reach out to?** Consider your broader network of colleagues, mentors, friends, community members, and family for support, guidance, connections, and inspiration.

TIP

For more information on professional fellowships, such as where and how to find them, plus a personal anecdote of a client who used a fellowship to enhance his career opportunities, see Chapter 5.

If you plan to start your own business or pursue self-employment as a service provider or freelancer, you may consider steps like

>> Exploring the U.S. Small Business Administration to develop a comprehensive business plan

>> Purchasing *Starting a Business All-in-One For Dummies* by Eric Tyson and Bob Nelson (Wiley) or *Starting an Online Business All-in-One For Dummies* by Joel Elad and Shannon Belew (Wiley) to help you navigate the entire process

>> Researching potential grants that can help you finance your business

REMEMBER

If you're pursuing something new, you'll experience a learning curve. Embracing a sense of curiosity will help you enjoy the learning process. View your action steps as small experiments that provide valuable information about what you do and don't like. You can apply this learning to tweak and adjust your action plan, gaining clarity and increasing alignment in the process. The following anecdote provides an example of a client who took this approach to exploring self-employment.

ANECDOTE

Heidi used her interests, strengths, and circumstances (living in Guatemala) to brainstorm ideas for self-employment. She didn't want to return to life as an employee, so she considered several options, giving herself time to see what worked. She began a small export business, working with local designers to source unique items. She also explored Airbnb hosting and managing, medical interpreting, and vacation planning. Some ideas took root, whereas others didn't, but for each idea she focused on the small steps she could take to grow the business. She signed up for courses, hired a coach (yours truly), used her network, and said yes to interesting and unexpected opportunities. The single most important step she took to grow a successful business was showing up before she felt completely ready and letting people know how to hire her.

If you're interested in heading into full-time employment with a new employer, you can consider any of the following steps (also, check out Chapter 14 for tactical steps to find a great job and impress potential employers):

>> Hiring a career coach to fine-tune your job search, interview skills, and career story arc to land a dream job

>> Researching companies to learn more about their business and culture via sites like LinkedIn and Glassdoor

>> Updating your resume and sharing it with a recruiter, expert, or AI tool for feedback and suggested improvements

TIP

If you're returning from a career break lasting more than two years, you can also consider more formal returnship programs with companies like Amazon, Intuit, Johnson & Johnson, and Microsoft. These are basically internship programs for returning workers that provide structure and support for those returning to the workforce after a longer hiatus.

ANECDOTE

When I was clear on my new goal (becoming debt-free), I decided to pursue a return to corporate life to achieve this goal as fast as possible. Because my break had changed my perspective and pushed me to think bigger and expect more from life, I focused on jobs that felt more aligned with my personal values and desired lifestyle than my pre-break job. My action steps to land a new and well-suited opportunity included working with a recruiter, updating my resume, networking with friends and past colleagues, searching LinkedIn for job openings, and listing the highlights and lessons from my break so I could incorporate them into my interview process.

Chapter **14**

Securing Job Offers after Your Career Break

Returning to the job market after a career break is a notably different experience than searching for a different job while working — and this can be a good thing! If you're worried about struggling to find a job when your break is over, it may surprise you to know that a break can actually help you land a fantastic new opportunity.

You can land a great job *because of* your break, not in spite of it. In this chapter, you'll discover how to use your break to create an advantage and land offers that you're excited to accept. I'm sharing the same process I used to land five job offers in five weeks, including a dream job, after my 20-month break.

ANECDOTE

When it was time to begin searching for a new job, I leveraged my break to help me become a standout applicant. By only searching for jobs that felt aligned with my new goal and values, I showed up as a genuine and well-prepared candidate, which helped me connect with my interviewers. I highlighted my break on my resume and dove into specifics in my cover letters. Most importantly, I held on to the belief that I was much better for having taken a break, which meant that my future employer was going to benefit from my break as well. Five weeks after updating my resume and beginning my job search, I landed five offers and went on to accept a dream job.

WARNING

This chapter is most effective if you take time to reflect on your career break experience and clarify your new goal. If you haven't had a chance to do this, please visit Chapter 13 and give yourself a bit more time to prepare before you launch into job-search mode and put this chapter's suggestions into action.

Crafting Your Break Story for Potential Employers

One of the places where I see career breakers struggle the most is in explaining their break to potential employers — both in interviews and in their job search materials (resumes, cover letters). What I share in this section makes it a lot easier to talk about your break and let it be an asset in the job search process.

If you position it well, your break can give you an edge over other applicants, but this advantage hinges on your belief. Believing in the value of your break is potent magic. If you have belief, doors will swing open for you. If you don't, they will remain closed.

Think about the energy of a candidate who shows up after a six-month break feeling desperate to find a job and self-conscious about their decision to take a break. They might downplay their experience and avoid talking about their break altogether. Now compare that to a candidate who is clear on the benefits they received from their break and is excited to show their potential employer how they can apply these benefits in the new role. Your thoughts about your break matter, and they can make or break your re-entry experience.

REMEMBER

For many people, a career break is a foreign concept. Because others aren't sure what to think about taking a break, they'll look to you for guidance. Your thoughts and beliefs will help them determine if it's a good thing or a bad thing. You have the power to influence their opinion and help them see your break as meaningful and valuable.

Your default reaction might be to downplay your break or skim over it, but this can actually hurt your chances of finding a great job. Instead, focus on promoting the benefits of your break and providing context. This creates fertile ground for appreciation. Your future employer can't appreciate the magnitude of what you've done if you don't give them a chance to know any of the details!

Authentically hyping up your break

Because belief is critical to your success, strengthening your belief is the first step to crafting a winning career break story that will help you create a successful outcome. Framing this experience in a positive light helps others see the value of your break. During interviews, the hiring teams asked a lot of questions about my break. You may experience this, too. By first building up belief that my break was immensely valuable and interesting, I could view the interviewers' questions as coming from a place of genuine curiosity and interest. I didn't feel the need to defend my decision, which allowed me to share more details with sincerity, confidence, and enthusiasm.

There's no magical combination of words that will make people want to support your break. Your confidence will do the heavy lifting here. Instead, focus on emitting an energy that says, "Yes, I took a break. Can you believe it? How incredible is that?! I'm a better person for having taken it, and I can't wait to tell you about it." How you feel about your break heavily influences how others feel about it, so cultivate belief and confidence in your decision.

This activity helps amp up your belief and build your confidence. Write a list of 25 benefits you've received from your break. Yes, 25! Reflect on goals you've achieved, fun things you've done, ways you've stretched your comfort zone and grown as a person, and gifts you've received from your break. This activity is meant to stretch you, so take your time completing it. Save your answers — you'll want them for the next activity.

It's important to remember that post-break you has the same qualifications, job experience, and network as pre-break you, plus all of the amazing benefits you outline in the previous activity. You are a more recharged and inspired version of yourself, and all of this goodness comes to the job market with you, making you a stronger candidate than you were before the break. You aren't like every other applicant who comes in to interview for the job. Your break and the goals you've achieved while on it will make you a more impressive and memorable candidate.

It's time to start crafting your break story! This activity helps you understand and articulate how your break has positively impacted you and your candidacy and can potentially benefit your future employer as well. The following structure helps you develop a thoughtful and compelling story about your break to feel clearer and more confident in sharing it, *but it's not a script*. Work through the following prompts and review them to internalize your answers and feel more prepared to share your story with others:

>> **I took a break to [*positively framed purpose statement*].**

See Chapter 7 for examples.

>> **To achieve this purpose, I focused on [*your break themes*].**

See Chapter 4 for examples.

>> **What I learned through this experience was [*top insights and lessons*].**

See your answers from the previous activity.

>> **This made me an even stronger candidate for this role because [*ways your insights and benefits could benefit the employer*].**

>> **And I'm excited to work with you because [*ways you're aligned with the job description and/or company values and mission*].**

When it came time to start searching for work after my 20-month career break, I wasn't sure how long it would take to find my next job. I fully believed that my break made me a better candidate, so I highlighted it on my resume and shared more details in my cover letters and interviews. I eventually landed a dream job, where my manager later confessed that he knew he'd found the person he'd been searching for when he saw my cover letter and resume come through the system.

Handling disapproval

If you show up in full belief and confidence, the vast majority of people will support you and see the value of your break, but not everyone will "get it." There will likely be a few who are stuck in old ways of thinking and doubt the wisdom and benefits of your decision. But the great news is that it doesn't matter; you don't need everyone to agree that your break was a good idea to land a great job (or jobs).

If you encounter a naysayer or doubter who threatens your confidence, revisit your list of 25 benefits and recommit to the belief that a better you emerged because of this break (visit Chapter 7 for additional support). Remember that they are projecting their own limiting beliefs about what's possible for *them* onto you. They live in a world where miracles like breaks don't exist. Have compassion (a world without breaks is a sad and exhausting place) and reject their fears and doubts. Let them keep their limiting beliefs while you focus on the places and people who can see the value of what you've accomplished.

WARNING

If potential employers and team members can't see the value of your break, take it as a sign that the opportunity and the culture weren't a good fit for you. However, if you receive the same critique from multiple sources, review the feedback for opportunities to improve your approach. For example, you may want to strengthen your candidacy by reworking your resume, honing your interview skills, reframing the message around your break, or developing a complementary and relevant job skill.

ANECDOTE

During my re-entry period, I reconnected with a recruiter who'd reached out to me at the beginning of my break. While she was excited to work with me, she confessed that my break was a "red flag" to future employers and that I should be prepared to accept a demotion and reduction in salary. She assured me I could eventually build back up to where I once was, but that I needed to lower my expectations if I wanted to find a good job after my break. I chose not to work with her and rejected her suggestion. It was just an opinion, not a fact. I believed that anyone who hired me was getting a great deal. I didn't lower my standards, and I didn't settle. Of my five offers, one was for a dream job that paid a similar salary in a better location and another was for a role that came with a 30 percent raise and a promotion. I proved her wrong, but if I'd been willing to buy into her limiting beliefs, I would have settled for much less.

Creating your professional toolkit

As you prepare to re-enter the job market, you need to set aside time to update key job search materials. Your resume, online profile, and cover letters offer companies a first impression of you, so how you represent yourself and your break matters. Investing time to thoughtfully update and tailor your materials before you start the application process will pay dividends, helping you land a great job much sooner.

These materials provide an opportunity for you to tell a compelling story about your time away, bridge the gap between your break and the desired role, and emphasize your achievements and expertise. A strategically highlighted break helps you stand out, so don't neglect this opportunity to shine a light on the benefits of your break and signal to your future employer that you're excited and ready to dive into your next challenge.

Updating your CV or resume

Your resume or CV provides a great opportunity to highlight your break experience. Here you can frame your break in a positive light and give some insight into your character and values, which is important information for potential employers. The secret to nailing this part is sharing a few nuggets that help you stand out from the crowd and leave hiring teams curious to know more. When it comes to highlighting a break on your resume, you can include it in either the Additional Information or Experience section. The approach you take depends on the length of your break and the number of experiences you want to highlight. The longer your break, the more important the additional context is for your resume and cover letters.

When I updated my resume, career breaks were pretty taboo, so I chose to mention my break in the Additional Info section and lean into more detail in my cover letters.

Here's how I referenced my break in the Additional Information section on my resume and succinctly hinted at using that time to do some really cool things:

> Recently completed a 1-year trip around the world. Certified yoga instructor. Passionate about health & nutrition. Conversational in Spanish. Passed Actuarial Exams 1-4. Pro Bono Consultant. Active in corporate diversity recruitment.

If you've had an extensive break (six months or longer) or have activities and/or accomplishments you'd like to highlight, the Experience section is a great place to share an overview of your break. For this approach, you need to do the following:

1. **Create a title or short description that summarizes the purpose of your break.**

   Examples include Family Sabbatical, Learning Sabbatical, Personal Sabbatical, Planned Career Break, Travel Break, and Wellness Sabbatical.

2. **List the dates of your break.**

3. **Share a few key experiences and achievements.**

   Consider including things like the following: relocation, gaining a certification, traveling or starting a creative pursuit like blogging or podcasting, courses taken or fellowships completed, independent projects, newly acquired skills, noteworthy personal projects, and volunteer experiences.

Figure 14-1 provides several examples of how to share your break in the Experience section.

Updating my resume was the most painful part of my post-break job search, but longer breaks aren't nearly as taboo or unusual as they were in 2013 (when I started my break), which is an advantage for you. Now you have access to amazing resources like career coaches and AI tools that will help you develop top-notch, tailored resumes.

TIP

If you need or want support in updating your resume (and other job search materials), you can source helpful feedback from career coaches, resume experts, online templates, and/or AI resume writing tools.

Refreshing your online presence

Having a strong online presence can boost your visibility and success rate during the job search. As part of your preparation, consider updating your information on platforms and in online spaces that are most aligned with your current career goals. Here are some ideas:

>> **Blog:** Pull together articles (previously written or newly created) that highlight your knowledge and expertise and/or shed more light on the journey and learning you've acquired during your break.

Travel and Wellness Break,
July 2023 – Present

- Embarked on a solo backpacking journey across Southeast Asia, eating my way through six countries and gaining valuable insights into global perspectives.
- Pursued a personal passion for photography, documenting my travel experiences and honing my skills as a visual storyteller.
- Committed to personal well-being and pursued an intensive health and fitness program, ran my first marathon and significantly improved my overall fitness.

Planned Career Break with Entrepreneurial Pursuits,
Jan. 2023 – Nov. 2023

- Founded and managed a small online business, designing and selling handmade jewelry through e-commerce platforms.
- Developed a personal blog and social media presence to share my experience and inspire others to pursue their passions—grew to more than 2k followers in just 90 days.
- Launched and hosted a self-produced podcast, *Adorned & Inspired*, featuring interviews with top makers and artists, focused on marketing and innovation.

Family Sabbatical,
April 2023 – Present

- Temporarily relocated to the countryside of Tuscany, Italy, embracing a slower-paced lifestyle and immersing our family in local culture and traditions.
- Engaged in a homeschooling adventure, blending educational curriculum with hands-on experiences, such as exploring ancient ruins, studying Renaissance art, and mastering the art of making homemade pasta and gelato.

FIGURE 14-1: Examples of highlighting your break in the Experience section of your resume.

>> **Social media:** Curate your profile to highlight the benefits and achievements from your break while announcing your return to the job market.

>> **Website:** Create a space to share a portfolio of your work and sample of your talents. You can also highlight client testimonials here.

TIP

LinkedIn is a helpful social media platform for job seekers. Here, you can share your expertise, connect with a broad network, and search for jobs. LinkedIn also includes a feature that lets you easily share your career break status. Access this feature by updating your experience and selecting Add Career Break. From here, you can choose from 13 types of breaks and provide context about your experience.

Figure 14-2 shows an example of how to use the LinkedIn career break feature for a high-level summary of your break experience.

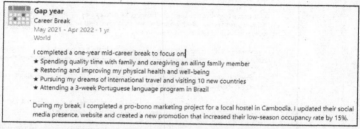

FIGURE 14-2: An example of using LinkedIn's career break feature to share high-level details about the break.

By contrast, Figure 14-3 provides an example of how to use the LinkedIn career break feature for a more detailed overview of your break experience.

Highlighting your break in a cover letter

When you're returning from a break, cover letters are your friend (and a necessary part of the job search process), because they provide an opportunity for you to own the narrative around your break and create a positive association. Here, you can showcase its value and explain how it made you a stronger job candidate than you would have otherwise been. By sharing this part of yourself, you are also highlighting your character, values, and willingness to seek personal growth and alignment — qualities many employers admire.

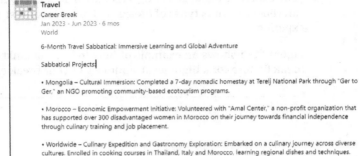

Travel
Career Break
Jan 2023 - Jun 2023 · 6 mos
World

6-Month Travel Sabbatical: Immersive Learning and Global Adventure

Sabbatical Projects

• Mongolia – Cultural Immersion: Completed a 7-day nomadic homestay at Terelj National Park through "Ger to Ger," an NGO promoting community-based ecotourism programs.

• Morocco – Economic Empowerment Initiative: Volunteered with "Amal Center," a non-profit organization that has supported over 300 disadvantaged women in Morocco on their journey towards financial independence through culinary training and job placement.

• Worldwide – Culinary Expedition and Gastronomy Exploration: Embarked on a culinary journey across diverse cultures. Enrolled in cooking courses in Thailand, Italy and Morocco, learning regional dishes and techniques.

• Personal Wellness Pursuit – Explored holistic well-being through attending local yoga, breathwork and meditation retreats, deepening my practice and understanding.

Through this sabbatical, I pursued personal exploration and professional development. Each chapter contributed to my growth, allowing me to blend newfound passions with existing expertise, ultimately leading to a broader understanding and more well-rounded perspective.

FIGURE 14-3: An example of using LinkedIn's career break feature to share more in-depth details about the break.

TIP

As you begin outlining your cover letter, list any notable achievements, developments, and new skills or certifications you've acquired during your break. Narrow your list down to the most relevant items, which may vary by application, and incorporate them into your cover letters to highlight your desirability.

A cover letter should include why you're applying for the role (what makes it so appealing to you), an overview of your professional background, and an explanation of why you're uniquely qualified for the role. This is also your opportunity to explain your break in a bit more detail, while leaning in to why you think you're an ideal match for the job.

When it comes to explaining your break, weave in highlights of your break (see the previous activity for help with this) and be sure to mention aspects of your break that align with the company's mission and values or that supported your development in a relevant way.

The following is a general structure you can follow for your post-career break cover letters.

>> **Intro:** State the position you're applying for and how you learned about it. Convey your interest and enthusiasm for the role and company.

>> **Body:** Address your break by sharing a few highlights from your career break story that demonstrate relevant values, strengths, and/or passions. Move on to connect your background and previous accomplishments with the requirements of the current job. Be sure to explain what makes you the perfect candidate, providing a couple of brief examples that bring these qualities to life.

>> **Close:** End your letter expressing gratitude for "the company's consideration and clarifying any potential issues with your candidacy or resume.

REMEMBER

Taking a break demonstrates your commitment to growth, making brave decisions, and taking a sustainable path toward your professional success. These are great qualities that help make you an attractive job candidate. If your break had an involuntary start, please know that stepping up to create a positive experience that yielded many benefits after a challenging start is an impressive skill.

TIP

If you get stuck or want help developing your cover letters, seek out templates, support, and feedback from career coaches, career-focused websites, and AI models like ChatGPT.

ANECDOTE

Because career breaks were uncommon when I began searching for jobs, I used my cover letter to really sell the value of my break. I essentially said, "You might notice this gap on my resume. Let me tell you about how amazing it was, and why it made me an even better candidate for this role!" In the past, I'd avoided cover letters at all costs, but I was able to land five job offers in five weeks because I wrote cover letters that connected the dots between my break and becoming a top candidate for each job I was applying for. I represented myself as a passionate person with relevant experience and skills, plus a newfound clarity on what I wanted in my next role.

Launching Your Post-Career Break Job Search

After you've built up your confidence, crafted your career break story, and started putting together your job search collateral, it's time to launch your search. This section covers how to approach it with clarity so you create a successful outcome. You find out how to use your break to make networking easier and explore options that align with your current goals and values. I also offer some tips to help you zoom ahead and crush your interviews.

Networking after a break

Networking is one of the most productive activities to focus on when you're searching for a new opportunity after a break. If the word *networking* makes you want to cringe or roll your eyes, don't skip over this section just yet! Your break provides an easy entry point for outreach and an engaging starting point for your conversations. People will be very receptive to connecting and curious to hear about your break. Many will admire your journey and be happy to make connections and suggestions to support your re-entry.

This is a great time to lean into networking, even if networking isn't normally your thing. Your break creates a natural and compelling opening to connect (or reconnect) with people in your orbit. These conversations can be low-pressure chats that help you

>> Explore your interest in adjacent (or completely different) roles than you've previously held

>> Learn about new and interesting opportunities and roles that might not have existed before your break

>> Refresh yourself and get up to speed on relevant and/or emerging topics in your industry

>> Understand the lay of the land for a company, industry, or role after time away

Figure 14-4 shows a great example of announcing your return from a break and beginning the networking process.

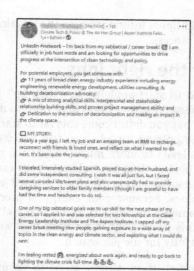

FIGURE 14-4: A LinkedIn post announcing the end of a career break.

REMEMBER

As you begin searching for your next role, be open to connecting and sharing with your extended network. The support and advice you'll receive can be invaluable in landing your next opportunity.

TIP

Don't overcomplicate your outreach. Lean into the interest and intrigue your break stirs up as you reach out to your extended network. Be sure to personalize your message, expressing interest in other people and what they're up to.

Beyond sourcing helpful information and potential opportunities, connecting with your network can also help you land referrals. Because many positions receive a lot of applications, having a referral can make a big difference in your job search. They can move you to the front of the line and help you stand out in a sea of qualified candidates. In the United States, research has shown that referrals account for 30 to 50 percent of all new employees, and referrals are four times more likely to be offered a job than website applicants.

TIP

As you find new companies you're interested in, check to see if you know someone who works there. LinkedIn is a great resource for this. If you do, consider reaching out to connect. If that goes well, you can make the bigger ask for a referral. The person may also be able to connect you with other people within the company who could give you additional information on the position and/or tips for the interview process.

Searching for the right jobs

You may feel tempted to start applying to "back up" jobs that you aren't really interested in. Your brain may want to direct you toward the easy wins, but you didn't come this far to start settling right out of the gate. Applying for jobs you feel like you should want but really don't leads to more misery down the road. The end of a break is the perfect time to recalibrate your career path and ensure you're pursuing options that are aligned with your current goals and values. Because your energy is precious and finite, you need to channel it into opportunities that you're genuinely interested in. This keeps your motivation high and allows you to show up powerfully for the job search.

Here, I walk you through three simple steps to ensure you're applying for the right jobs (and avoiding the wrong ones).

Know what you're looking for

Even if you're open to many possibilities, as you begin your job search it's helpful to have some clarity about what you're looking for. You might have a list of things you're hoping for in your next role or a list of things you desperately want to avoid. Whichever starting point you choose, the next activity helps you think through some important aspects of your future job, so you can feel clearer about your ideal job situation (which is vital to landing a job you want to keep!).

ACTIVITY

Reflect on the following list and take note of your preferences. Rate each as a 1 (top), 2 (mid), or 3 (low) priority to organize them by level of importance and help you evaluate your opportunities:

>> Benefits (healthcare, 401k, equity, sabbaticals)

>> Company details (size, public vs. private entity)

>> Level of intellectual stimulation

>> Location (on-site, hybrid, remote, commute)

>> Paid time off (vacation, illness, disability, family leave)

>> Provided learning opportunities

>> Salary and compensation (current and future potential)

- » Schedule (rigid, flexible, spacious)
- » Sense of meaning and contribution
- » Team culture
- » Values alignment

Determine your nonnegotiables

It's likely that your perspective on work and life has shifted over the course of your break. You may feel open to new possibilities and have a sense of deep reprioritization as you begin searching for your next role. To honor this change and sustain your new perspective, I highly recommend determining the nonnegotiables for your next role. This makes your evaluation and decision processes much easier and helps you ensure you feel aligned with your next opportunity.

Your nonnegotiables create a new standard for your work life and next chapter. They provide guardrails to help you evaluate your opportunities. Specifically, getting clear on your nonnegotiables helps you

- » **Avoid analysis paralysis when comparing opportunities:** Because you want to make the best choice possible, your brain might want to compare and contrast every detail and possible trajectory for each option. But it can't predict the future (as much as it might want to) and this approach leaves you fixating on details that aren't significant. When you can simplify and filter your options through this lens, you avoid feeling overwhelmed by trying to account for every possible nuance.

- » **Filter out a bad fit that seems very appealing:** Sometimes a poor fit can come wrapped in a very attractive package. When this happens, you may be tempted to ignore the red flags and justify the sacrifices you'd need to make. Using this approach helps you evaluate exciting opportunities and ensure they meet your minimum requirements to set you up for success.

- » **Recognize hidden opportunities you might otherwise overlook:** This approach helps you spot great opportunities in disguise. It can be easy to dismiss things that are unfamiliar and different from what you're used to, but maybe you'll discover an opportunity that you wouldn't have previously considered.

Be sure to set your nonnegotiables before you begin pursuing opportunities. Things can get a bit murky if you develop them after your brain has attached itself to a new possibility. It may want to ignore red flags or overemphasize something that's no longer as important to you. Avoid this trap by determining your three nonnegotiables right away.

To help you start to think through your nonnegotiables, I'm including several examples from past clients:

>> **Access to a healthier lifestyle:** If you desire freedom and autonomy in your schedule to help you balance your physical well-being and pursue a healthier lifestyle

>> **Adequate parental leave:** If you're planning to have a child in the future

>> **Affordable quality health insurance:** If you or a family member is dealing with a critical and potentially expensive health situation

>> **Minimum level of compensation:** If you're returning from a break concerned about your financial situation

>> **Supportive team and culture:** If you thrive in collaborative environments and want to avoid an overly competitive culture or want to work where you can stretch your wings and grow

>> **Time to pursue hobbies and outside interests:** If your break helped you realize that you heavily value time to cultivate other aspects of your life

ACTIVITY

Determine your three nonnegotiables. There are no right or wrong answers. Be honest with yourself and embrace your answers. Consider what seems critical for your next step. What do you need to feel good about your decision and know that your biggest needs and desires are being met? Choose three things your new situation absolutely has to have or three things it absolutely can't have (or a mix of both!). Whatever your answers, your three nonnegotiables are the new minimum requirements for your next opportunity, so choose wisely and hold fast to your new standard as you begin evaluating your options.

REMEMBER

It's worth noting that your new nonnegotiables may be remarkably different from your previous ones. Be careful not to mindlessly default back to your old priorities. Give serious consideration to what currently matters most in your life and what you want for your next chapter. Post-break you may have outgrown certain aspects of your old life. For example, maybe you're ready to trade in your corporate ladder climbing for more balance and autonomy. Be sure to reflect on what you need to feel satisfied and fulfilled in this current stage of life.

WARNING

Three is the magic number when it comes to nonnegotiables. This tool is useful because of its simplicity. Adding more than three items to your list quickly complicates things. You may have to devalue items on your list or prioritize some over others, defeating the purpose of this exercise. If something doesn't meet your nonnegotiables, it should be a non-starter, and it's easier to enforce this when you only have three.

ANECDOTE

One of my clients was searching for an opportunity that would allow enough time to pursue her artistic passions outside of work. When she was approached with a part-time job, her immediate thought was to turn it down. But as she reflected on her nonnegotiables, she realized that it met all three, including her requirement for balance between work and her personal life, and was something she could seriously consider. She eventually accepted the job and quickly grew within the organization, while managing to dedicate time to pursuing her passion.

Explore aligned opportunities

Hot off the heels of your break, you may enter the job search wanting to create more alignment in your next chapter. If this is your goal, this section covers how to achieve it as you begin searching for your next opportunity.

To be an aligned opportunity, a job doesn't necessarily have to be a dream job (although it definitely could be!), but it does have to be an opportunity that genuinely interests or excites you. There may be some aspects of your new job that truly light you up and others that you're indifferent about — this is still alignment. Think of alignment as heading in the right direction. Does the job move you closer to the life you want or farther away? The benefit of taking this approach, beyond finding an opportunity you're excited to accept, is that you'll come across as a more authentic and compelling candidate.

REMEMBER

Don't pressure yourself to land your dream job immediately after your break. It's OK if your next role doesn't completely match your new vision for your life. Using the activity in the section "Knowing what you're looking for" can help you prioritize your preferences and ensure you find a more aligned role. Your next job may be a steppingstone to your ideal life, and that's great news. It means things are moving in the right direction!

When you're ready to begin searching for aligned opportunities, you want to start with companies or roles that "speak to you" for one reason or another. From this starting point, you give yourself permission to explore new possibilities and dig deeper into companies, roles, or opportunities that spark your interest. To help you get started, here are four ways to approach aligned job searching:

>> **Research businesses or organizations that you believe in and/or want to contribute to:** Explore company websites and articles that cover organizations that align with your values and interests. See what positions they're currently hiring for to learn whether there are opportunities you may want to consider. You could also pursue a volunteer opportunity to learn more about them and experience their culture firsthand.

>> **Explore roles that intrigue and interest you:** Using a job search platform like Indeed or LinkedIn, use keywords to find roles that utilize your strengths and align with your interests. You may discover new or emerging roles that are adjacent to your expertise and a better fit for your future goals. From here, you can start searching for companies and businesses hiring for those types of roles.

>> **Look at companies that you admire, that share your values, and/or that provide products or services that you love and appreciate:** Start with brands you like and admire. Peruse their websites and job boards to see what positions they're currently hiring for. You may discover adjacent roles that some minor upskilling or intentional networking can unlock. You can also use a networking tool like LinkedIn to search for potential connections who may be able to give you the inside scoop on the company and its job openings or refer you for an open position.

>> **Search for opportunities in highly desirable locations and/or that provide the lifestyle that you want to live (digital nomad, remote worker):** If location or lifestyle is important to you, explore businesses that align with your

goals. If you want to move to a new city, check out which companies are headquartered there or search for fully remote companies that would allow you to work from home. You can also search for top jobs or companies that hire digital nomads or remote employees.

ANECDOTE

One job I applied to at the end of my break was located in Baltimore, Maryland. This apparently wasn't a selling point for most job applicants. However, I was genuinely interested in moving closer to my family in West Virginia. So, during my interview, I leaned into this aspect of alignment to convey my genuine interest in relocating to Baltimore. Because they sometimes struggled to retain employees due to their location, they were excited to have a candidate they believed would stick around if offered the job. While not everything about this opportunity was aligned with my post-break goals, I truly would have loved the opportunity to be closer to my family. This allowed me to authentically show interest and create another selling point for hiring me (and, yes, they did end up offering me a job . . . with a big raise and promotion!).

Acing your interviews

As you move through the job search process, you need to prepare for addressing your break and highlighting the benefits in your interviews. Your success in interviews comes from confidence and belief in your decision to take a break and being able to frame it in a positive light that showcases how it's increased your potential value to the company. Don't forget the value of focusing on jobs that align with your values and goals; lean into this alignment to share a compelling reason why you want the role and connect more authentically with the interviewer.

TIP

Be prepared for and open to discussing your break during your interviews. Think about tying your answers (when relevant) to benefits the employer may value or also benefit from. To fully prepare, complete the activity for crafting your career break story in "Authentically hyping up your break" earlier in this chapter.

Almost half of my interviews contained questions about my break, some born of spontaneous curiosity and others conducted as a strategic assessment. In both cases, I leaned into my enthusiasm for the break and, when I was able to, I did my best to tie my answers back to tangible ways my break made me an even stronger candidate for the desired role and company.

ACTIVITY

List 25 benefits you've received from your break (see the activity in the "Authentically hyping up your break" section for more details) and consider it from an employer's perspective. How might they benefit from your experiences, achievements, and activities? Considering "what's in it for them" will help you convey the value of your break in a meaningful way during the interview process.

To help you get started, here are a few examples of break benefits that can improve your professional desirability:

>> Arriving flush with new ideas and innovative solutions

>> Becoming more skilled and resourceful (studying a language, completing courses or certifications)

>> Feeling clearer about how you'd like to contribute and inspired to positively impact others

>> Returning physically restored, well-rested, and fully recharged

TIP

You can use an AI model, like ChatGPT, to significantly enhance your interview preparation. It can provide question prompts based on job descriptions and interview topics, give instant feedback on your interview responses, and help you mine your specific work examples and career break experience to create strong, tailored responses.

As you prepare for your interviews, it's helpful to reflect on your stories with stellar results. Using this approach, you'll create an opportunity to share your strongest stories and examples, highlighting your skills and strengths. So, if you're prompted to share a big challenge you've overcome, you can retrofit your answer to include one of your best examples, instead of using an example that fits the "biggest challenge" requirement but produced only mediocre results. If you'd like to take this approach, follow these four steps:

1. **Brainstorm which stories you'd most like to share with potential employers.**

   What are the amazing wins and experiences that highlight your skills and talents, both in your career and during your career break? Have you won any awards or received any special recognition?

2. **Refresh yourself on key details, jotting down a few key bullet points for each, so you can relay them in a cohesive framework (like the STAR method) during your interview.**

   - STAR stands for Situation, Task, Action, Result. The following article provides more information about this common interview technique (www.themuse.com/advice/star-interview-method).

3. **Pull together common interview questions you might be asked.**

   Here are two examples:

   - Describe a situation where you had to work with a difficult team member.
   - Tell me about a time when you had to meet a tight deadline or handle a high-pressure situation.

4. **Review your examples and note which questions or prompts they could apply to.**

It's likely that your best stories apply to several different prompts or scenarios. After you've followed this process, you'll have a cheat sheet of killer examples that you can use to answer questions or prompts in any interview!

» **Allowing the new version of you to emerge**

» **Creating a vision for life after the break**

Chapter **15**
Thriving Beyond the Break

As you near the end of this thrilling ride, it's time to start thinking about your life beyond the break — not just what you'll do for work but also how you want to experience life. In this chapter, you discover how to embrace the new you that's emerging and how to carry forward the positive changes and benefits you've created through your break. You'll end this experience on a high note and learn how to create a lasting change that will ripple through the rest of your life.

Sustaining the Benefits of a Break

After a restorative and freedom-filled break, you might be wondering how you'll return to work without sacrificing the positive changes and benefits you've just experienced. Maybe you're worried about reverting back to an unsustainable pace or unhealthy lifestyle when the work demands start piling on. Well, I have good news: Returning to a life full of responsibilities and professional obligations doesn't have to jeopardize the peace and balance you've just created. In this section, I walk you through a four-step approach that will help you continue thriving and reaping benefits from your break, even after you've returned to work.

Establishing supportive routines and habits at the beginning of your next chapter will help you preserve your well-being and avoid defaulting back into unhealthy habits and patterns. (Undesirable habits are 100 times harder to break if you let them take root and then have to undo them again.) So, don't hesitate to start the process I'm about to lay out for you.

Celebrating your journey

Cue the confetti. The next phase of your life starts with celebration! Before you start to design your next chapter and integrate your new self into that design, first celebrate the journey you've just been on. Your brain will want to downplay your accomplishment now that the adventure's behind you. (Brains are sneaky like that — they like to raise the bar on us after we've achieved a big goal.) Avoid the urge to gloss over your accomplishment. Make time to celebrate your courage and affirm that you can do hard things, even when there's a ton of uncertainty involved.

Many people wish they could do what you've just done. You are an inspiration. You overcame fear, doubt, and discomfort to follow your heart and approach life in a new way. You shed old identities that no longer fit and explored new possibilities. What you've just accomplished is worthy of celebration.

To help the magnitude of your accomplishment sink in, revisit your break, noting the highlights and challenging moments you've overcome. Reflecting on your progress will help you achieve a deeper level of celebration. Here are a few ways you can recap your journey in preparation for the celebration:

>> If you journaled during your break, reread your entries or social media posts and reflect on your growth and how you've overcome fear and uncertainty to arrive at this very moment.

>> If you took a break with someone else, set aside time to reflect and reminisce together. This will provide an even better recap of all that you've done.

>> Relive the highlights and bright spots of your break by reviewing your timeline and calendar or itinerary. Take note of the high points and growth you've experienced along the way.

>> Revisit old photos, starting from the planning phase of your break and moving through the entire experience. Remember how overwhelming this break once felt, as you reflect on how far you've come.

TIP

Once you've finished reflecting on your journey and acknowledging your wins, consider sharing your experience to encourage others. You can share your biggest lessons and celebrate your accomplishments via a blog or social media post and inspire others to consider taking a break too.

ACTIVITY

After you've taken it all it, it's time to celebrate! Make a plan for how you will do this. You can do it alone or with others to amplify the positive energy. (I recommend both!) You could throw yourself an "end of break" party, go out for a celebratory meal, take a special day trip or hike, or curate a quiet moment of reflection to celebrate during your final days. However you choose to mark the occasion, be intentional about embracing a spirit of celebration and appreciation.

Incorporating what worked well

If you want to sustain the positive impact of your break and take it into your next chapter, you need to create a plan for incorporating the most beneficial aspects of your break into your new reality. I have a simple four-step approach to identifying the benefits and lessons you want to carry forward and developing a plan to infuse them into your next chapter.

WARNING

Don't delay in starting this process! Waiting until you feel comfortable and settled in your new role to thoughtfully reflect on what you'd like to incorporate from your break makes it much harder to establish the new habits and routines that support your overall well-being.

Reflect on your experience

Reflecting on the lessons, benefits, and personal growth you've experienced helps you understand what worked well and uncovers what you want to leave behind as you begin your next chapter.

This process will also help you set better boundaries and protect your well-being. Here are five questions to reflect on and some examples for each:

» **What important lessons have I learned from my break?**
- I thrive with autonomy and flexibility.
- Being socially connected is important for my mental health.
- I no longer want to be an accountant.

» **What worked well for me in regard to my break lifestyle?**
- Daily movement improved my energy.
- Having clear boundaries with my schedule made my life feel calmer and more joyful.

» **What aspects do I want to keep, even if I have to modify them?**
- Going to bed before 11 p.m.
- Having 20 minutes of stillness every morning
- Turning my email notifications off during the weekend

» **What am I no longer willing to accept in my life as I return to work?**
- Working after 6 p.m.
- Not having at least one responsibility-free day each week
- Not seeing my family at least three times each year

» **What will I intentionally not allow myself to re-create in my next chapter?**
- Working full-time on-site — must have a hybrid or remote work option
- A life without hobbies — must spend time pursuing interests weekly

Create a clear list of benefits

When you have an understanding of what worked well and what didn't, distill your answers down to a clear list of benefits that you want to sustain when you return to work. It's OK if these are general; you get more specific in the next step. Here are some examples to help you get started:

- Adequate downtime and rest
- Better work-life balance than before the break
- Consistent healthy habits and routines
- Deeper and expanded connection with others
- Incorporating more travel and adventure
- Living by a new measure of success
- Pursuing hobbies, interests, and passions
- Self-care practices
- Time for creative pursuits
- Time for learning and exploring

Make your list accessible

Now it's time to make your list actionable. This is where you need more specificity. The goal of this step is to strategize how you'll incorporate and nurture the aspects of your break that you want to bring with you into your new life. For every benefit on your list, you need to do the following:

- **Create a specific target or goal.** If you chose "work-life balance" as a benefit to keep, get specific on what that looks like for you. Is it ending work by 6 p.m.? Never working on weekends? Having a complete morning routine before you begin your work day? Or, if you chose "time for creative pursuits," you can decide which creative pursuits you'd like to explore and how often you'd like to pursue them (weekly, semiweekly, and so on).

- **Make it accessible.** After you've set your goals, you need to make sure your list is accessible. Work takes up a significant amount of time, so it's important to be realistic and set an attainable goal so you can create a sustainable practice you can keep up with. If you find you have too many initiatives, prioritize your list and start with your top three.

Hold yourself accountable

To stay on track, you can schedule future check-ins. Pull out your calendar and determine your check-in cadence (I recommend at least monthly). Set reminders so you won't forget, and plan to revisit your list during each check-in. It's OK if your priorities change or your schedule demands a modification.

WHAT TO DO WHEN YOU'VE CHANGED BUT THE PATH YOU'RE RETURNING TO HASN'T

If you're planning to return to a similar role, company, or career path, you may question how you'll maintain the new version of yourself while operating in a familiar environment. Will all of your progress be erased by a pull to default to old patterns, like neglecting your health or deprioritizing your life outside of work?

Although the path ahead will feel familiar, the changes you experienced during your break can create an entirely different reality. Not only can you choose to continue embracing the positive changes from your break, you also may realize you're showing up with a new perspective, a new attitude, and a new approach to work and life. And this change can lead to benefits, like increased enjoyment at work, improved performance, better work-life balance, and more innovative ideas. If you follow the four-step process outlined in this section, you'll be able to create an entirely new experience of your professional life.

TIP

Set yourself up for success by creating an affirming ritual around your check-ins. Finding ways to make them more fun and rewarding will help you stay consistent and increase your enjoyment. Whether you do your check-in at your favorite cafe or treat yourself to a pedicure or a walk through a park once it's over, sprinkle some goodness into your check-in routine to create a positive and motivating experience.

TIP

Be sure to set realistic expectations for yourself. Your goal isn't to achieve a perfect balance; it's to continue learning, growing, and moving along a path that feels aligned. If you notice something isn't working, you can always update your approach to make it more approachable and sustainable.

Inspiring others with your story

One of the best long-term benefits of taking a break is having the opportunity to inspire others to chase their own dreams. When you share your story with others, you're providing an example of what's possible and planting seeds for them to do the same.

Your ability to courageously step away from the familiar markers of success and prioritize your own happiness and well-being will make you an inspiration to others.

Allowing your break to encourage and inspire others will bring more meaning to your experience and help solidify the positive impact your break has had on your life. You expand the positive impact of your break by extending it to others.

Be prepared. You'll likely face a lot of questions about your experience. Try to frame it as curiosity (and not judgment). Most people are truly awestruck by your decision to take a break.

Back in 2011, when I started planning for a one-year break, I didn't have social media or online communities to draw from for inspirational stories and examples. But I was hungry for firsthand experiences and the opportunity to ask a ton of logistical questions. When my friend Rachel heard about my new goal, she happily connected me with Jen, who'd recently completed a travel break with her partner. Jen became an invaluable resource and source of inspiration for me. When things felt impossible or I was swimming in doubt, I reminded myself that Jen did it, and I could, too. Don't underestimate the impact your break can have on others. After your break, you have the opportunity to inspire others and show them what's possible.

Embracing the New You

Returning to a variation of your old life may initially feel uncomfortable and a bit unsettling. You'll likely start to notice how you've changed in new ways, which means some parts of your pre-break life might not fit as well as they once did. In this section, I explain how you can accept and embrace the new version of you that's emerged and map out a vision for an aligned next chapter.

Be prepared for things to feel a bit wonky as you end your break and return to work. It can be surreal to return to "regular life" and be surrounded by pieces of your past while feeling like a different person with a new perspective. If this is you, I want you to know that this feeling is completely normal and temporary. You will adjust and find a new normal.

Accepting the changes

As you return from your break, be prepared to see life through a different lens. A break creates space for a clearer and stronger you to emerge, and it can shift your priorities and desires in the process. It's normal to feel like you've outgrown aspects of your old life after a break. Whether you want to forge a completely new path or continue along the previous one with a new approach, I encourage you to embrace the new you and the changes that you're desiring.

REMEMBER

Some of your friends or loved ones may initially struggle to understand the changes. They might expect everything to return to "normal" now, but if you've changed, it's likely that your definition of "normal" has changed, too. This is all OK. Remember that your break was once a big goal that some couldn't understand . . . and look at you now!

Outgrowing people or aspects of your pre-break life can be very uncomfortable and disappointing. But it's also evidence of your growth. If you could snap right back into your old life without any tension, it would be a sign that not much has changed. If growth was one of your goals, take the discomfort as proof that you've achieved it. And remember that when you eliminate or reconfigure things to align with your new priorities and values, you're also creating space for more aligned relationships and opportunities to come into your life.

TIP

Don't fight the changes or try to force yourself back into the old box to feel more harmony with your pre-break life. Part of creating a lasting and positive change through a break is being able to accept the differences. If you stay curious and open and honor your new values and priorities, you'll create a new experience of life that feels even better than before.

ANECDOTE

After studying abroad for a year, Kristen made the bold decision to find a job in her new country. She was excited but also nervous about coordinating the logistics. She was also worried about the pushback she might receive from loved ones, who assumed she'd return after her break. This was a much bigger goal than pre-break Kristen would have dreamed up, but after more than a year of extending her comfort zone and achieving big goals (like taking a one-year break to study abroad), she felt ready to tackle becoming an expat. Ultimately, she secured a job and was able to continue following her exciting new path.

Setting a vision for your next chapter

As you move into your next chapter, taking a moment to set an intention and vision for your future will get you much closer to your ideal experience. You don't need to have all the details figured out, but (similar to planning for a break) being clear about your overall vision will make it easier to achieve. After you've set a vision, you'll be able to make decisions that support and align with your ideal life.

Don't shrink your dreams. As you start to develop a vision for your future, you may feel empowered to set bigger goals than pre-break you would have been comfortable with. Don't be alarmed. Your imagination, comfort zone, and expectations of what's possible are growing, and this is a great thing!

Work your way through the following list and score each aspect of life based on your current satisfaction level (with 1 being complete dissatisfied and 10 being completely satisfied). Next, revisit the list and describe what a 10 would look like for each aspect. Your answers will paint a clearer picture of your ideal life.

>> Career

>> Community

>> Friends and Family

>> Fun

>> Health

>> Learning

>> Money

>> Romance

Now you're going to visualize your ideal life. Set a timer (for 5 to 10 minutes) and allow yourself to slowly walk through your ideal day. Then extend the visualization into your ideal week. Notice what you're doing, where you're doing it, and how you feel as you move through the various parts of your day. It's OK if some parts feel vague or blurry; just focus on the details that you do know to paint a picture of your ideal day and week. Reflect on your answers and jot down the key things that come up in your vision.

Once you've uncovered the key characteristics of your ideal life, be sure to keep them top of mind when making decisions about where to invest your time and energy. Incorporating these characteristics into your life will bring you closer to your ideal experience.

Considering another break

I need to make a confession. This book should have come with a warning label. Once you've broken free of the rat race and tasted the freedom and possibility of a break, it's likely that you'll want to take another one, because now you know that they aren't life-ending, career-ruining adventures. In fact, you return from them feeling better than before — and that's some pretty potent stuff.

I've tried to refrain from referring to a break as a once-in-a-lifetime experience in this book for this very reason. Even before their first day back at the office, the majority of my clients declare plans to take another break in the next three to five years. And many have become break advocates who encourage and support coworkers and friends to take breaks, too.

Taking breaks can become a gateway to a more sustainable and enjoyable approach to life, and you may decide to do this all again (just like I did). When you allow yourself to dream bigger and beyond the obstacles you see in front of you, the sky becomes the limit, and you set yourself free to accomplish very big things.

6
The Part of Tens

Discover the basic ground rules for creating a successful and life-changing career break experience.

Get a glimpse of ten incredible, real-life examples of what you can do on a career break.

Chapter **16**
Ten Ground Rules for a Successful Break

I f I had to simplify my best advice for knocking your break out of the park, it would come down to the ten suggestions in this chapter. From the preparation stage to re-entry, these are the ground rules to follow to ensure you have a successful break. These rules will help you build a solid foundation and navigate your break with more joy and ease. And when you're ready to return to work after your break, these rules will make sure you land on both feet.

Creating Your Own Definition of Success

"If success is not on your own terms, if it looks good to the world but does not feel good in your heart, it is not success at all."

—ANNA QUINDLEN

This statement rings especially true when it comes to designing your break. Having a successful break hinges on your ability to understand what a successful break means to you. Having a clear purpose statement allows you to get what you came for — a break that fulfills you. (Check out Chapter 4 for two questions that will help you unlock your purpose statement.)

WARNING

Don't try to replicate someone else's experience. Just because it looks good or worked for them doesn't mean the same experience will give you what you need. Designing a break to meet your own unique needs and desires is the recipe for success.

Planning for a Re-Entry Period

You need to be proactive when it comes to setting yourself up for a successful return to the workforce. Trust me, you don't want to rush back into the job market feeling desperate and disoriented. Incorporating a re-entry period into your plan ensures you have time to process your experience, set your next goal, and create a smooth transition.

Chapter 4 includes the 1 for 6 rule that helps you dedicate enough time and money to this transition period.

Knowing Your Numbers

I can't overstate the importance of assessing your financial landscape before taking a break. At a minimum, you should calculate an overall estimated cost for your break and develop a rough budget, which will help you stay on track and avoid running out of money during your break. Chapter 5 guides you through both of these steps and helps you feel more financially grounded.

If you're still saving for a break, following these two steps helps you see exactly how far you are from your goal as of now. This critical information can help you stay motivated and reach your savings goal much faster. Chapter 5 also provides several steps to reach your savings goal faster.

Leaving Your Job on Great Terms

Did you know it's possible to leave your job on great terms and without burning bridges when you decide to take a break? Sharing your news in the right way can create more professional opportunities for you in the future and create advocates who want to cheer you on and support your break.

When it's time to give your notice, you'll want to confidently express your purpose statement and frame it in a positive light, focusing on what you hope to achieve through the break. Check out Chapter 7 for guidance on what to say and when to say it as you're giving your notice.

Disconnecting from the Working World

It may be difficult at first, but one of the best things you can do for yourself is to fully disconnect from your work life when you start the break. Your brain might want to panic about being out of the loop, losing touch with your network, and falling behind in your career. But that's what the re-entry period is for. (See Chapter 4 for more on this topic.) You can reconnect with everyone and everything after you've achieved the main goals of your break. Otherwise, staying connected to work through your entire break makes you less likely to focus on your personal goals and more likely to stress about what comes after the break. Creating a full separation deeply restores you and allows you to be present in your nonwork life.

If you're on a sabbatical, fully disconnecting can be challenging at first. You may have to break deeply ingrained habits, like checking your email 249 times a day, but I know you can do it! Letting go of work frees up so much mental space and allows you to achieve a deeper level of rest and restoration.

Putting the Focus Back on You

Sometimes career breakers try to shrink from the light of their own break. For instance, they might focus on making their break "productive" and try to design a break that makes them a better worker (that is, more desirable to future employers). Others might lose themselves in their caregiving duties and forget to give equal weight to their own needs.

If this is happening to you, I want you to put the focus back on YOU. Don't worry about becoming a stronger candidate. If you explore new interests, take good care of yourself, and have some fun, a more desirable version of you will naturally emerge. And if you're incorporating caregiver duties, be sure to carve out time to fulfill your own needs and desires, too. You can proactively set boundaries and expectations with other caregivers or partners involved to avoid potential conflicts and ensure everyone's on the same page. Remember, everybody wins when you prioritize taking care of yourself.

Giving Yourself Some Grace

This rule can be one of the most challenging ones to follow. Your break will be an exciting and bumpy adventure full of growth, highs, and lows. You will learn as you go, so you're bound to stumble a time or two (or more). Don't judge yourself for it and don't make yourself wrong if it takes some time to adjust to being on a break. As magical as it may sound, a break can initially feel uncomfortable (especially if you struggle to give yourself permission to rest and relax).

Ease into your break over the first two months and don't try to overplan your experience. Leave space for ease, rest, growth, and spontaneous magic to occur. Chapter 10 walks you through how to navigate the first two months of your break and the ups and downs that are sure to follow.

Approaching Life Differently

Have you been longing for a change? Maybe you wish life would slow down and give you some breathing room or simply that you could feel more joyful along the way. If your old approach wasn't working, I encourage you to embrace the idea of approaching life differently during your break.

You will likely encounter your biggest and most life-changing lessons when you're stepping outside of your comfort zone and trying something new. For example, if your default is to keep yourself busy, don't be afraid to lean into stillness and discover why you've been resisting it. Your break offers you a chance to create an identity that is separate from your productivity, job, or level of busyness, and this gift can improve your overall quality of life.

TIP

Curiosity is a great tool that allows you to make discoveries and observe without judgment. If you approach your break with a spirit of curiosity and experimentation, you can avoid making yourself wrong when things don't go according to plan. Instead, you can view it as an opportunity to learn something new, curiously explore what didn't work, and apply that learning to create a better result next time. If you want to create different results, you have to be willing to do things differently, with a few stumbles along the way. Be kind to yourself and stay curious in your pursuit of finding a better way.

Slowing Down for Extended Travel

Travel can be one of the most exciting parts of taking a break. If you have big travel plans, you're in for a treat. . . as long as you don't burn yourself out.

If this will be your first time pursuing long-term travel, you may need to adjust your expectations. Extended travel won't feel like an extended vacation for long. The vacation pace and approach to travel isn't sustainable when you're on the road for many weeks or months at a time. Constantly unpacking and repacking, learning new transportation routes and customs, finding time to deal with admin issues . . . it all can become overwhelming when you're traveling for an extended period of time. You'll want to include days for rest, ample downtime (just like at home), and a slower approach to your itinerary. For more long-term travel tips and resources, be sure to check out Chapter 9.

Hyping Up Your Break Experience

Your break is going to give you a special advantage when it comes time to re-enter the workforce . . . if you use it! One of the biggest mistakes you can make when it comes to taking a career break is downplaying or shying away from mentioning your break.

You can highlight your experience to enhance your desirability and strengthen your applications. You don't have to accept the belief that your break is a red flag. Getting clear on the benefits it's provided you can actually make it a green flag. Many people won't be sure what to make of it, so proactively and positively framing the narrative helps them realize your break's value. In Chapter 14, I explain exactly how to do this and how to craft your career break story so you can secure great job offers when your break is over.

Chapter **17**

Ten Great Examples to Inspire Your Break

This chapter was inspired by incredible things I've seen my clients do during a break. Some traveled halfway across the world, and others ventured out to the local pottery studio. I have clients who went financially all out and others who stuck to a modest budget. There's no right way to do a break. This chapter will inspire you with a wide variety of anecdotes. Use the examples in this chapter to spark new ideas and create even bigger dreams for yourself.

Traveling in a New Way

Have you ever wanted to explore a nomadic lifestyle or temporarily relocate to a new country you've always felt drawn to? A break provides a low-stakes opportunity to experience travel in a new way. You can use a career break to test drive a geographic change without making a long-term commitment, or explore new ways of wandering through the world. If you love travel, consider this an opportunity to experience travel in an exciting new way.

Rita used her break to test out remove work. During her break she began freelancing as she slowly made her way through Costa Rica, Cornwall, and Israel. Another client, Damien, used his break to temporarily relocate his family to Spain. Desiring the contrast of a more laid-back culture, they spent two years enjoying a life filled with siestas.

Learning a Language through Immersion

If learning a language or gaining proficiency is high on your list, consider doing language immersion. This can be a time-intensive endeavor, so a break is a great time to give it a try. During immersion, you'll learn more quickly and be more deeply exposed to the culture. You can even live with a host family for a true local experience. Being in country gives you a big boost toward your language goals, and planned outings and a small-group atmosphere can make immersions even more enjoyable, especially when you're traveling solo.

Stephen's interest in learning Spanish grew as his break progressed. He was able to approach learning in several different ways, with a highlight being his language immersion in Guatemala, where he lived with a lovely host family. Twila took a different approach and did her immersion through a formal program in the United States. She pursued her dream of learning Mandarin through an eight-week immersion at Middlebury College.

Tackling a Time-Intensive Goal

With work demands and a limited amount of paid time off, it can be hard to go for big personal goals or scratch items off your bucket list. (And if you're like me, your list seems to grow every year.) Well, I've got great news — a career break is the perfect opportunity to pursue your time-intensive goals. During a break, you'll have the time to thoughtfully prepare and can give your dreams the time and attention they require. You no longer need to keep telling yourself you'll do things "someday." When you're on a break, today can be the day!

ANECDOTE

One of my married couples chose to hike 400 miles of the Camino de Santiago in Spain. They spent several weeks making this trek and created a lot of memories along the way. My client Kisha used her break to finally get her novel out of her head and onto the page. Being on a break helped her make significant progress toward her dream of writing a book.

Pursuing a New Version of an Old Dream

It's never too late to pursue your dreams, even the ones you think you've outgrown. If you're worried that you've missed your chance, a break can grant you the opportunity to make it happen. You may have to adjust or modernize your goal to fit you as you are today, but with a little resourcefulness and creativity, you can revisit an old dream and make it come to life in a new way.

ANECDOTE

Kristen was in her late 30s when she made the bold decision to move to France to study abroad for a year. There were challenging moments, but Kristen impressed herself with her ability to adapt, build community, and excel at her studies. Another client of mine followed her intuition to pick up a new sport (tennis) and discovered she was really good. She became a competitive player at age 42.

Spending Quality Time with Loved Ones

Creating more time to connect the most important people in your life can be a great reason to take a break. Maybe you feel like you're missing the important moments of those closest to you, or maybe you'd like to be more present for someone you love. You can use this time off to pour into yourself *and* those you care about, making memories and creating an impact that will last a lifetime. My clients have used their time off to

>> Be more present in their children's lives and daily activities

>> Reconnect with their partner and find new ways to enjoy time together

>> Caretake and brighten the spirits of an aging parent

>> Help a loved one through a difficult time

Using Your Passion to Make a Big Impact

Following your passions and interests is rewarding on its own but can also benefit those around you and create a positive ripple in the world. If making a positive contribution or impact on others is important to you, a break can give you time to fulfill this desire. You can set yourself free to explore and put the things you're learning and talents you're discovering to good use.

ANECDOTE

Jessica followed her passion for animals, especially horses, to the U.K. where she earned a diploma in Equine Healing & Communication during her break. She doubled down on this passion when she became a practicing energy healer and launched an animal sanctuary for aged animals. Many felt the positive impact of Jessica's break.

Sparking Your Creativity

Creating simply for the sake of expressing yourself can be a cathartic experience. It's likely that your pre-break life didn't afford much time for this. But with a break, you can explore your creative side and pursue activities that spark your creativity. And if sharing is your thing, you double the benefit by sharing your creations and inspiring others.

ANECDOTE

Juliana poured her time and energy into creating a blog to reflect on and share her career break experience. She offered advice, travel tips, and personal reflections to inspire other midlife women on a similar journey. Brittany chose to pursue a budding interest in pottery. She purchased a membership at a local pottery studio and began discovering a new talent.

Restoring Your Health and Well-being

If you find yourself struggling with a health issue, you can use your career break to get things back on track. Taking a break provides the time and space you need to get to the bottom of an unexplained illness or to address lingering health issues more fully.

Being on a break makes it much easier to take excellent care of yourself and to restore your health. You'll also have more energy to advocate for your well-being and get important answers to your medical questions.

ANECDOTE

One of my clients started her break much earlier than planned due to her declining health. She'd been suffering from a mystery illness, which was later diagnosed as Lyme disease. It was a long journey to find answers, but she credits her break with saving her health and allowing her the space and time to get the answers she needed. Sometimes the healing is mental — like when you lose a loved one and need more time to process your grief and restore your spirits.

Discovering New Hobbies and Interests

Discovering new interests and talents can be a lot of fun and remind you that you're never done learning and growing. Your break is a great opportunity to experiment with new interests that pique your curiosity. By allowing yourself this opportunity, you'll discover new (or long forgotten) parts of yourself and appreciate your talents more deeply. You don't have to go far, travel abroad, or take on a massive adventure to indulge your inner explorer. You just have to get curious and be willing to discover new things to enjoy.

ANECDOTE

Chad took the opportunity to help out a neighbor who raised chickens and kept bees. He got to explore his curiosity and discovered a new hobby — raising chickens. After his break, Chad began raising his own.

Getting a Fresh Start

Are you long overdue for a change? If life's been feeling stale and you feel ready to make a dramatic change, you can use your break to recalibrate and create a fresh start. Whether it's starting a new career, launching a business, or relocating to a new region or country, you can use the momentum of a break to support other big changes and set yourself up for an exciting new chapter.

ANECDOTE

Misha sold her home, moved across the country, and relocated to the Pacific Northwest during her break. Not having to focus on work gave her time to adjust to her new city and develop a great community of friends. Heidi used her break to relocate to Guatemala, where she purchased a home. This exciting adventure paved the way for her to pursue new opportunities.

Index

length of break and, 130

long-term financial goals, 56

numbers detox, 249–250

objection that breaks are unaffordable, 17–18

order of priorities

break-design first, cost-setting second, 104, 132–133

cost-setting first, break-design second, 105, 131–132

professional financial advisors, 56, 119–120

recurring expenses, 162–163

red zone number, 244–246, 248

savings, 17, 55, 59, 104, 120

spending

giving yourself permission to spend, 246–250

spending wisely, 125–126

tracking, 122–124, 184–185, 240

start date, 135–137

tax breaks, 120

travel, 183–187

accounts, 186–187

goals, 185

homebase, 183–184

points and miles programs, 187–189

priorities, 185–186

tracking spending, 184–185

travel speed, 106–107, 183–184

flaneuring, 203–204

friends and family. See also caregiving and caretaking

connecting, reconnecting, and deeper connections, 13, 36, 40, 101, 178, 207, 229, 252, 264, 331

handling naysayers, 152–153

health insurance, 165

loneliness, 229

as motivation for career break, 13

re-entry stage, 101

reflection point to consider relationships, 34

responsibilities, 15–16, 58, 259–260

sharing news of your break, 145–154, 159–160

travel with, 208–209

G

gap years, 11–12

golden gap years, 11

H

health

burnout, 13–14, 30

jeopardizing by not taking break, 64

maximizing employer-provided benefits, 170

mental and emotional well-being, 30–37

as motivation for career break, 13–14, 332–333

physical well-being, 26–30, 37, 39

self-care, 14

travel, 204–205

health insurance, 11, 62, 69, 163–166, 170, 304

home, handling while on break, 166–167

I

interviews, 307–309

J

journaling, 39, 85, 237, 255–256, 270

L

leaves of absence, 12–13

LinkedIn, 297

About the Author

Katrina McGhee is a career break and sabbatical expert and Master Certified Life Coach with an MBA and 15+ years of corporate experience. She specializes in helping midcareer professionals create happier, more fulfilling lives by designing bold and transformational breaks.

After saving $40k in 18 months, Katrina sold her possessions and left her corporate job for a 20-month break to travel the world. Informed by her own successful experience, Katrina's Break Blueprint guides her clients to create life-changing career breaks and sabbaticals. On their time off, her clients have traveled the world, launched businesses, changed careers, and more.

Her advice on career breaks, money, and travel has been shared in leading online media outlets such as Forbes, Smarter Travel, Thrive Global, and Yahoo.

As an enthusiastic world traveler and digital nomad, Katrina is always on the hunt for new ways to use points and miles to her advantage. She's passionate about food tours and enjoys starting her mornings with a hot cup of Earl Grey.

The journey doesn't have to end here. Stay up to date on Katrina's newest offers, free career break resources, and latest adventures by joining her mailing list (www.kmcgheecoaching.com/join).

Dedication

I dedicate this book to my late brother, Phillip, for being my original and biggest fan and for always seeing my full potential. Thank you for being the best brother I could have asked for. You are always in my heart. And to my parents for always supporting me, even when I choose to do things my own way. Mom, thank you for always welcoming me back home and keeping me well-fed. Dad, thank you for showering me with special treats that keep me going and make me feel special. I love you both. Thank you for everything you've done to help me get here.

Author's Acknowledgments

Writing this book was one of the biggest challenges I've pursued, and I am so grateful for the village of support that ushered me along this journey.

Thank you to my amazing cheering section who poured into me so that my cup was never empty. Missy Ammerman, thank you for being a steady presence in my life and for always being there to listen. Majida Sherriff, thank you for always creating space for me to say what's in my heart. Jenny Dobson, thank you for offering me a place to call home and for being an amazing source of support and validation anytime I needed it. Krista Lorio, Mike Buchwald, and Liz O'Hara, I appreciate your continued support so much and am so grateful to have you in my corner. Finley McGhee, thank you for picking up your dad's torch and being a fantastic cheerleader. And to my sisters, Abby and Theresa, thank you for supporting me on this journey.

Elizabeth Gilbert, I'm one of the many who are grateful that you decided to share your story with the world. You planted a seed in me that eventually led to this book. Thank you for helping me see my only limitation was my imagination.

To my life coach, Ann Carter, who helped me realize the world was full of possibility: Thank you for helping me quiet my mind to hear the truth — that I really needed a break — and for supporting me in the early stages of that journey.

Thank you to my biggest sources of inspiration who helped me see that traveling around the world was actually possible. Nomadic

Matt (Kepnes), your resources were invaluable. Travis Sherry at Extra Pack of Peanuts, thank you for the great information and for allowing me to share my story when I was first starting out as a career break coach. Jodi Ettenberg at Legal Nomads, your stories inspired my imagination and helped me feel brave enough to travel the world with a gluten allergy. Ayngelina Brogan at Bacon Is Magic, thank you for sharing your journey and your passion for great food. And to Jen Bruntlett, thank you for being my real-life example of what was possible and for helping me feel brave enough to make the leap.

I want to acknowledge my past managers who supported my unconventional journey. Eric Pierce, thank you for seeing the value in my break and for offering me a dream job when it was over. And to Marilyn Weiss and Cindy Blackstock, thank you for letting me go part-time so I could continue investing in my dream. You helped me change lives.

Nic Windschill, thank you for being my partner in crime all those years ago. You helped me through the hardest time in my life, and your support helped me salvage my break and turn it into something truly wonderful and life-changing.

My very first career break client, Becky Drinnen, thank you for helping me see that my crazy idea could really work.

Thank you to my amazing clients. Without you, this book would not exist. Thank you for your trust and for letting me ride shotgun with you and helping me learn so much about career breaks along the way. You have been my inspiration to keep believing in this vision, even when it felt impossible.

And a big thank you to acquisition editor Jennifer Yee, who contacted me to write this book. Thank you for believing in this idea and in my ability to write this book. Your encouraging words and support made this crazy goal feel possible. Thanks to my incredibly supportive writing coach, Vicki Adang, who helped me realize I could actually do this, and my talented (and patient) development editor, Charlotte Kughen — I'm grateful for your skillful corrections, improvements, and words of encouragement. And finally, to my supportive and talented technical editor, Lyndall Farley, thank you for your time and support in making this book the very best it could be. Your thoughtfulness, care, and wisdom were an invaluable gift. I so appreciate you.

Publisher's Acknowledgements

Acquisitions Editor: Jennifer Yee

Project Editor: Charlotte Kughen

Copy Editor: Kelly Henthorne

Technical Editor: Lyndall Farley

Production Editor:
Saikarthick Kumarasamy

Cover Image: © mavo/Shutterstock

Leverage the power

Dummies is the global leader in the reference category and one of the most trusted and highly regarded brands in the world. No longer just focused on books, customers now have access to the dummies content they need in the format they want. Together we'll craft a solution that engages your customers, stands out from the competition, and helps you meet your goals.

Advertising & Sponsorships

Connect with an engaged audience on a powerful multimedia site, and position your message alongside expert how-to content. Dummies.com is a one-stop shop for free, online information and know-how curated by a team of experts.

- Targeted ads
- Video
- Email Marketing
- Microsites
- Sweepstakes sponsorship

20 MILLION PAGE VIEWS EVERY SINGLE MONTH

15 MILLION UNIQUE VISITORS PER MONTH

43% OF ALL VISITORS ACCESS THE SITE VIA THEIR MOBILE DEVICES

700,000 NEWSLETTE SUBSCRIPTION TO THE INBOXES OF *300,000* UNIQUE INDIVIDUALS EVERY WEEK

# of dummies

Custom Publishing

Reach a global audience in any language by creating a solution that will differentiate you from competitors, amplify your message, and encourage customers to make a buying decision.

- Apps
- Books
- eBooks
- Video
- Audio
- Webinars

Brand Licensing & Content

Leverage the strength of the world's most popular reference brand to reach new audiences and channels of distribution.

For more information, visit **dummies.com/biz**

PERSONAL ENRICHMENT

Staying Sharp
9781119187790
USA $26.00
CAN $31.99
UK £19.99

Facebook
9781119179030
USA $21.99
CAN $25.99
UK £16.99

Guitar
9781119293354
USA $24.99
CAN $29.99
UK £17.99

Investing
9781119293347
USA $22.99
CAN $27.99
UK £16.99

Beekeeping
9781119310068
USA $22.99
CAN $27.99
UK £16.99

Digital Photography
9781119235606
USA $24.99
CAN $29.99
UK £17.99

Meditation
9781119251163
USA $24.99
CAN $29.99
UK £17.99

Pregnancy
9781119235491
USA $26.99
CAN $31.99
UK £19.99

Samsung Galaxy S7
9781119279952
USA $24.99
CAN $29.99
UK £17.99

iPhone
9781119283133
USA $24.99
CAN $29.99
UK £17.99

Crocheting
9781119287117
USA $24.99
CAN $29.99
UK £16.99

Nutrition
9781119130246
USA $22.99
CAN $27.99
UK £16.99

PROFESSIONAL DEVELOPMENT

Windows 10
9781119311041
USA $24.99
CAN $29.99
UK £17.99

AutoCAD
9781119255796
USA $39.99
CAN $47.99
UK £27.99

Excel 2016
9781119293439
USA $26.99
CAN $31.99
UK £19.99

QuickBooks 2017
9781119281467
USA $26.99
CAN $31.99
UK £19.99

macOS Sierra
9781119280651
USA $29.99
CAN $35.99
UK £21.99

LinkedIn
9781119251132
USA $24.99
CAN $29.99
UK £17.99

Windows 10
9781119310563
USA $34.00
CAN $41.99
UK £24.99

SharePoint 2016
9781119181705
USA $29.99
CAN $35.99
UK £21.99

Fundamental Analysis
9781119263593
USA $26.99
CAN $31.99
UK £19.99

Networking
9781119257769
USA $29.99
CAN $35.99
UK £21.99

Office 2016
9781119293477
USA $26.99
CAN $31.99
UK £19.99

Office 365
9781119265313
USA $24.99
CAN $29.99
UK £17.99

Salesforce.com
9781119239314
USA $29.99
CAN $35.99
UK £21.99

Coding
9781119293332
USA $29.99
CAN $35.99
UK £21.99

Learning Made Easy

ACADEMIC

9781119293576
USA $19.99
CAN $23.99
UK £15.99

9781119293637
USA $19.99
CAN $23.99
UK £15.99

9781119293491
USA $19.99
CAN $23.99
UK £15.99

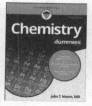

9781119293460
USA $19.99
CAN $23.99
UK £15.99

9781119293590
USA $19.99
CAN $23.99
UK £15.99

9781119215844
USA $26.99
CAN $31.99
UK £19.99

9781119293378
USA $22.99
CAN $27.99
UK £16.99

9781119293521
USA $19.99
CAN $23.99
UK £15.99

9781119239178
USA $18.99
CAN $22.99
UK £14.99

9781119263883
USA $26.99
CAN $31.99
UK £19.99

Available Everywhere Books Are Sold

Small books for big imaginations

9781119177173
USA $9.99
CAN $9.99
UK £8.99

9781119177272
USA $9.99
CAN $9.99
UK £8.99

9781119177241
USA $9.99
CAN $9.99
UK £8.99

9781119177210
USA $9.99
CAN $9.99
UK £8.99

9781119262657
USA $9.99
CAN $9.99
UK £6.99

9781119291336
USA $9.99
CAN $9.99
UK £6.99

9781119233527
USA $9.99
CAN $9.99
UK £6.99

9781119291220
USA $9.99
CAN $9.99
UK £6.99

9781119177302
USA $9.99
CAN $9.99
UK £8.99

Unleash Their Creativity